FIGHTING SLAVERY IN CHICAGO

Abolitionists, the Law of Slavery, and Lincoln

TOM CAMPBELL

AMP&RSAND, INC.

Chicago, Illinois

ISBN 978-0-9818126-2-5

Design
David Robson, Robson Design

Published by
Ampersand, Inc.
1050 North State Street
Chicago, Illinois 60610
www.ampersandworks.com

Printed in Canada

To Dianne

{ ACKNOWLEDGMENTS }

SEARCHING FOR THE footprints of the Chicago abolitionists, whose story this is, became a several year odyssey that led me to spend many hours in the Research Center of the Chicago History Museum where I was ably assisted by Leslie A. Martin, Olivia Pi-An Chen and AnneMarie Chase. I also delved into the collections of the Lincoln Library (Springfield, Illinois) where Jane Ehrenhart and Byron C. Andreasen lent their expert assistance. I was helped by Ken Frew at the Historical Society of Dauphin County (Harrisburg, Pennsylvania) where the papers of Simon Cameron are preserved; and was assisted by helpful staff members at the Library of Congress, the Newberry Library, the United States Archives and Records Administration, the National Archives of the United Kingdom, and the Alton Area Historical Society (Alton, Illinois).

Several people who were kind enough to read and comment on my draft manuscript deserve special thanks. These include: Mathew Bird, Douglas Carlson, Gary Johnson and William J. Lynk. Encouragement and helpful suggestions from Vincent Buonanno, Vera Clark, Clark Fetridge, Doris Kearns Goodwin, Bill Kurtis, John Lovejoy, Jane Ann and William Moore, Elizabeth Richter, Bruce and Betsy Wagner, Lisetta White, and Christopher Wren are gratefully acknowledged.

My esteem for the Chicago abolitionists was heightened by the insightful seminar on the Lincoln-Douglas debates taught by Rev. Robert Sprott at the Newberry Library in the Fall of 2004, and William Miller's *Arguing About Slavery*.

Finally, Suzanne T. Isaacs helped transform my manuscript into a published book.

{ CONTENTS }

{ ILLUSTRATIONS }

EXPLAINING CHICAGO'S ROLE in the fight to end slavery requires telling three overlapping stories covering the period from 1835 to 1865.

The first story traces the activities of Chicago's *abolitionists* who founded Chicago's Anti-Slavery Society, published newspapers that advocated the abolitionist cause, formed political parties, and ran a vibrant branch of the Underground Railroad, helping over a thousand runaway slaves escape to freedom.[1] The Chicago abolitionists helped form the Republican Party of Illinois, and, in 1860, gave crucial support to Abraham Lincoln that led to his nomination for President. They campaigned for Lincoln and later advanced the cause of emancipation while serving in the Lincoln Administration.

The second story is about *the law of slavery* and how it developed as the population grew. The Constitution accepted slavery. The Northwest Ordinance made Illinois a "Free State." Nevertheless, in the Free States, slavery was still tolerated as the Free States sought to accommodate the legitimacy of slavery in sister States. (Illinois shares hundreds of miles of border with Kentucky and Missouri, both Slave States before the Civil War.) In Illinois, between 1835 and 1860, there were constant court battles over slaves, their status, attempts to reclaim fugitives and whether someone helping a slave escape to freedom should be prosecuted criminally. The Illinois Supreme Court issued a number of opinions on these issues and Lincoln and every other practicing lawyer in Illinois studied these opinions. Among the many cases he handled in his legal practice before becoming the Republican candidate for President, Lincoln handled at least four runaway slave cases at the trial level and one appeal that went to the Illinois Supreme Court.

In 1854, the Nebraska Act repealed the Missouri Compromise and threatened to open up the territories to the expansion of slavery. The Dred Scott decision further advanced the States' Rights position holding that Congress could not exclude slavery from the territories. The state of the law presented a challenge to opponents of slavery. Lincoln crafted a position that drew on the Declaration of Independence, the Constitution and the Northwest Ordinance claiming that the founders of our nation envisioned that slavery should be limited and set on the course to its ultimate extinction. Lincoln expounded this thesis in his House Divided Speech, the seven Lincoln-Douglas debates and his Cooper Union Speech. This became the Republican platform and carried him to victory at the 1860 convention and in the election.

The third story is *Lincoln's position on slavery* — where did he stand and how, if at all, did his position on emancipation change? Some have said Lincoln did not initially label the Civil War as the war to end slavery and that he was reluctant to embrace emancipation because he was a racist and did not support abolition.[2] It is true that Lincoln paid lip service to the prevailing attitudes of white supremacy. It is also true that he put off issuing the Emancipation Proclamation until he found an opportune occasion. However, Lincoln took advantage of the opportunities that arose to pursue his agenda to set slavery on the road to its ultimate extinction. When the entire record is examined, the acts reflecting an unwavering commitment to abolishing slavery outweigh the episodes that Lincoln's detractors point to. Lincoln took measured steps that led in only one direction.

Together, these three stories explain how fighting slavery in Chicago resulted in slavery being abolished.

PART I

1835–1850:

The Era of the Acceptance of Slavery

The Role of Chicago
in the Fight against Slavery

WHEN THE DELEGATES of the newly formed Republican Party gathered at the Wigwam in Chicago in 1860 and ultimately nominated Abraham Lincoln as their candidate for President, the nation finally was poised to decide the great unresolved question of the day: Could the country any longer endure "half slave and half free?"

Lincoln was nominated on the third ballot. The Republicans won the election. Fort Sumter was fired upon. The nation was soon embroiled in a horrific civil war. It would be five long years before the issue was settled and slavery was eradicated for good. But Chicago did more to end slavery than host the convention that nominated Lincoln. Long before open warfare broke out, the battle for freedom was being waged in Chicago by a group of courageous citizens who opposed slavery and fought to end it – in defiance of laws upholding slavery – both openly and under ground.

Outraged by the murder of an abolitionist newspaper editor by a mob in Alton, Illinois on November 7, 1837, Charles Volney Dyer, one of Chicago's first physicians, rented a hall and called a public meeting to protest the murder.[3] Dr. Dyer was uncertain whether some, sympathetic to slave owners, might try to disrupt the meeting, so he took the precaution of hiring a guard to maintain order. It turned out to be unnecessary. The meeting did not provoke any open opposition. What it did do was bring together those citizens of Chicago who viewed slavery as evil, who were incensed by what the mob had done in Alton and who were ready to play a role in the fight to end slavery.

To stir the public conscience, these firebrands founded newspapers advocating the abolitionist cause, wrote letters, gave speeches, held public meetings, formed an "Anti-Slavery Society," defended runaway slaves in court, and promoted anti-slavery candidates and political parties. All of that was in the open. They also carried on a *secret* enterprise – operating the Chicago station of the Underground Railroad that helped fugitive slaves escape to Canada and freedom. Because they were violating the laws upholding slavery, this activity had to be covert. But the people who were behind it was an "open secret." A public brawl with slave-catchers from Kentucky trying to reclaim their "property" (*i.e.*, a fugitive slave), the obstruction of a trial claiming two men were runaway slaves, and other run-ins with those who would enforce the Fugitive Slave Act confirmed the suspicions of everyone as to the identity of those behind the Underground Railroad in Chicago.

Chicago became a hotbed of abolitionism. In the 1850s, Chicago would be at the forefront of the forces that threatened to unravel the carefully constructed policies to compromise on slavery that were fashioned by Senator Stephen A. Douglas. Douglas led the effort to expand the Union. To win Southern Senators' votes to admit new States into the Union, Douglas employed various measures to mollify them on the slavery issue. One such measure was the Fugitive Slave Act of 1850. Douglas reasoned that a strong federal law requiring the return of runaway slaves would reduce the friction between the Slave and Free States. Another was the doctrine of "Popular Sovereignty," the idea that new Territories and States should decide for themselves whether to be Slave or Free. A skillful politician whose rise in Illinois had been meteoric, Douglas had become a nationally known leader of the Democratic Party in the 1850s. Naturally, he hoped the alliance of Northern and Southern interests he had forged would propel him into the Presidency.

The Chicagoans who wanted to end slavery had other ideas. They openly defied the Fugitive Slave Act. They held public meetings to protest the compromise measures. They continued to help runaway slaves operating the Chicago arm of the Underground Railroad at full steam despite enhanced penalties and more rigorous enforcement of the Fugitive Slave Act. They formed a chorus of voices calling for a political party that would not compromise on slavery. In short, they helped set the stage for the rise of Abraham Lincoln to national prominence, the birth of a new national party opposed to the expansion of slavery, and

The Old Chicago Wigwam, where Lincoln was nominated for
the Presidency on May 18, 1860. (Chicago History Museum)

the slating of Lincoln as a Presidential candidate at the
1860 Republican Convention held in the Wigwam,
the building Chicago's business leaders had erected to
attract the convention to Chicago.

The abolitionists, with their willingness to break
the law to achieve their ends, were viewed as extremists even in the North. Lincoln had to be careful not to
be identified too closely with the abolitionist cause. He
crafted a stance that exposed the danger of Douglas's
positions, sounding the alarm that Popular Sovereignty
could lead to the spread of slavery and its legitimiza-
tion everywhere. In 1858, in their famous confrontation two years before the presidential election, Lincoln
refined his attacks on Douglas's policies through seven
exhausting debates. The two skilled debaters caused
citizens of Illinois and the nation to face the issue
which many ingenious compromises could no longer

obscure. Lincoln charted a course that was a shrewd
political calculation, explaining how Douglas's policies
would lead to the expansion of slavery, yet refusing to
endorse emancipation for the slaves, or any version of
equal rights for free blacks, a position the nation was
not ready for in 1858. It was a policy of containment
designed to preserve the Union.

Douglas beat Lincoln and won the Senate seat
they were contesting in 1858. The larger contest over
whether slavery would be contained or allowed to
expand was not over. The election of 1860 would be
the next battleground. The Republican Party would
decide who its candidate would be at the convention
in Chicago. Lincoln had had a hand in crafting the
party's platform. His positions fit perfectly with the
final product. He was naturally the favorite son of the
Illinois delegation. New York's William Seward was

the front runner. Lincoln's campaign strategists sought to persuade other delegations to make Lincoln their second choice and to switch to Lincoln after the first ballot. The success of this strategy depended on creating alliances with other delegations to persuade them to join a "Stop Seward" movement.

Several months before the convention, the Chicago abolitionists, led by Dr. Dyer, formed a club to support Simon Cameron, a rival of Lincoln's who would come to Chicago as the favorite son of Pennsylvania. Originally called "the Cameron Club," and later renamed "the Cameron-Lincoln Club," a 50 member delegation from the Club's 300 members greeted the Pennsylvania delegation when it arrived in Chicago. When the Pennsylvania delegation switched to Lincoln on the second ballot the momentum it created assured Lincoln of the nomination. Even then Lincoln's election did not mean that slavery would be abolished when he was sworn in. Lincoln would win with less than 40 percent of the popular vote.[4] There would be more to do and the Chicagoans would continue to play an important part.

The Legitimacy of Slavery

Openly opposing slavery in the 1830s meant being branded a fanatic. Slavery was not just tolerated, there were laws that actually commanded every citizen to uphold it. This was the legacy from the uneasy compromise struck at the birth of the nation. Five of the first seven Presidents of the United States – George Washington, Thomas Jefferson, James Madison, James Monroe and Andrew Jackson – were slaveholders.[5] So were a number of other "Founding Fathers." And the man President Jackson appointed to be Chief Justice of the Supreme Court in 1836, Roger Brooke Taney, had been a slaveholder.[6] Slavery was embedded deeply into the fabric of the nation.[7]

The Constitution presented an obstacle for those who wanted to end slavery through the passage of laws. Even though the delegates to the Constitutional Convention carefully avoided expressly mentioning the word "slavery" when drafting the nation's charter in 1787, that document carried the tacit agreement among the delegates that slavery existed, that it should not be disturbed, and that the legal rights of slaveholders should be respected.

This "agreement" was expressed in a round-about way. The government established by the Constitution was one in which slavery was legal and citizens were commanded to accept it. This was the result of two seemingly innocuous provisions. First, there was the apportionment provision with the now notorious "three-fifths clause." In Article I § 2, the membership in the House of Representatives was constituted based on an apportionment of one member for every 30,000 persons,[8] determined by counting as follows:

The whole Number of free Persons, including those bound to Service for a Term of Years, and excluding Indians not taxed, three fifths of all other Persons.

Who were these "other persons?" "Other" had to be something different than "Indians" or "free Persons." This was an indirect way of describing slaves.[9] (Lincoln called it "covert language."[10]) Then, in Article IV § 2 there was an even more draconian provision, one that gave slave owners a right to obtain the "return" of their "property" (*i.e.,* runaway slaves) if they escaped to another (Free) State:

No Person held to service or Labour in one State, under the Laws thereof, escaping into another, shall, in Consequence of any Law or Regulation therein, be discharged from such Service or Labour, but shall be delivered up on Claim of the Party to whom such Service or Labour may be due.

The language "shall be delivered up" seemed to command every citizen to uphold slavery.[11] Whatever compromise may have made sense to bring the 13 States together at the birth of the nation, the bargain struck a balance between Free and Slave States that would ultimately prove to be untenable. Slavery was already under attack around the world,[12] and it was just a matter of time before the cause of freedom engulfed the nation in a bloody civil war.

A Nettlesome Question

IF SLAVERY WAS constitutionally sanctioned, how could anyone hope to eradicate it? Where to start?

The American Colonization Society, formed in 1817, advocated *gradual emancipation*. The idea was to persuade slave owners to *manumit* their slaves voluntarily and the Society would help the released slaves emigrate to the new African nation of Liberia. (Manumit, the word meaning "to free from bondage," was a legal term familiar to Americans in the 1800s. Derived from Latin, the word itself was a reminder that the rights of slaves and slave owners were governed by laws since at least the time of the Romans.) The concept of gradual emancipation attracted the support of many politicians including Whig politicians Henry Clay and Abraham Lincoln. But it was an ineffectual policy. In 1833, John Greenleaf Whittier authored a pamphlet, *Justice and Expediency* that pointed out the obvious shortcomings of the colonization policy:

> *Let facts speak. The Colonization Society was organized in 1817. It has two hundred and eighteen auxiliary societies. The legislatures of fourteen states have recommended it. Contributions have poured into its treasury from every quarter of the United States. Addresses in its favor have been heard from all our pulpits. It has been in operation sixteen years. During this period nearly one million human beings have died in slavery, and the numbers of slaves have increased more than half-a-million, or in round numbers, 550,000;*
>
> *The Colonization Society has been busily engaged all this while in conveying slaves to Africa; in other words, abolishing slavery. In this very charitable occupation it has carried away of manumitted slaves: 613.*
>
> *Balance against the society: 549,387!*[13]

Recognition that colonization – gradual emancipation – was not working set the stage for a new policy – *immediatism*. William Lloyd Garrison, the editor of the *Liberator*, a Boston anti-slavery newspaper, together with Whittier and other like-minded men met in 1833 in a convention in Philadelphia in the Adelphi Building.[14] The Adelphi Convention produced the American Anti-Slavery Society. The delegates issued a declaration that excoriated slavery and slave-owners and called for the immediate end of slavery. Garrison authored the declaration adopted by the Convention. This document, in addition to labeling slavery immoral and criminal, called for *immediate* emancipation. It not only rejected the idea of compensation to the slave owners, but stated that if compensation were paid to anyone, it should be the freed slaves.[15] The delegates committed themselves to establishing Anti-Slavery societies everywhere to promote the cause.[16]

Proselytizing for this cause was not greeted with open arms. In fact, it became dangerous to advocate the abolition of slavery – as would be proven in Illinois in short order.

In the Southern States the slave owners recognized the threat posed by the abolitionists and formed Committees of Vigilance.[17] The fear of a slave rebellion was heightened after Nat Turner's rampage in Virginia in 1831 in which 60 white people were killed, including women and children.[18] Calling for abolition was equated with fomenting rebellion. A Congressman from South Carolina, Waddy Thompson, Jr., called abolitionists murderers:

> *They [Abolitionists] are murderers, accessories before the fact, and they know it, of murder, robbery, rape, infanticide.*[19]

The rhetoric of opponents to abolition went beyond just name-calling. If abolitionists were "murderers," would killing such a murderer be justified? Another Congressman from South Carolina, James Henry Hammond, thought so. He warned abolitionists not to come south preaching their cause:

And I warn the abolitionists, ignorant, infatuated, barbarians as they are, that if chance shall throw any of them into our hands he may expect a felon's death.[20]

Was this just rhetoric? Were these idle threats? Hardly. In the South, suspected abolitionists were tarred and feathered. The *Liberator* and other anti-slavery publications were banned. Prices were put on the heads of the signers of the Adelphi Declaration.[21] It was not long before the debate turned lethal. In fact, the first death – a murder by a mob – occurred in Illinois, when a daring newspaper editor refused to bend to the demands that he cease agitating for emancipation.

Elijah Lovejoy – Illinois's Abolitionist Editor

AFTER GRADUATING IN 1826 from Colby College in Maine, Elijah P. Lovejoy came west and worked for newspapers in St. Louis. Though he grew up in a religious family, he had never experienced a personal conversion. He liked his work but was restless, searching for a greater purpose. In 1832, he attended a religious revival which profoundly affected him. Reverend David Nelson – Dr. Nelson – attacked sin, and directly associated condoning slavery with sin. His message was that the sale of human beings or one man owning another was as sinful as adultery or murder.[22]

For Lovejoy, this was it. He had found a new purpose to his life. He decided to attend the Theological Seminary in Princeton, New Jersey where he studied for the ministry. Afterwards, he returned to St. Louis to start up a religiously sponsored newspaper, the *St. Louis Observer*.[23] At the age of 30, he embarked on the career of newspaper editor, feeling that this would be the most effective way for him to influence people on the moral issue he had decided would become his personal crusade.

Almost immediately Lovejoy was embroiled in controversy. He editorialized against slavery. Though he took the moderate position of advocating the gradual emancipation doctrine, his advocacy roiled the waters. The State of Missouri permitted slavery and his positions were viewed as dangerous to the public order where the practice flourished.[24] He disagreed with a group of St. Louis citizens who proclaimed that slavery was sanctioned "by the sacred scriptures." He wrote fiery editorials regularly invoking biblical imagery to denounce slavery:

At present, Slavery, like an incubus, is paralyzing our energies, and like a cloud of evil portent, darkening all our prospects. Let this be removed, and Missouri would at once start forward in the race of improvement….[25]

He analogized slavery to a vampire:

In every community where it exists, it presses like a night-mare on the body politic. Or, like the vampire, it slowly and imperceptibly sucks away the life-blood of society, leaving it faint and disheartened to stagger along the road to improvement.[26]

It was not long before Lovejoy was accused of distributing abolitionist publications. He defended his position by arguing that gradual emancipation was not "abolitionist propaganda" and that, in any event, the Constitutions of the United States and the State of Missouri guaranteed freedom of the press and freedom of speech. This did not quell the furor. A committee of citizens demanded that he be silent on the issue of slavery. He refused to bow to what he considered censorship. The "citizens' committee" issued a not-so-subtle threat that they would destroy the newspaper.

When Lovejoy went out of town to attend a convention, the owners of his newspaper sought to appease his opponents by promising to be silent about slavery. The announcement they published made it clear the nature of the threat they thought they faced:

The proprietors of the St. Louis "Observer" having heretofore expressed their determination that nothing should be advanced in the columns of that paper, calculated to keep up the excitement on the Slavery question ... have heard with astonishment and regret, that certain evil disposed persons have threatened violence to the "Observer Office." We call upon all prudent men to pause and reflect upon the probable consequences of such a step – there is nothing to justify it.

We believe this to be a momentary excitement arising out of the apprehension of the white men who stole Major Dougherty's Negroes, and who have been dealt with according to the new code by several of our more respectable citizens....[27]

The "new code" was a reference to the rise of mob law and vigilantism that had taken hold throughout the South. In the case referred to, two white men, Fuller and Bridges, were taken on suspicion of having "decoyed away" some Negroes. They were brought "by illegal violence" from Illinois and, as determined by the "committee," whipped 100 to 200 times each.[28] When the committee deliberated to decide on this punishment, there were actually some among these "respectable citizens" who voted to lynch the suspected miscreants.

On his return Lovejoy learned of the capitulation of the paper's owners. He immediately resigned. But the person holding the mortgage on the *St. Louis Observer's* press over-ruled the owners, hired Lovejoy back and insisted that he be given free reign over editorial policy.

Passions were on the rise. Other troubling reports of mob action revealed how matters could turn lethal. In May of 1835, Lovejoy reported on the action of a mob that broke into the St. Louis jail, dragged out a mulatto named Francis MacIntosh who was awaiting trial, chained him to a tree and burned him alive. MacIntosh had been apprehended after killing a policeman in the course of a brawl. Lovejoy wrote an editorial describing this event and citing other incidents where "citizens committees" had acted, saying: "And now we make our appeal ... is it not time to stop?"[29]

But things got worse. First, the judge who presided over the Grand Jury that was empanelled to inquire into the death of MacIntosh gave a speech to the Grand Jury excusing the conduct of the mob. That

One of Elija Lovejoy's presses for his *Alton Observer* newspaper. (Chicago History Museum)

was a strong hint to return no indictment. That is what they did. Worse still, he lambasted Lovejoy and blamed him for inciting Negroes to revolt. The judge's screed sounded like an open invitation for a mob to go after Lovejoy.[30]

Only a few months before, at the age of 35, Lovejoy married Celia Ann French, who was 21. For his personal safety and that of his new family, Lovejoy was counseled by his friends to move the paper from St. Louis across the Mississippi River to Alton, Illinois. Illinois was a "Free State" and presumably a more hospitable place from which to publish the views he espoused. But the move did not turn out the way Lovejoy's well-wishers had hoped. The day of the move, his press was brought across the river and left by the bank of the river over night to be delivered to his new office in the morning. When morning came, Lovejoy found his press destroyed.

The people of Alton were outraged. They held a public meeting to deplore the act and they pledged to pay for a new press.[31] Lovejoy bought a new press. For a while afterward the paper was published without incident and circulation grew to 2,000. It was a voice well beyond Alton. But Lovejoy's denunciation of slavery caused him to be viewed by some of his neighbors as a menace and the threat of mob action to silence his voice was constantly hovering overhead.

Lovejoy considered moving away for the sake of his young family. But speaking freely in Alton was also a priority weighing on his conscience. He stayed. And he continued to express his views about slavery. When a fellow preacher suggested that "where religion flourishes, slaves are well treated," Lovejoy responded that the Gospel required fair treatment of the Negro, not as a slave, but as a man. Lovejoy's stance inflamed the slaveocracy.

In June of 1837, the Anti-Slavery Society that Whittier and Garrison had started with the Adelphi Convention asked Lovejoy to provide the names of two people in every county in Illinois who would circulate petitions that could be submitted to Congress asking it to abolish slavery in the District of Columbia.[32] Whittier and Garrison were seeking to arm John Quincy Adams, who, after his defeat for re-election as President, became a Member of Congress, and led the effort to use the Right of Petition, one of the rights guaranteed in the First Amendment to the Constitution, to limit slavery. Adams introduced petitions from citizens asking Congress to contain slavery by not allowing it in new territories and to end it in the District of Columbia, where Congress had the power to do so.[33] Lovejoy published this request. In fact he went further. He editorialized: "[L]et every free man in the republic remember, that so long as slavery exists in the District of Columbia he is himself a slaveholder."[34] And he asked whether the time had come to form an Anti-Slavery Society in Illinois.[35] This turned out to be the spark that ignited the powder keg.

On July 8, 1837, handbills were circulated calling for a public meeting. Resolutions were adopted demanding that Lovejoy observe a pledge not to discuss slavery that he supposedly made earlier when he moved his press to Alton. A committee of five citizens was appointed to call on Lovejoy to ascertain "whether he intends to disseminate … the doctrine of abolition." Instead they wrote him, and he wrote back defying their demands:

I cannot consent … to recognize you as the official organ of [the] public…. But as individuals whom I highly respect, permit me to say to you, that it is very far from my intention to do anything calculated to bring on an "unwise agitation," on the subject of Slavery…. I hope to discuss the overwhelmingly important subject of Slavery, with the freedom of a republican and the meekness of a Christian.[36]

Rocks were thrown through his windows. On August 21, 1837, on his way home, he was intercepted by a mob that threatened to tar and feather him. He did not turn and run. He stood his ground. He calmly asked that one among them take the medicine he was carrying to his wife without explaining why he would be delayed. This request was granted. But then his tormentors lost their nerve. They let him go. Later that night his office was broken into and his press destroyed – *again*.

Lovejoy ordered another press – his third. Before it arrived, another public meeting was held and there were again demands that he cease editorializing. He refused.

The new press was shipped to Alton. It was to arrive on Monday, November 6, 1837. Expecting trouble, the young Mayor, John M. Krum, arranged for it to be housed in a warehouse and enlisted 40 to 50 men with muskets and rifles to guard the warehouse under the supervision of a town constable. At 10 o'clock, several left. At 3:00 A.M., the press arrived. A sentinel for the trouble-makers sounded the alarm. Horns blew throughout the city. The Mayor oversaw the unloading of the press, told the defenders to stay inside the warehouse and keep quiet unless they were needed.

Mob attacking Gilman's Warehouse, Alton, Illinois 1835.[41]
(Chicago History Museum)

However, due to the lateness of the hour, the trouble-makers were unable to muster sufficient numbers to harass the guardians. They threw a few stones. The press was safely unloaded and moved inside. Lovejoy had not been present. Heeding warnings of possible harm to himself and his family, he had taken them to a friend's home to safeguard them.

On Tuesday night, November 7, 1837, the defenders reassembled but with fewer numbers in light of the fact that there had not been any trouble the night before. This time Lovejoy was with them. At 10:00 P.M., "the drinkeries and coffee-houses began to belch forth their inmates and a mob of about 30 individuals, armed, some with stones, some with guns and pistols, formed themselves into a line" at the south end of the warehouse.[37] In time their numbers grew to 150. Worse, 50 to 80 of them were armed.[38]

Gilman, one of the owners of the warehouse, shouted out, "What do you want?" The leader of the mob, William Carr, replied: "the press." Gilman said it would not be given up, that they wished their neighbors no harm, but were authorized to defend the property and would do so "with our lives."

The mob threw stones and broke some windows. Then they fired their guns into the building. The defenders returned fire wounding several rioters. One was carried off to a doctor's office. The gunfire checked the efforts of the mob and they pulled back. But, "after a visit to the rum-shops," they were back. This time they came with ladders and headed to the side of the warehouse that had no windows, with shouts of "Burn them out!" Their numbers were formidable.

The Mayor had returned to the scene and tried to broker a truce. He thought it would be foolhardy for the outnumbered defenders to resist the mob and asked Lovejoy and his cohorts whether they would give up the press on a promise of safe conduct through the mob. Knowing that this might be a fatal decision, Lovejoy declined. He asked whether they should defend their property with arms and the Mayor said they had a perfect right to do so.

The Mayor reported back to the mob that the defenders would not yield. Word had also reached the mob that their wounded comrade who had been carried off earlier had died.[39] All of this just added to their fury.

The mob set upon the building with a roar shouting, "Burn them out. Shoot every abolitionist!" It was near midnight but the moon shown brightly. The ladders were thrown up against the windowless wall. One of the rioters scampered up and kindled a fire on the roof. Five defenders came out of the building, came around the building and fired their guns. They drove the men with ladders off.

There was a lull. The five defenders returned to the warehouse. Lovejoy stepped to the doorway to peer out and determine the number and position of the besiegers. He was unaware that one of the attackers had concealed himself behind a wood pile near by.

The assassin fired from virtually point-blank range. Lovejoy was mortally wounded. He dragged himself into the building but died a few moments later. Lovejoy had been assassinated. His voice was silenced for good.[40]

The death of Lovejoy sent shock waves that reverberated across the country. It was the call to action that galvanized opponents to slavery. In Chicago, Dr. Dyer roused his fellow citizens to protest the action of the mob. The meeting he called was just the first step. This frontier doctor would soon lead other like-minded citizens to raise their own voices and act against slavery to "prove that you cannot bury the truth by burying its messenger."[42] Lovejoy had been an abolitionist and a fanatic to those supporting slavery and to those content to leave the situation as it was. But his murder did not just strike a blow to the opponents of slavery, it struck at the freedom of the press and the right to free speech – something fundamental to Americans. To kill a man for speaking or publishing his views was an offense against the machinery of democracy. Lovejoy's death was a watershed. The truth about slavery would still be told – but now it would have to be told by Lovejoy's successors.

Chicago's Response

THE FIRST STEP down the path to activism and resistance was a simple public meeting in 1837. Dr. Dyer, one of Chicago's first physicians, rented a hall and called for a public demonstration protesting the action of the mob in Alton.[43] What emerged from this meeting was recognition that Illinois needed a voice in the debate over slavery. Dr. Dyer quickly identified the other Chicagoans who would help promote the cause and stand with him. The next step was the obvious one of holding an anti-slavery meeting and forming a Chicago Chapter of the Anti-Slavery Society. In early 1838, another meeting was held at the "Saloon Building," at the corner of Lake and Dearborn. This was the building that regularly hosted meetings, lectures and entertainments in early Chicago.[44] The Society was formed and its leaders were Dr. Dyer, Rev. Flavel Bascom of the First Presbyterian Church, Philo Carpenter, Robert Freeman and Calvin De Wolf.[45] It would not be long before they started a new paper to pick up Lovejoy's torch. And they soon realized that to effectively combat slavery they had to take certain steps covertly.

Chicago in 1838

AT THE TIME of this meeting, Chicago was the fastest-growing city in the United States. It had grown from a population of less than 100 in 1832, to 2,000 in 1835. The Indians were gone. The Pottawatomie staged their last war dance during the summer of 1835; they had come to Chicago to receive their last annuity and prepare for their migration.[46] Chicago would boast 4,000 inhabitants by 1840 and 6,000 by 1842.[47] What spurred this surge?

Before becoming a State in 1818, Illinois had been a territory ruled first by France and then by England before becoming part of the territory owned

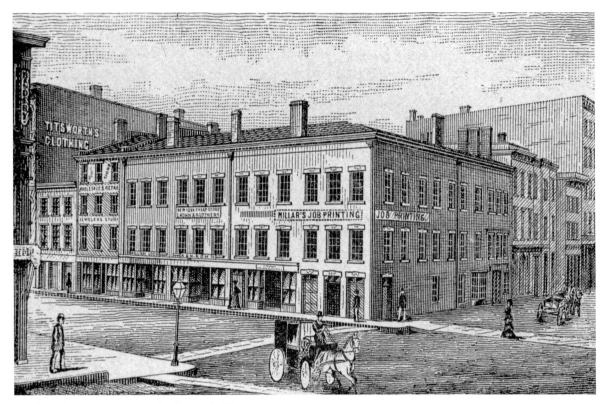

The Old Saloon Building where Dr. Dyer called for
action to protest the attack on Gilman's Warehouse.
(Chicago History Museum)

and governed by the United States. The Indians
who hunted, fished, camped on the shores of Lake
Michigan were probably oblivious to the territorial
claims of the colonial powers when they first encountered and started selling furs to traders. But that would
soon change. The powers claiming to be sovereign over
the territory could and did affect the lives of its inhabitants. The first upheaval came with the French and
Indian War. Illinois was part of the Upper Louisiana
Territory claimed by France. In that war, the French
and the Indians allied with them were defeated. The
territories France claimed east of Mississippi, including what became Illinois, were ceded to England in the
Treaty of Paris in 1763.

In 1783, 20 years later, England lost this territory in
the War of Independence and ceded it to the United
States in another Treaty of Paris.

Virginia laid claim to the territory but ceded it to
the United States in 1784 at which time it became part
of the "Territory of the United States Northwest of the
River Ohio," or "the Northwest Territory."

Throughout the changes in sovereignty, the ownership of the tiny settlement that would become Chicago
was swept along as territories changed hands. Chicago
began its life on August 3, 1795 when a tract of land,
approximately six miles square, was deeded to the
United States in the treaty made at Fort Greenville
(later Greenville, Ohio) by General ("Mad") Anthony
Wayne with the Pottawatomies and other tribes who
ceded the parcel "at the mouth of the Chikajo River."[48]
Before then, it had been an Indian village. In 1804, a
military post was established and the American Fur
Company set up a trading post. At the time of the
War of 1812 with Great Britain, the United States garrison abandoned the Fort and was massacred by the

An ORDINANCE for the GOVERNMENT of the TERRITORY of the UNITED STATES, North-West of the RIVER OHIO.

BE IT ORDAINED by the United States in Congress assembled, That the said territory, for the purposes of temporary government, be one district; subject, however, to be divided into two districts, as future circumstances may, in the opinion of Congress, make it expedient.

Be it ordained by the authority aforesaid, That the estates both of resident and non-resident proprietors in the said territory, dying intestate, shall descend to, and be distributed among their children, and the descendants of a deceased child in equal parts; the descendants of a deceased child or grand-child, to take the share of their deceased parent in equal parts among them: And where there shall be no children or descendants, then in equal parts to the next of kin, in equal degree; and among collaterals, the children of a deceased brother or sister of the intestate, shall have in equal parts among them their deceased parents share; and there shall in no case be a distinction between kindred of the whole and half blood; saving in all cases to the widow of the intestate, her third part of the real estate for life, and one third part of the personal estate; and this law relative to descents and dower, shall remain in full force until altered by the legislature of the district. —— And until the governor and judges shall adopt laws as herein after mentioned, estates in the said territory may be devised or bequeathed by wills in writing, signed and sealed by him or her, in whom the estate may be, (being of full age) and attested by three witnesses; —— and real estates may be conveyed by lease and release, or bargain and sale, signed, sealed, and delivered by the person being of full age, in whom the estate may be, and attested by two witnesses, provided such wills be duly proved, and such conveyances be acknowledged, or the execution thereof duly proved, and be recorded within one year after proper magistrates, courts, and registers shall be appointed for that purpose; and personal property may be transferred by delivery, saving, however, to the French and Canadian inhabitants, and other settlers of the Kaskaskies, Saint Vincent's, and the neighbouring villages, who have heretofore professed themselves citizens of Virginia, their laws and customs now in force among them, relative to the descent and conveyance of property.

Be it ordained by the authority aforesaid, That there shall be appointed from time to time, by Congress, a governor, whose commission shall continue in force for the term of three years, unless sooner revoked by Congress; he shall reside in the district, and have a freehold estate therein, in one thousand acres of land, while in the exercise of his office.

There shall be appointed from time to time, by Congress, a secretary, whose commission shall continue in force for four years, unless sooner revoked, he shall reside in the district, and have a freehold estate therein, in five hundred acres of land, while in the exercise of his office; it shall be his duty to keep and preserve the acts and laws passed by the legislature, and the public records of the district, and the proceedings of the governor in his executive department; and transmit authentic copies of such acts and proceedings, every six months, to the secretary of Congress: There shall also be appointed a court to consist of three judges, any two of whom to form a court, who shall have a common law jurisdiction, and reside in the district, and have each therein a freehold estate in five hundred acres of land, while in the exercise of their offices; and their commissions shall continue in force during good behaviour.

The governor and judges, or a majority of them, shall adopt and publish in the district, such laws of the original states, criminal and civil, as may be necessary, and best suited to the circumstances of the district, and report them to Congress, from time to time, which laws shall be in force in the district until the organization of the general assembly therein, unless disapproved of by Congress; but afterwards the legislature shall have authority to alter them as they shall

at an earlier period, and when there may be a less number of free inhabitants in the state than sixty thousand.

Article the Sixth. There shall be neither slavery nor involuntary servitude in the said territory, otherwise than in punishment of crimes whereof the party shall have been duly convicted: Provided always, that any person escaping into the same, from whom labor or service is lawfully claimed in any one of the original states, such fugitive may be lawfully reclaimed and conveyed to the person claiming his or her labor or service as aforesaid.

Be it ordained by the authority aforesaid, That the resolutions of the 23d of April, 1784, relative to the subject of this ordinance, be, and the same are hereby repealed and declared null and void.

DONE by the UNITED STATES in CONGRESS assembled, the 13th day of July, in the year of our Lord 1787, and of their sovereignty and independence the 12th.

Cha Thomson Secy

The Northwest Ordinance of 1787 provided for settling, incorporating and governing western lands and addressed the issue of slavery directly. It ranks third in importance after the Declaration of Independence and the U.S. Constitution. (Library of Congress)

The Northwest Territory, created by Ordinance of the
Continental Congress, July 13, 1787, effective on passage.
The area included land that was eventually incorporated
into the states of Ohio, Michigan, Indiana, Illinois, Wisconsin
and Minnesota. (Chicago History Museum)

Indians. It was rebuilt in 1817 and it went on the map as Fort Dearborn. From then until 1830 Chicago was "the residence of the soldier and the Indian trader."[49]

But then the growth came. In 1833, Chicago was incorporated as a town. In 1837, it was incorporated as a city. In 1838, Stephen A. Douglas, a rising public figure, made his first political speech in Chicago at the age of 25.[50]

The growth that came in the 1830s happened because of the blueprint for development of this territory that the Continental Congress drew in the Northwest Ordinance of 1787.[51] This document ranks third in importance after the Declaration of Independence and the Constitution. It is the charter that provided for the settlement and incorporation of western lands, an area of approximately 265,000 square miles. It not only spelled out how the territory was to be governed, how people living in the territory would participate in their government, how new States could be organized and admitted to the Union, but it also addressed slavery – and, unlike the Constitution, it did so *directly*.

A "Free State"

WHEN LOVEJOY MOVED his press across the Mississippi River he had expected a friendlier climate for expressing his ideas about emancipation. Illinois was a "Free State." What did that mean? Remarkably, the same Continental Congress that drafted the Constitution also drafted the Northwest Ordinance which *banned* slavery in the new territory. This time there was no beating about the bush. In the articles that provided a bill of rights to the citizens of the new territory, there was an express prohibition on slavery:

Article 6. There shall be neither slavery nor involuntary servitude in the said territory, otherwise than in punishment of crimes whereof the party shall have been duly convicted: Provided, always, That any person escaping into the same, from whom labor or service is

lawfully claimed in any one of the original States, such fugitive may be lawfully reclaimed in any and conveyed to the person claiming his or her labor or service as aforesaid.

While the command of the Northwest Ordinance that "there shall be no slavery" appears clear, there were continuous efforts to undermine or evade it. Of course, there was the proviso that recognized the rights of slaveholders to reclaim "fugitives." But other inroads were carved out as the Northwest Territory evolved into the State of Illinois. And the nasty business of "reclaiming" fugitive slaves would embroil Illinois citizens in numerous controversies in the period from 1830 to 1860.

With respect to governance and the evolution from territory to State, the Ordinance provided that Congress would appoint a governor and judges; that once there were 5,000 free male inhabitants of voting age, they would elect a territorial legislature and send a non-voting representative to Congress; that once the population reached 60,000 the legislature would submit a State constitution to Congress; and that once that was approved, the new State would enter the Union on an equal footing with the existing States.

Dr. Dyer's Vermont Heritage

CHARLES VOLNEY DYER, the future abolitionist, was born in Vermont, June 12, 1808. He was one of 11 children. His father, Daniel Dyer, was a prominent farmer in Clarendon and a veteran of the Revolutionary War. His mother was Susannah Olin. Dyer worked on his father's farm in Vermont as a boy. An avid reader with an inquiring mind, his parents sent him to Castleton Academy. He was attracted to medicine and graduated with a degree in medicine from Middlebury in 1832.[52] He tried practicing medicine briefly in Trenton, New Jersey but the prospect of life as a doctor there was too tame. He set off for the frontier, landing in Chicago in 1835. He was one of the first physicians to practice in Chicago. He became the physician to the militia at Fort Dearborn which helped him establish a viable medical practice in the fledgling town quickly.

Dyer had abolition in his blood. He was related on his mother's side to an extraordinary figure in Vermont's history, Theophilus Harrington, who was elected a Judge of the Supreme Court of Vermont in 1803 and served on that court for 10 years. Harrington was not a lawyer. He was a plain farmer, but his quick mind and incisive reasoning more than made up for his lack of formal legal training. He had a strong sense of justice and made common sense decisions that people recognized as rendering substantial justice.

The case that made him a legend was one in which a New Yorker sought to reclaim a fugitive slave under the original fugitive slave law. (New York was then a Slave State.[53]) The slave had escaped to Vermont and sought to establish a home. He was pursued by his former owner. The owner hired an attorney who sought a warrant for the extradition of the Negro he claimed as a slave. The matter came before Judge Harrington. The attorney presented papers to establish that the New Yorker was the owner of the Negro. He "rested," believing he had made a *prima facie* case – that he had presented enough evidence for the warrant to issue. Judge Harrington shook his head negatively and told the attorney that the proof he had offered was not sufficient to establish title to the supposed fugitive slave. The chastened attorney offered additional proof of ownership. To show a chain of ownership going further back, he presented proof that the Negro and his ancestors had belonged to the New Yorker and his family for "time out of mind of man." Still the judge shook his head and indicated that there was some defect in the title. The exasperated attorney asked: "Will your honor be good enough to suggest what is lacking to make a perfect title?" Judge Harrington thundered: "I REQUIRE A BILL OF SALE FROM THE ALMIGHTY!"[54]

Dr. Dyer relished telling this story about his famous relative. And he certainly was in agreement with the stance Vermonters took with regard to slavery – refusing to become its enforcers. The spirit of abolition was

Monument to Theophilus Harrington, Judge of the Supreme Court of Vermont and an ardent abolitionist. Chippenhook Cemetery, Clarendon, Vermont. (Private Collection)

vibrant in Vermont and that State wrote a Constitution that expressly forbade slavery. In fact, Vermont joined the Union as the fourteenth State after submitting its Constitution – which prohibited slavery – to Congress for approval. When Dr. Dyer came to Chicago, he carried with him the strength of his Vermont boyhood – both physical strength (to be expected of someone raised on a farm) and that strength of character of his Vermont forebears. He would draw on both when fighting slavery in Chicago.

The Illinois General Assembly Condemns Abolitionist Societies

THE SOUTHERN STATES, in response to the formation of abolition societies asked Northern States to pass resolutions affirming the legitimacy of slavery and condemning the formation of abolitionist societies. The Illinois General Assembly, under the control of the Democrats, complied. The resolution introduced on January 20, 1837 provided:

Resolved *by the General Assembly of the State of Illinois, That we highly disapprove of the formation of abolition societies, and of the doctrines promulgated by them.*

Resolved, *That the right of property in slaves, is sacred to the slave-holding States by the Federal Constitution, and that they cannot be deprived of that right without their consent.*

Resolved, *That the General Government cannot abolish slavery in the District of Columbia, against the consent of the citizens of said District without a manifest breach of good faith.*

Resolved, *That the Governor be requested to transmit to the States of Virginia, Alabama, Mississippi, New York, and Connecticut, a copy of the foregoing report and resolutions.*[55]

Though the report of the select committee lamented "the unfortunate condition of our fellow men, whose lot are cast in thralldom in a land of liberty and peace," the Senate passed the resolutions unanimously and the House passed them with six votes against.

Abraham Lincoln was a member of the Illinois General Assembly in 1837, serving his second term. By virtue of clever stump speeches, he had been elected as a Whig in a strongly Democratic district.[56] Lincoln voted against the resolutions and his efforts to amend them failed. He then filed a protest which he and Dan Stone, another representative of Sangamon County, were the only two who signed. The protest expressed the view that slavery was wrong but also mildly chided the abolitionists for causing "agitation:"

Resolutions upon the subject of domestic slavery having passed both branches of the General Assembly at its present session, the undersigned hereby protest against the passage of the same.

They believe that the institution of slavery is founded on both injustice and bad policy; but that the promulgation of abolition doctrines tends rather to increase that to abate its evils.

They believe that the Congress of the United States has no power, under the constitution, to interfere with the institution of slavery in the different states.

They believe that the Congress of the United States has the power, under the Constitution to abolish slavery in the District of Columbia; but that that power ought not to be exercised unless at the request of the people of said District.

The difference between these opinions and those contained in the said resolutions, is their reason for entering this protest.[57]

The Illinois resolutions approving the slave holding States' position on slavery reflected the prevailing attitude not just of the members of the General Assembly but also most of their constituents. Lincoln's protest was based on the view that slavery was wrong. At the same time he accepted that Congress could not interfere with it in the States where it existed. These became two pillars of the position he would construct on slavery. At a time when abolitionists were regarded with contempt, to stand alone asserting a position of conscience – that slavery was wrong – was a courageous act.

The Underground Railroad – The Beginning

Z EBINA EASTMAN, WHO became editor of Chicago's abolitionist newspaper, *Western Citizen*, would later recount that the first passenger on the Underground Railroad to pass through Chicago was a young black from Alabama who had been a plantation blacksmith. The year was 1839. Eastman then lived in Lowell, Illinois in LaSalle County, 50 miles southwest of Chicago. He heard from a farmer that there was a strange person down by the river bank who had pointed a shotgun at him and warned him off. The farmer thought he might be some kind of fugitive. Eastman asked the farmer to go back and, if the man was a Negro, to tell him he was among friends and bring him to Eastman. Soon Eastman was looking upon a "strange, famished and terrified Negro"[58] who told him that he had wandered for nearly a year, by night, under the guidance of the North Star, on his way to Canada, equipped with a crude knife he had fashioned out of a scythe and a "rough-looking" gun.[59] Up until he encountered Eastman, he had avoided talking to people. He was uncertain whether he should acknowledge to Eastman that he was a runaway slave.

Eastman and some friends took him in, fed him and determined to pass him along through other friendly hands to Dr. Dyer in Chicago. They realized that some of their neighbors might see their duty differently, so they proceeded cautiously. They stayed off the main roads, hid their passenger in wagons, moved at night. They worked out a route, paralleling the Illinois and Des Plaines Rivers, that was used frequently later – Ottawa to Northville to Plainfield to Lyons and on to Chicago.

Dr. Dyer was already well known as one of the founders of the Anti-Slavery Society of Illinois. But this act was not about holding a meeting or debating the political leanings of various politicians of the day. There was danger to those who assisted runaways to

DR. CHARLES VOLNEY DYER

Dr. Charles Volney Dyer. June 12, 1808–April 24, 1878. (Chicago History Museum)

escape. Dr. Dyer took the young boy in. Later, he talked to Captain Blake who commanded the steamer *S.S. Illinois* then plying Lake Michigan between Chicago and Detroit, Michigan. Blake was willing to help but he also knew that he could put his business into jeopardy if he were to openly run a slave to Canada and get caught. He also had to be wary of other passengers on board, never knowing whether some might be opposed to the abolitionists' cause.

But Capt. Blake was as intrepid as his friend Dr. Dyer and he devised an appropriate ruse. He hid the boy on his boat and then, when he neared the Canadian shore, he made a tour of the hold and pretended to "discover" a stowaway. He made a tremendous show of being disgusted that someone would put a runaway slave on his boat. He loudly cursed abolitionists. He ordered his boat pulled to the nearest shore so that he could cast the unwanted cargo off his boat. This was done with great fanfare. Of course, the nearest shore by then was Windsor, Canada.

Mission accomplished!

Zebina Eastman, editor of *The Genius of Liberty*, which succeeded Lovejoy's *Alton Observer*. Dr. Dyer lured Eastman to Chicago to become editor of the *Western Citizen*, Chicago's abolitionist newspaper. *Western Citizen* ultimately became the *Chicago Tribune*. (Chicago History Museum)

This was the beginning of an enterprise that would grow over the years. The *S.S. Illinois* and a companion steamer, the *S.S. Great Western*, were "under constant patronage" by Dr. Dyer.[60] As time went on Capt. Blake found other ways to transport fugitives without the charade. Other Chicagoans who were later identified as operators of the Underground Railroad included: Eastman, Philo Carpenter, Alan Pinkerton, L.C.P. Freer, James H. Collins, Calvin DeWolf, Rev. L.F. Bascomb, S.D. Childs, H.L. Fulton, N. Rossiter and J.B. Bradwell.[61]

Of course the "Underground Railroad" was not a subterranean railway train. There were no tunnels or underground tracks. In an era when railroads were carving routes across the land, the name was an apt metaphor. Runaway slaves were handed off from safe house to safe house as they made their way north to freedom. The code was simple: safe houses were referred to as "stations," the anti-slavery sympathizers who helped the fugitives were "conductors" and the runaway slaves were "passengers." The various branches of this network of safe houses and sympathizers operated independent of each other. There was no central governance. It was critical to maintain secrecy. There were laws prohibiting helping slaves escape bondage and there was the danger of encountering "slave-catchers" – bounty hunters who sought the rewards offered for the return of runaways. The Chicagoans learned how to move runaways along their routes staying clear of trouble.

But this activity attracted the attention of slave owners. Worse, it spurred them to enlist allies where they could – and it was an activity that gave momentum to the Southerners' demands to write tougher laws to give them the upper hand when it came to "reclaiming" fugitives. It would not be very long before Dr. Dyer was playing cat and mouse with the local sheriff.

The Case of Phoebe

THE ANTI-SLAVERY SOCIETY met, debated and passed resolutions condemning slavery. Then they published their proceedings in an effort to persuade others that the threat of slavery had to be confronted. One position they took was that if a slave was brought into Illinois by a slave-owner, voluntarily, then the slave should be deemed free. After all, if Illinois was a "Free State," and if the slave was not a fugitive, what other result could there be?

This was not an academic question. Slave-owners brought slaves into Illinois with some regularity. But the answer was not as simple as the Anti-Slavery Society members might have liked. Unfortunately, there were a number of laws that conflicted, many pointing in exactly the opposite direction from the answer that the abolitionists wanted. In fact, the issue produced lawsuits that called forth the State's ablest lawyers. Abraham Lincoln, for example, handled at least four cases involving "runaway slaves." In two cases he represented the side of the "runaway." In the other two, Lincoln represented the slave-owner. How could Lincoln, or any lawyer in Illinois, for that matter, take the side of the slave-owner and suggest that Illinois, a "Free State," allowed slavery?

Back in 1828, the Illinois Supreme Court had decided the case of *Phoebe, a woman of color, versus William Jay.*[62] Phoebe sued Jay claiming battery and false imprisonment. Jay's defense was that in 1814 she had *agreed* to serve as an indentured servant to Jay's father for a period of forty years. Jay's father had died and he was his father's heir. To compel her to perform her duties, "he had necessarily to use a little force and beating...."[63]

Justice Samuel D. Lockwood wrote the opinion for the Court that decided the case. The first issue that he had to consider was whether a law passed by the Indiana Territory's legislature, during the time Illinois was part of the Indiana Territory, was valid. (On May 7, 1800, Congress had split the Northwest Territory into two sections. Everything west of the western border of present-day Ohio became the Indiana Territory.) The Indiana Territory's legislature passed an *Act Concerning the Introduction of Negroes and Mulattos into the Said Territory*, on September 17, 1807. When Illinois became a separate territory in 1809, and later, in 1818 when it became a State, the un-repealed laws of the Indiana Territory were continued in effect.

This law was one of those efforts to evade the command of the Northwest Ordinance that "there shall be no slavery" in the Territory. It provided that a slave-owner could bring a slave into the Territory and appear before the clerk of the court within 30 days and ask the Negro or mulatto to agree that he or she would voluntarily serve as an indentured servant for a term of years.[64]

In deciding the first issue, Justice Lockwood considered this Act to be repugnant to the Northwest Ordinance. He said, "Nothing can be conceived farther from the truth, than the idea that there could be a voluntary contract between the Negro and the master. The law authorizes the master to bring his slave here, and take him before the clerk, and if the Negro will not agree to the terms proposed by the master, he is authorized to remove him to his original place of servitude." This was not a voluntary agreement. It was a choice between two evils – service for a term of

years (probably beyond his or her lifetime) or return to perpetual servitude. But the defect Justice Lockwood grounded his decision on was that the territorial legislature, a creature of the Northwest Ordinance passed by Congress, could not abrogate to itself the power to undo what Congress had done. Justice Lockwood held the provision void because it violated the Northwest Ordinance's command.[65]

But that was not the end of the matter. It was one thing to strike down the law of the territorial legislature when it conflicted with an Act of Congress, but what about the provision in the Illinois Constitution that mimicked that provision?

Lockwood was confronted with the problem that the Constitution of the State of Illinois, adopted on August 26, 1818 in the convention at Kaskaskia, contained virtually the same obnoxious provision, grafted onto the "no slavery" command borrowed from the Northwest Ordinance:

> *Neither slavery or involuntary servitude shall hereafter be introduced into this state, otherwise than for the punishment of crimes ... nor shall any ... person ... be held to serve any person as servant, under any indenture hereafter made,* unless such person shall enter into such indenture while in a state of perfect freedom, and on condition of a bona-fide consideration received....[66]

There were two reasons that this provision was more problematic for Justice Lockwood. First, he viewed a constitution as establishing the fundamental law, the "fixed will" of the people acting in their sovereign capacity. Whatever condition is assigned to any portion of the people (*i.e.,* slaves reclassified as indentured servants) he viewed as "irrevocably fixed, however unjust in principle it may be."[67] The second problem was that the State constitution was submitted to Congress and accepted when Illinois applied for Statehood. If Congress could outlaw slavery in a Territory, as it did in the Northwest Ordinance, it could repeal that provision, which is what it effectively did when it admitted Illinois as a State.[68] Phoebe's fate was to continue to be an "indentured servant," a euphemism for being a slave, the "voluntary" kind of slavery that Illinois would tolerate.

There were other possible avenues that Justice Lockwood considered that might have led to a decision favorable to Phoebe. The indenture could have been found void under the Indiana territorial law and not revived by the Illinois Constitution. Or, he could have determined that proof of its voluntariness was deficient, *a la* Judge Harrington (the Vermont jurist who declared the proof insufficient to issue a warrant). He did neither. Clearly Lockwood regarded the ritual of a voluntary agreement to become an indentured servant to be a fiction. He felt compelled to give effect to another provision in the Illinois Constitution, one that commanded that "voluntary indentures" be honored:

> *Each and every person who has been bound to service by contract or indenture in virtue of the law of Illinois Territory … without fraud or collusion, shall be held to a specific performance of their contracts or indentures; and such Negroes and mulattoes as have been registered in conformity with the aforesaid laws, shall serve out the time appointed by said laws.*[69]

Thus, Lockwood upheld the voluntary indenture claim.

So, as of 1828, the "Free State" of Illinois recognized and enforced slavery when a slave-owner could plausibly claim compliance with the "voluntary indenture" exception.[70]

Lockwood was well aware of strength of the sentiment in Illinois that favored slavery. He was Attorney General in 1821 and an ally of Governor Edward Coles. (Coles had been private secretary to President Madison from 1809 to 1815.) Coles and Lockwood led the fight to defeat the call for a constitutional convention in 1824 that was aimed at making Illinois a Slave State. The call for the convention was defeated 6,640 to 4,972.[71] Illinois narrowly escaped becoming a Slave State.

Here was the legal intersection between Free and Slave States. Illinois lawyers like Lincoln would study these decisions intently. They not only needed to be able to craft arguments in court when representing a runaway or a slave-owner, they also had to navigate a path for clients whose business activities crossed borders or whose dealings brought them into contact with others who did.

Between 1825 and 1860, the Illinois Supreme Court decided at least 18 other cases involving slavery. As in the *Phoebe* case, Illinois considered slaves "persons" and gave them access to the State's court system. But the results in these cases were mixed, reflecting the confusion created by laws that pointed in opposite directions. Sometimes the Court sided with the slave; sometimes with the slave-owner.[72]

Other Illinois Supreme Court Decisions on Slavery Prior to 1850

PRIOR TO 1850, when Congress passed a strengthened Fugitive Slave Act, which essentially preempted the States' ability to tinker with rules governing runaway slaves, the Illinois Supreme Court decided a series of cases concerning the status of "indentured servants," whether they could be sold to satisfy a debt and what the consequences were if someone helped a slave escape. In one early case, also in 1828, the Court held that "Nance, a girl of color" (*i.e.*, a slave) was "property" that a judgment creditor could execute against. The sheriff could sell her to satisfy a debt.[73] Similarly, the Court decided that the right to an "indentured servant's" services could be assigned.[74] Indentured servants could be rented out.

On the other side of the ledger, in one case, the Court affirmed a judgment based on a jury's verdict *finding for* "Moses, a man of color," who sued for false imprisonment, assault and battery.[75] He was awarded $30. The Court considered Moses "by virtue of our constitution … a free man, [who] had a right to hire himself to whom he pleased." He was entitled to sue for services rendered.[76] In the 1836 case of *Choisser v.*

Hargrave, the Court recognized that slave-owners could claim the right of service from properly registered indentured servants, but held for "Hargrave, a man of color," because Choisser (the owner) could not prove he had complied with the requirement that he register the indenture within 30 days.[77] Hargrave went free.[78]

In the case of *Boon v. Juliet*, the Court was confronted with the question of whether the children of properly registered indentured servants were born free or owed service because of the proviso in the Illinois Constitution that decreed that children born of indentured servants "shall become free, the males at the age of 21 years, the females at the age of 18 years."[79] Did this provision mean that children owed service before reaching respectively 21 years of age or 18? No. The Court held that children were born free, reasoning that the proviso was intended to limit any supposed greater period of service. The proviso did not create an obligation of service.

Then, in *Jarrott v. Jarrott*, the Court held that any person born in Illinois after the Northwest Ordinance was enacted was born free, even though descended from slaves owned by one of the original French settlers, who had resided in Illinois in 1769 (before the Ordinance).[80] While the French permitted slavery in the province of Louisiana (per an edict of Louis XV in 1723), as did Great Britain and Virginia, Congress could abolish slavery, as it did in the Northwest Ordinance. It had the power to do this irrespective of the stipulation that the "titles and possessions, rights and liberties" of the French settlers were guaranteed to them in the deed by which Virginia ceded its claim to the Illinois Territory to the United States.[81]

The *Jarrott* case closed a loophole: the practice of considering "French Negroes" – *i.e.*, those descended from the slaves of French settlers residing in Illinois before the Northwest Ordinance – to be slaves irrespective of the Ordinance.

The abolitionists could take comfort in the fact that putative indentured servants – slaves – were given access to the Illinois court system. They could also take comfort in the fact that juries and judges would, on occasion, find for a plaintiff such as "Moses, a man of color," or "Hargrave, a man of color." They could also

rejoice that children of slaves born in Illinois would be deemed to be free. That result fit perfectly with the sentiments of the gradualists. However, the fact remained that the State's judicial system was in the business of enforcing the institution of slavery. While the Illinois Supreme Court decided only a handful of cases involving fugitive slave issues, because only a fraction of cases filed and litigated are appealed and reach the high court, there were obviously many more cases in the trial courts. Cases involving slaves, and the collateral legal issues arising from the ownership of that kind of "property," were a staple of the lawyer's practice. This explains how it was that Lincoln, like many other Illinois lawyers, handled this type of case.

Harboring Runaway Slaves

ILLINOIS MADE HARBORING a runaway slave a crime. In 1843, in the case of *Eells v. Illinois*, the Illinois Supreme Court was called upon to decide whether: (1) this law was constitutional, (2) whether it conflicted with the federal enactment covering the same subject, and, if the Court got past those issues, (3) what evidence was needed to convict.[82] Dr. Richard Eells of Quincy, Illinois, had been accused of harboring a slave who had run away from his Missouri owner to Adams County, Illinois. Eells was convicted in a trial before Judge Stephen A. Douglas, another Illinois lawyer who would soon have a much bigger role to play in the battle over how, if at all, slavery should be limited.

The trial was fairly straightforward. Eells was essentially caught red-handed. On August 21, 1842, a slave named "Charley" escaped from his master in Monticello, Missouri.[83] He swam across the Mississippi River! A free Negro named Barryman Barnett who was a look-out for the Underground Railroad took him to Dr. Eells's home four blocks from the river. Eells hurriedly hitched up his carriage to drive him out of town ahead of the posse that was coming and gave him a change of clothes. (The Missourians had seen the escape attempt and lost no time coming after the fugitive.) When Eells saw the posse coming after them, he told the Charley to run for it through a corn field. Charley hid in Samuel Pearson's stable. Eells drove home. A few hours later, the fugitive was cornered in a barn and taken back to Missouri. His fate remains unknown. The sheriff came after Eells. In the excitement, Eells had neglected to throw out Charley's wet clothes. The sheriff found the wet clothes in Eells's carriage and a lathered horse. So, at trial, Eells was convicted based on identification of his carriage (which had been seen by the pursuers), the wet clothes, the lathered horse and the change of clothes Charley was found in (which were traced to Eells). Eells was fined $400.

Eells's appeal to the Illinois Supreme Court did not dispute the facts. Eells's lawyer, George C. Dixon, made an argument that the Anti-Slavery Society members surely applauded. He argued that "Free States are under no legal obligation to furnish the legal means to reclaim fugitive slaves." He reasoned that Illinois was not under any "constitutional obligation to lend her courts and judges, or magistrates, to aid a law of Congress concerning fugitive slaves."

The Attorney General for the State of Illinois, J.A. McDougall, responded that the last argument was "an absurdity" because the federal constitution was the supreme law of the land and it placed "an obligation … upon the entire government, and each and every of its integral parts; to aid in the enforcement of that right [of an owner to pursue and recapture his slave]."

A divided court upheld the conviction. Justice Shields, writing for the majority, held that the Illinois law did not conflict with the federal law. In fact, he cited an earlier United States Supreme Court opinion by Chief Justice Taney who, in concurring, had construed the Constitution's "shall be delivered up" phrase to imply a duty on the States to pass laws like the Illinois law:

> *The words of the article directing that the fugitive shall be delivered up, seem evidently designed to impose it as a duty upon the people of the several states to pass laws to carry into execution, in good faith, the compact into which they thus solemnly entered with each other.*[84]

Eells stood convicted of "harboring and secreting" under Illinois law.[85]

The Illinois law on harboring fugitives was not the only peril that someone helping a runaway slave faced. Dr. Eells was also *indicted* by the Grand Jury of Lewis County, Missouri for abducting slaves, and that State sought to extradite him from Illinois.[86] The Grand Jurors said the act was committed in Missouri, though Eells claimed he had never been in Missouri. A warrant was issued by the Governor of Missouri asking the Governor Ford of Illinois to arrest Eells and deliver him to the Missouri authorities. Eells was tipped off that this was under way and fled – *on the underground railway* – to Chicago. (He may have been "harbored" by Dr. Dyer, but there is no record one way or the other.) Fortunately, the Governor of Illinois was persuaded to quash the warrant and Eells returned to Quincy.

As to his conviction for "harboring," Eells sought to appeal to the United States Supreme Court. The $400 fine was not a crippling amount to him. He was a substantial land owner. But there was a principle that he wanted to vindicate. Like the other abolitionists in Illinois, he chafed at the idea that citizens of Illinois could be *compelled* to help recapture fugitive slaves. This is what he thought the law against harboring fugitives did. He thought the Illinois law should be struck down as unconstitutional so that Illinois could decide for itself whether to be Slave or Free and what the consequences of choosing to be Free meant. As a Free State, Eells thought Illinois should be a haven.

Eells hired Salmon P. Chase to argue his appeal. (Chase, a staunch abolitionist, later was Lincoln's rival for the Presidential nomination in 1860, then Secretary of the Treasury in Lincoln's cabinet and, ultimately, appointed by Lincoln to be Chief Justice.) Unfortunately, this quest did not succeed. The appeal took 10 years, dissipated Eells's resources, and contributed to his declining health.[87] The Supreme Court affirmed his conviction in 1852.[88] This was a little late, for Eells had died in 1846. Earlier in that year, the Illinois branch of the Liberty Party, the first political party formed by the abolitionists, nominated Eells as its candidate for Governor of Illinois. Eells was nominated "without a dissenting voice, and with the hearty concurrence of the friends in all parts of the State, as evidence of their attachment and confidence in, and sympathy for him in the persecutions he had been called to endure."[89]

During Eells's lifetime, Quincy was a cauldron of abolitionism. The town was aptly named after John Quincy Adams, who led the cause to limit slavery for many years. Eells's home at 415 Jersey Street was sometimes called "Stop Number One" on the Underground Railroad on the way to Chicago.

There were other incidents at the southern end of the railroad reflecting the constant friction between the Missouri slave owners and their Quincy neighbors. The Anti-Slavery Society's resolutions in 1842 included a condemnation of Missouri for imprisoning three citizens of Illinois – Allison Work,[90] George Thompson and James E. Burr. Thompson and Burr were missionaries in training at the Mission Institute, two miles east of Quincy. (Mission Institute was founded by David Nelson, the fiery abolitionist preacher who had influenced Lovejoy when Nelson was in St. Louis. The Institute was considered a breeding place for abolitionists.) Work was the father of children who attended the school. He and the other two had crossed the Mississippi River in an attempt "to assist some slaves to obtain their inalienable rights."[91] They had previously made several trips to preach to slaves. On this occasion they were supposed to meet two slaves and take them across the river. Instead they were lured into a trap. When they met the slaves and started toward the river the slaveholders rose out of the grass with rifles pointed at them. They were marched off, tied up and locked in a jail to await trial. There was no law on the books in Missouri expressly prohibiting preaching to slaves or encouraging them to escape, but this did not slow matters down. The "Quincy Three" were indicted for stealing slaves and attempting to steal slaves. They were tried and convicted of "Grand Larceny."[92] Tempers were so hot that a scaffold had been erected near the courthouse.[93] They were sentenced to 12 years each in the Missouri Penitentiary.[94] This episode became a cause célèbre for Chicago's abolitionist newspaper *Western Citizen*, the spiritual successor to Lovejoy's *Alton Observer*, which thought Missouri's "Lynch Code" an abomination for making criminal what *Western Citizen* regarded as free speech. The way *Western Citizen* saw it, Missouri made it criminal "to tell a man when your opinion is asked, that you think he will better his circumstances by removing into the State of Illinois, and offering to convey him across in your own boat…."[95]

If this prosecution was supposed to curb the activities of the abolitionists and terrify would-be fugitives, it had the opposite effect.

That is probably why, on March 8, 1843, some proslavery men from Missouri crossed the river and set the Mission Institute on fire. They managed to touch off a cache of gunpowder being stored in the chapel, causing an enormous explosion, lighting the night sky for miles.[96] The symbolism was unintended, but this episode confirmed what the Illinois abolitionists already knew – abolitionism was an incendiary issue.

The Chicago Harboring Evasion

D R. DYER WAS clearly aware of the Illinois law. If he was going to help slaves escape, he had to be prepared to answer to it. He came up with his own ingenious solution. The Illinois law provided:

If any person shall harbor or secrete any Negro, mulatto, or person of color, the same being a slave or servant, owing service or labor … [he] shall be deemed guilty of a misdemeanor and fined not exceeding five hundred dollars, or imprisoned not exceeding six months.[97]

Taking the extreme view that "harboring" meant "fraudulent concealment," Dr. Dyer's answer was to *openly* house his "visitors." In fact, he would pay his guests, employing them to run errands for him while they awaited transit on to Canada. (The steamer *Great Western*'s schedule had it departing from Chicago approximately every two weeks for Buffalo, New York.) There was then nothing "secret" about where they were. So, arguably, he was not "harboring" a runaway slave.[98]

This worked for a while. But there were other perils from this openness, as Dr. Dyer would soon discover.

Lincoln's Path to Becoming a Lawyer

ABRAHAM LINCOLN ACTIVELY practiced law from 1836 to 1861. The extent to which the laws upholding slavery were then part of the warp and woof of a lawyer's practice is exemplified by the cases he handled.

That Lincoln became a lawyer – and such a prominent one – was an extraordinary feat. His father was illiterate.[99] As a youth, he was expected to work his father's farm and handle the laborious chores piled on him. In fact, his father hired him out to work for others. From 1816 to 1830, from the age of seven until Lincoln reached the age of 21, the family lived on a farm in Southern Indiana, 16 miles north of the Ohio River near Little Pigeon Creek in Perry (later Spencer) County.

Lincoln had less than a year of formal schooling. His mother, Nancy Hanks Lincoln died in 1818 of "milk sickness," a disease contracted from drinking the milk of cows that had ingested white snakeroot, a toxic weed. Lincoln was nine years old.

In 1819, Thomas Lincoln married Sarah Bush, a widow, and the family continued to live in Indiana until 1830 when they moved to Illinois about 75 miles east of Springfield. Sarah was the one who inspired young Abe in his quest to learn, encouraging him to read. In the time he could spare, he devoured every book that he could get his hands on. Thus, he read and re-read, the Bible, *Aesop's Fables*, the poetry of Robert Burns,

The Grave of Nancy Hanks Lincoln, Mother of Abraham Lincoln, Lincoln State Park, Indiana

Abraham Lincoln's mother, Nancy Hanks Lincoln, died in 1818, when he was nine years old. (Private Collection)

GEOGRAPHICAL, STATISTICAL, AND HISTORICAL MAP OF INDIANA.

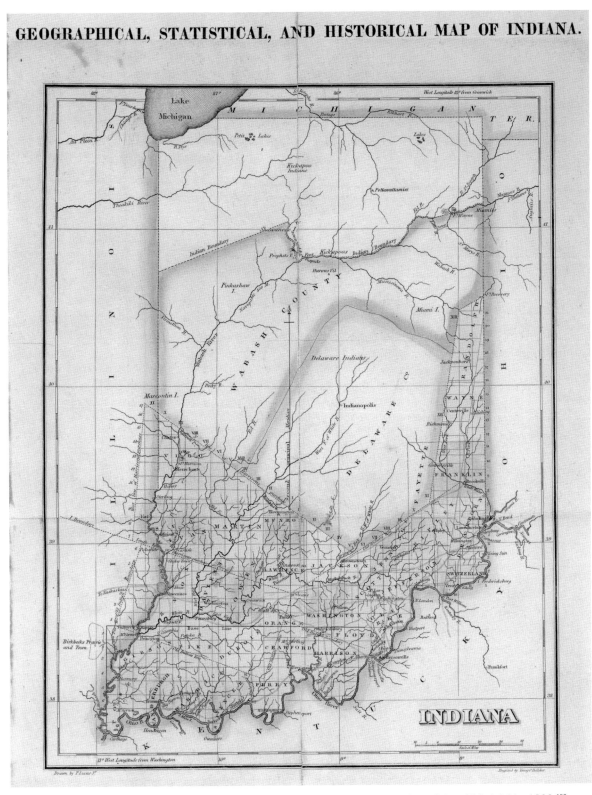

Abraham Lincoln and his family lived near Little Pigeon Creek in Perry County, Indiana from 1816 to 1830 when he moved to Illinois. Map from Carey & Lea, Philadelphia, 1822.[100] (Chicago History Museum)

Thomas Lincoln, Abraham Lincoln's father. (Courtesy of the Abraham Lincoln Library and Museum of Lincoln Memorial University, Harrogate, Tennessee)

Sarah Bush Johnston Lincoln was a widow when she married Thomas Lincoln in 1819. She is the one who encouraged young Abe to read. (Chicago History Museum)

and the plays of William Shakespeare. He even borrowed a copy of the *Indiana Revised Statutes* which he pored over. This gave him a chance to read and ponder the meaning of the Declaration of Independence, the Constitution, the Northwest Ordinance, and the laws of the Indiana Territory.[101]

When the family moved to Illinois in 1830, Abe was 21 and it was time to strike out on his own. He began by organizing a flatboat trip to New Orleans, ferrying merchandise down the Sangamon, Illinois and Mississippi Rivers. He returned to New Salem and settled into the life of that community with an assortment of jobs. Here he began his study of the law in earnest. He was encouraged by John T. Stuart and would ride to Stuart's office in Springfield, 20 miles away, to borrow books on the law. He borrowed *Blackstone's Commentaries on the Law of England*, and, similarly, read this exposition of the common law until he thoroughly understood the principles involved. These were his guideposts. He was entirely self-taught. He was granted a license to practice on September 9,

1836 and admitted to the bar by the Illinois Supreme Court on March 1, 1837.

Lincoln became a trial lawyer and he excelled at trying cases. Arguing to juries and making an occasional appellate argument called forth his penchant for telling a good story, a skill he had honed in his youth when he mimicked the stories told at family gatherings and recited Shakespeare to the delight of other youngsters. He learned how to frame the issue that the jury was asked to decide. He recognized early on that how the question is framed can influence what the answer will be.

Lincoln traveled on a circuit, as did the other trial lawyers of his day, regularly appearing in different court houses. Twice a year he traveled to the 14 counties that made up the Eighth Judicial Circuit.[102] The circuit consisted of 14 counties in the center of the State – Sangamon, Tazewell, Woodford, McLean, Logan, DeWitt, Piatt, Champaign, Vermilion, Edgar, Shelby, Moultrie, Macon, and Christian.

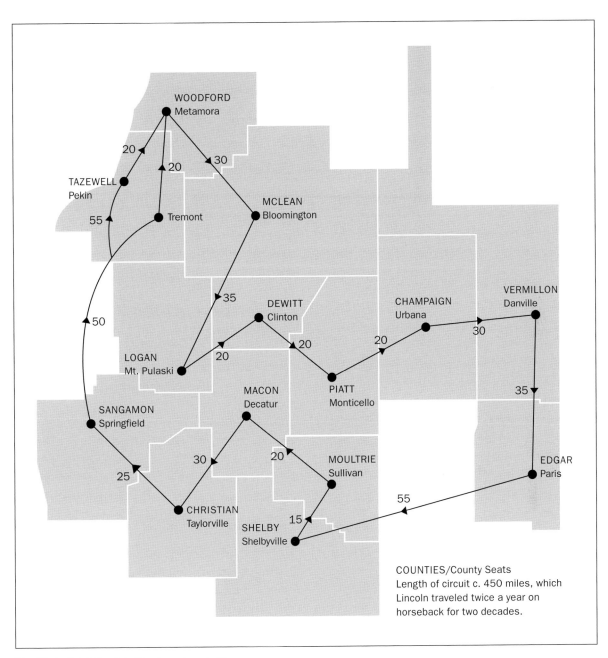

The 8th Judicial Circuit in Illinois as traveled by
Abraham Lincoln in 1850.[103] (Private Collection)

To travel around the circuit entailed a trip of approximately 450 miles. As his reputation grew, he was sought out by litigants across the State.

Lincoln's Role in Fugitive Slave Cases

LINCOLN HAD SOME involvement with at least six cases involving fugitive slaves. His law partner, William H. Herndon, whom Lincoln called "Billy," was involved with two others. Here is the known record:[104]

In 1845, Lincoln signed the sheriff's return on a writ of *habeas corpus* in an action known as *Ex Parte Warman*. (A writ of *habeas corpus*, known as the Great Writ, is a judicial command to a prison official that a prisoner be brought before the court so that it can be determined whether he is imprisoned lawfully or should be released from custody.) Warman, a Negro, was arrested while traveling through Illinois, on suspicion of being a runaway. The court ruled in his favor on the petition for the writ of *habeas corpus* and he was freed. Lincoln's role, beyond signing the return, is unknown.

In *People v. Pond*, also in 1845, Lincoln and Herndon were retained by Pond, who was accused of harboring the fugitive slave John Hauley. Pond was found not guilty. Lincoln and Herndon received $5 for their legal services.[105]

The cases in which Lincoln represented the slave-owner were *In re Bryant* and *Martin v. Rutherford*.

Abraham Lincoln,   W. H. Herndon.
LINCOLN & HERNDON, Attornies and Counsellors at Law, will practice in the Courts of Law and Chancery in this State.

Abraham Lincoln and William H. Herndon announced their law practice in Illinois. (Private Collection)

Lincoln was retained by Matson who brought five slaves into Illinois in 1845. In 1847, he planned to take them back to Kentucky. Jane Bryant and her children claimed they were free because they had been brought to a Free State. Matson enlisted the sheriff to arrest them as fugitives. Bryant had sought refuge from Ashmore and Rutherford. Ashmore filed a petition for *habeas corpus* on Bryant's behalf. Lincoln, representing the slave-owner, argued that the slaves were "in transit" and that under the doctrine of "comity," slave-owners could use their slaves for labor in Illinois and then take them back to, in this case, Kentucky. (Apparently, Matson had not registered his slaves as indentured servants and could not rely on the indentured servant exception to the Illinois ban on slavery.) In the Bryant case, the court ruled for Bryant, setting her and her children free.[106] So, Lincoln lost.

In 1848, in *Matson v. Rutherford*, Lincoln again represented Matson, who had sued Rutherford for harboring five slaves. The case was dismissed, probably based on Matson's lack of success in the companion case.

Lincoln also handled cases on appeal and argued one case involving slavery in the Illinois Supreme Court. In *Bailey v. Cromwell*,[107] Lincoln represented Bailey, who sought to avoid paying on a note. Bailey argued that the note was part of a transaction in which he had purchased a slave from Cromwell and that, as part of the transaction, Cromwell had agreed to provide proof that "Nance" was his property, lawfully bound to serve him as a slave or indentured servant. Nance had been delivered to Bailey but Cromwell died never having delivered any papers to show she was his property. Later, claiming she was free, Nance took off. The administrator for Cromwell's estate sued to collect on the note. At trial Cromwell's administrator was awarded $431.97. But the Supreme Court reversed, agreeing with Lincoln's argument, based on the Northwest Ordinance, that Nance was to be presumed free and the burden was on the administrator to prove she was not.[108] While the Supreme Court's opinion was written by Justice Breese, Stephen A. Douglas was also a member of the court at the time and also agreed with Lincoln's argument.[109] Lincoln and Douglas would not be in agreement on the issue of slavery the next time they encountered one another.

There are two other cases, *People v. Kern* (1847) and *People v. Scott* (1847), in which Lincoln represented two men who were accused of harboring a slave. Lincoln argued that there was no proof that the Negro in each case was a fugitive slave, and he won both cases.[110]

Slaves "In Transit" and the Doctrine of "Comity"

THE ARGUMENT THAT Lincoln invoked in the *Bryant* case was actually one that the Illinois Supreme Court had recognized in an earlier decision in 1843. In *Willard v. Illinois*, the defendant was charged with "secreting a woman of color owing service to a resident of Louisiana."[111] Willard was convicted and sentenced to pay $20. Justice Scates, for the majority, wrote an opinion rejecting Willard's challenge to the constitutionality of the Illinois law. He held that it did not conflict with federal law and reflected a proper exercise of the State's police power:

> … *to preserve quiet and order in our own community, to protect us from vagabond, or pauper slaves; to punish or prevent them from entering our territory, if we think proper; to forbid it, or punish those who may encourage them to come, or harbor or secrete them….*

Justice Scates pointed out that Illinois had "hundreds of miles of contiguous boundary with Missouri and Kentucky" and needed to protect its citizens from brawls and breaches of the peace that might arise "from the influx of that unwelcome population."

The slave in question, Julia, escaped without her owner's consent when being brought from Kentucky, through Illinois, on the owner's way to Louisiana. If a slave "in transit" were to be declared free simply by traveling through Illinois, then Willard's

conviction could not stand. But the Court ruled otherwise. "Comity," the judicial doctrine that one State should respect another's laws, meant that Illinois must uphold the slavery laws of its sister States and enforce that right of a slave-holder to travel with his slaves through a Free State.

This was an especially controversial stance at the time and one that surely upset the Anti-Slavery Society members. Slavery was under attack around the world. The slave trade was outlawed as nations embraced the view that abducting people and relegating them to slavery was simple "piracy." If so, then it follows that to trade in slaves was to become an accessory after the fact to piracy. Illinois followed the common law of England and therefore cases decided by English courts were regularly cited as precedents that Illinois courts should follow if there were no existing precedent by an Illinois court. Justice Scates recognized that England did not enforce the doctrine of comity with regard to slavery. (In England, a slave reaching England was free and would not be returned to a country where slavery was legal.) But Scates concluded that allowing free and safe passage to slave-owners was not a violation of the Illinois Constitution's ban on slavery. It was not the "introduction of slavery" into the State. He thought a right of transit was essential to keeping the peace. To conclude otherwise would "destroy the common bond of union amongst us."

Justice Lockwood was clearly uncomfortable expanding the domain of slavery in Illinois. He reluctantly agreed that slaves "in transit" had to be another exception but took a different route to reach that conclusion. He thought the doctrine of comity gave judges discretion as to which laws of other States should be recognized and that there were other considerations that outweighed comity. He thought sustaining relations with our sister States should not be analogized to the law of nations. After all, the Constitution bound us into a Union. Lockwood took the view that "whatever injures one state injures the others. It is consequently our duty to consult the good of all the States, and so frame and administer our laws, that we give our sister States no real cause of offence." Lockwood's struggle to reach this result was a classic example of the dilemma facing the citizens of Free States who abhorred slavery: What accommodation to slavery was necessary and proper to maintain the union? How far did the citizens of Free States have to go?

So, by 1843, it was settled that Illinois would allow slavery (of a sort) where the "indenture" registration had been complied with and in the case of slaves "in transit."

How many people in Illinois were indentured servants or slaves? The decennial census reports for Illinois, between 1810 and 1840, recorded a slave population as follows:

1810   168
1820   917
1830   747
1840   331[112]

Do these numbers delineate the full extent to which slaves or "voluntary" indentured servants lived in Illinois? Not necessarily. There were other public records hinting at the size of this population – property tax records (slaves and indentured servants were taxed as property), registrations of indentures, probated wills devising indentured servants as property, divorce proceedings dividing up property, etc. As of 2004, Jesse White, the Illinois Secretary of State and State Archivist, had compiled a database of 3,400 names found in government records involving servitude and emancipation from 1722 through 1863.[113]

The "Free Negro" Population in Chicago in 1840

IN THE 1840 Census of Cook County, 11,055 people were counted. The census reported its count in three broad categories: Free White Male Persons, Free White Female Persons, and Negroes.[114] The count of the Negro population was further subdivided between: Free male persons of color of all ages, Free female persons of color of all ages, Indentured or registered servants and their children, and French Negroes and mulattos held in bondage. With regard to the Negro population, the tabulation showed 36 Free male persons of color, 28 Free female persons of color, no indentured or registered servants, and no "French Negroes." Most of the Negro population, according to the census, resided in Chicago in the second ward.

While Illinois could boast of a vibrant abolitionist community, an active Anti-Slavery Society and a cadre of people willing to help slaves escape bondage, the "Free Negro" faced many obstacles and was not welcomed with open arms. Justice Skates had intimated as much when he spoke of the need to pass laws to protect the citizens of Illinois from "the influx of *that unwelcome population*."

Dr. Dyer, his Medical Practice and his Vision for Chicago

HOW DID DR. Dyer avoid becoming a farmer in Vermont, the path his father and his brother Enos had followed? During his early years, working on his father's farm until he was 15, he showed a great aptitude and was sent to Castleton Academy. Possibly the family thought he should train for the ministry, or perhaps law. His mother's family included distinguished judges in Vermont's early days. But rather than study to become a preacher, he gravitated to the sciences and, as mentioned above, enrolled in the medical department at Castleton, graduating in 1832 with a degree from Middlebury College.[115]

Dr. Dyer had an early brush with a mob and "faced their shotguns" during his student years when the "Churchill riots" occurred. Students of anatomy in those days did not have a ready supply of cadavers to dissect for study. As a result, the old barbarous practice of robbing fresh graves flourished. A recently departed's remains would mysteriously disappear. As Dr. Dyer would later quip, it was a "grave offense."

In this case, some enterprising students stole the body of a recently deceased young lady named Churchill from Hubbardton, a neighboring town. There was no evidence that Dyer had a hand in the mischief. Her relatives and neighbors descended on the Academy with a fury. They had shotguns and muskets "that had not been fired since the revolution." They demanded to search the Academy. Their numbers and the fact that they were armed made any resistance futile. It was not long before the searchers discovered Churchill's body. But as the students panicked and tempers raged Dyer stood and faced the mob with a "do your worst" indifference that calmed everyone down.[116] This would not be the last time that Dyer's *sangfroid* served him well.

Dr. Dyer began medical practice in New Jersey, but he was too adventuresome to settle down to a staid medical practice there. He headed to the west and chose Chicago before others saw the inevitable growth that would come. He started as the physician to the garrison at Fort Dearborn which helped him establish a thriving medical practice. He boarded at the Tremont House and ate dinners there with two other doctors from the early days, Drs. Philip Maxwell and William Bradshaw Egan. The three doctors recognized the future potential of the city and each astutely bought and developed real estate. They developed rows of buildings on Dearborn and Clark Streets that soon housed lawyers, doctors, judges and other professionals, and undoubtedly housed shops as well. They made fortunes in 1833 and 1834.

Dr. Dyer's brother, Enos, in Vermont, noting his brother's success wrote and asked that he repay a loan. The doctor offered to give him a lot valued at $8 a foot on Monroe Street. Enos, a large landowner in Vermont, was offended to be offered this trifle. He responded that he bought land by the mile, but did not expect to be buying land in an Illinois mud-hole by the foot.[117] The debt was undoubtedly repaid, but not with Chicago real estate.

Dr. Dyer was a prominent member of the "Lyceum," Chicago's first library which was organized in 1834, had 300 volumes, and was the center of intellectual and social activities in the growing city.[118] "It was the

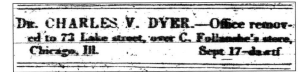

On July 14, 1846, Dr. Dyer announced his office move from State Street to Lake Street in the *Western Citizen*. (Chicago History Museum)

foremost institution in the city…. Not a man of note … who had any taste for intellectual and social enjoyment, who loved books, conversation and debate but who belonged to the Lyceum."[119] Dr. Dyer had a particular fondness for poetry and could quote long passages from memory.

In 1836, Dr. Dyer was financially ruined by the "Panic and Depression of 1836," as was just about everyone else in Chicago. This was the economic calamity that followed from President Jackson's refusal to renew the charter of the Second Bank of the United States and his executive order requiring that purchases of federal lands be paid for in gold or silver coin. His intention was to dampen rampant speculation, but the effect was to propel the nation into a depression as banks that had issued paper money could not back it up with gold or silver.

Dr. Dyer had his medical practice to fall back on and, over time, recovered.[120] In 1839, Dr. Dyer shared offices with another doctor, Levi D. Boone. In 1846, he moved his offices to 73 Lake Street "over C. Follansbee's store."

The practice of medicine meant combating fever and ague, usually with calomel and quinine. However, there were also occasional bouts of cholera which were inevitably deadly. Dr. Dyer was philosophical about the limits of his and the medical profession's knowledge of this disease. He told the story of the arrival of a ship with 18 cases of cholera aboard:

Deeming it requisite to establish a quarantine to prevent the introduction of the disease, we organized an amateur board of health, and hired a warehouse to be used as a hospital…. On viewing the sick, nine were decided to be beyond medical aid, and the remaining moiety were decreed to be favorable subjects for pathological skill; but unfortunately, the nine upon whom we lavished all the resources of science died, and those who were esteemed to be about in articulo mortis *all got well.*[121]

In spite of a mixed record of success, Chicago was destined to become a major center for the advancement of medical science. Rush Medical College had been granted a charter in 1837 and opened in 1843 with 22 students.[122] Dr. Dyer was a member of its faculty. County Hospital opened in 1847.

Dr. Dyer was one of the leaders of the medical profession who met in Springfield on June 9, 1840 and issued a call for a convention of physicians in the State to meet on December 1 to form a State medical society. In their open letter to members of the medical profession they excoriated the activities of "charlatan practitioners," declared war on "mountebanks" and dedicated themselves to improving the profession by "diffusing true and useful medical knowledge."[123]

In 1837, Dr. Dyer married Louisa M. Gifford, the sister of James T. Gifford, the founder of Elgin. She possessed "great energy, integrity and force of character, and exerted a strong influence over the doctor" aiding him in his anti-slavery endeavors. Between 1841 and 1851 they had six children, three of whom survived to adulthood (Stella, Charles G. and Louis). They also adopted a daughter, Cornelia.[124] He had a residence on State Street, near Randolph and to re-establish his real estate business, rented lots on Randolph Street, with a clause that allowed him to purchase the lots. There he put up inexpensive buildings for rent. He had a keen eye and continued to see opportunities others did not. He bet on the city expanding. He ventured to buy property beyond the existing confines of the city – and he prospered from his foresight. A fire swept away everything he built on Randolph Street and he was despondent. He thought he might be ruined. But the insurance proceeds and borrowing allowed him to rebuild. A second fire again destroyed his property. Once again insurance and borrowing allowed him to rebuild and he built sturdier buildings. He prospered from the rents and exercised his purchase clauses. Ultimately, he sold the lots to the United States government for a post office and customs house site. His foresight paid off. For the lots he bought where the post office was later built he paid $450. One year later, he sold the property to the United States government for $46,000![125]

He quipped that he had to be "ruined twice" to make his fortune.

Owen Lovejoy

WHILE DR. DYER and his friends in Chicago were fighting slavery by arranging transportation to Canada for fugitives that got to Chicago, they depended on a network of "stations" run by "conductors" to supply them with passengers. One prominent conductor was Owen Lovejoy. Stella Dyer, Dr. Dyer's daughter, said her earliest recollections as a child were visits by Owen Lovejoy to their home in Chicago.[126]

Born January 6, 1811, nine years younger than his brother Elijah, Owen joined Elijah in Illinois to help with the printing of the *Alton Observer* in Alton. After Elijah's death, he tried to get the American Anti-Slavery Society to raise money to keep the *Alton Observer* going. That did not happen. But the Society did commission a memoir to be written by Owen and Joseph Lovejoy recounting their brother's life. The brothers went to New York and authored *Memoir of the Reverend Elijah Lovejoy, Who Was Murdered in Defence of The Liberty of The Press at Alton, Illinois, November 7, 1837*. The volume included a forward by former President John Quincy Adams.

This memoir became an important milestone in the fight against slavery. Owen returned to Illinois with 1,000 copies, 500 intended for sale in Chicago and 500 in Alton.[127] He then embarked on studying to become an Episcopal minister. He was prepared to be ordained in Jacksonville in 1838. That never happened. On the day before his expected ordination the bishop asked that he sign a pledge not to discuss abolition. Lovejoy refused.[128]

The following labels appear on the map:

CHICAGO RIVER

PIER NO 1
PIER NO 2
PIER NO 3

S. WATER
LAKE
RANDOLPH
WASHINGTON
MADISON
MONROE
ADAMS
JACKSON
VAN BUREN
HARRISON
POLK
TAYLOR
12TH

S. MARKET
S. FRANKLIN
FIFTH
LASALLE
S. CLARK
DEARBORN
S. STATE
S. WABASH
MICHIGAN

SHERMAN
PACIFIC

HUBBARD PL.
PECK PL.
ELDRIDGE PL.
HARMON PL.

LAKE FRONT PARK

1. Ft. Dearborn
2. The Courthouse
3. The Saloon building
4. Site of The Wigwam
5. Mansion House
6. Site of Tremont House
7. Dyer's office
8. Dyer's residence
9. *Western Citizen*'s Offices
10. L.C.P. Freer residence
11. Calvin DeWolf residence
12. First Tribune Building
13. Zebina Eastman's residence

Chicago's First Ward as it appeared in the mid-1800s.

Owen Lovejoy, younger brother of Elijah Lovejoy, was a conductor for the Underground Railroad. (Chicago History Museum)

He went to Princeton, Illinois where he soon became a minister in the Hampshire Colony Congregational Church at a salary of $600 per year, a position he held for 17 years.[129]

Owen Lovejoy shared his brother, Elijah's, abhorrence for slavery and wasted no time putting his abolitionist convictions to work. He preached against slavery not just in Princeton, but in other churches to which he was invited. When the Third Presbyterian Church of Chicago split in the 1850s, Philo Carpenter led the dissenters to form the First Congregational Church of Chicago. This church was derisively called the "nigger church." Owen Lovejoy was proud to preach to its Negro and white congregation.[130]

With his abolitionist pedigree and his strong convictions it was no surprise that Owen Lovejoy was a conductor on the Underground Railroad. But he stood out from others because he flaunted his actions.

He courted danger by conducting this activity in the open. He maintained a "station" and regularly passed fugitive slaves on to Dr. Dyer, Carpenter and Eastman.

Lovejoy's Indictment

THROUGHOUT ILLINOIS AND in Bureau County, a county 90 miles to the west of Chicago, where Lovejoy lived, there were plenty of people who were not just unsympathetic to the abolitionists but were ardently proslavery. Lovejoy's activities and the vibrancy of the Underground Railroad galled them. In May of 1843, Norman Purple of Peoria pressed charges against Lovejoy for harboring slaves. Lovejoy was indicted for harboring Nancy and Agnes, supposed runaways. The States Attorney, Benjamin F. Fridley, was given the case. Purple told Fridley, "We want you to convict this preacher and send him to prison."

"Prison!" Fridley snapped back, "Lovejoy to prison! Your prosecution will a damn sight more likely send him to Congress."[131]

And, some years later, that prophecy came true.

The effect of the Lovejoy trial was the opposite of what its sponsors expected. Recognizing its importance, Lovejoy's supporters raised money to hire a famous abolitionist lawyer from Utica, New York, Alvan Stewart. When the case came to trial, Stewart was unavailable and James H. Collins of Chicago stepped in. Collins masterfully cross-examined the witnesses and contested every legal point. The prosecutor had eye witnesses whose testimony appeared to doom Lovejoy. One saw Lovejoy in his wagon with a Negro whom Lovejoy referred to as a runaway. Another testified that one of the runaways spoke at a public meeting.

But Collins elicited other testimony to show that the slaves had been brought to Illinois by their owners from Kentucky, ultimately intending to take them to Missouri. At the end of a week of trial, Collins asked for an instruction that by bringing them to Illinois the slaves were free. The judge agreed, instructing the jury: "By the Constitution of this state, slavery cannot exist here. If therefore, a master voluntarily brings his slave within the state, he becomes from that moment free...."[132] This result was celebrated by the abolitionists. But it was not a sweeping legal victory in light of the Illinois Supreme Court's decision in the other cases.[133]

As Fridley recognized, Owen Lovejoy was the last person who could be intimidated. Even while under indictment, Lovejoy was defiant. He placed an ad in *Western Citizen* proclaiming he would continue his activities:

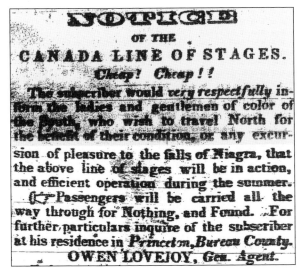

Notice from Owen Lovejoy, printed in the *Western Citizen* on June 1, 1843, where he openly invited men and women of color to contact him for free passage on the Underground Railroad.[134] (Chicago History Museum)

Lovejoy's open defiance of the laws against harboring set the stage for his entry into politics. He became one of the leading abolitionist voices, helped the abolitionist movement in Illinois make the transition to political action and ultimately served in Congress, propelled there by the notoriety of his trial, just as Fridley predicted.

Forming a New Political Party — The Liberty Party

BY 1840, SOME of the leaders of the abolitionist movement were calling for direct political action. The call to form a political party grew out of the conviction that "the slaveholders gain their advantage in national politics and legislation, and should be met in every move they make."[135] James Birney, a former slave-owner from Alabama, became a committed abolitionist, joined the American Anti-Slavery Society and tried to steer it into politics. He was rebuffed by William Lloyd Garrison, the publisher of the *Liberator* who had organized the Adelphi Convention that gave birth to the Anti-Slavery Society. Garrison and his followers were idealists, intent on using moral suasion to bring slavery to an end. They were reluctant to participate in the political process. The Garrisonians "could not see how anti-slavery people could justify holding office in a government that included slave-owners...."[136] Birney, Myron Holley and Gerrit Smith, at a meeting in Albany, New York, in 1840, broke with the Garrisonians and started the effort to organize a political party and christened it the "Liberty Party." The new party garnered only 7,000 votes in the 1840 election which elected William Henry Harrison president. Birney was the Party's candidate for President. In Illinois, he received 144 votes in Fulton County and only one vote was recorded in his favor from Cook County, though Zebina Eastman was sure that both Charles Volney Dyer and Calvin DeWolf had voted for Birney.[137] The organizers of the new party started preparing for 1844.

Many of the same Chicagoans who took the lead in the Anti-Slavery Society in Illinois formed the Illinois Liberty Party, a political party with an anti-slavery agenda.[138] On May 27, 1842, the Anti-Slavery Society held a meeting that was followed by the Convention of Liberty Voters. The Liberty Party eclipsed the Anti-Slavery Society and assumed the position as the hub of abolitionism. Though it continued until 1848, once the political party was formed, the Illinois Anti-Slavery Society was just an adjunct to the Liberty Party.[139] Given his passion, it was no surprise that Dr. Dyer was in the forefront of the organizing effort. He procured Chapman's Hall, a building on the southwest corner of Randolph and LaSalle Streets, as the place of the meeting.[140] The Cook County delegates included Dr. Dyer, DeWolf, Childs, Collins, Carpenter, and Henry Smith.[141] The Convention of Liberty voters explained that their motivation for forming a new political party was disgust with the two existing parties and the politicians who dodged the issue of slavery. Two resolutions they adopted at their first convention expressed their views concisely:

> Resolved, *That "Freedom or Slavery!" is the great question of this age and country – one which must be met, discussed, and settled on fair, just and consistent principles before prosperity can be expected again to smile on our land.*
>
> Resolved, *That the conduct of leading politicians of the Whig and Democratic parties preclude the hope that they will manfully meet and dispose of this question on its merits.*

Planning for 1844, the Illinois Liberty Party joined in nominating James Birney for President, and, in Illinois, it nominated Charles W. Hunter for Governor and Frederick Collins for Lieutenant Governor. It was at this meeting that Dr. Dyer was asked to lead the effort to establish a newspaper, which he did by devising a program to provide financial support to publish *Western Citizen*.

The Birth of Western Citizen

T O GIVE VOICE to their platform, the organizers of the new political party recognized the need to win the support of the abolitionist press. As Lovejoy's *Alton Observer* had shown, newspapers commanded the attention of the populace and galvanized public opinion. If slavery was to be defeated, it would require a broad base of support. The Illinois State Anti-Slavery Society was organized in Alton, Illinois in 1837, shortly before Elijah Lovejoy was murdered.[142] It held conventions annually, drawing representatives from across the State, and took positions on various issues. Lovejoy's *Alton Observer* stopped publication in April of 1837.

In 1839, at a meeting in Quincy, Illinois, the Illinois Society called for the establishment of a successor antislavery newspaper.[143] In response, in 1840, Zebina Eastman began publishing a newspaper called *The Genius of Liberty* in Lowell, Illinois. The Illinois Society commended *The Genius of Liberty* to the patronage of abolitionists. However, the Illinois Society did not offer to support the paper financially and Eastman was unable to publish it regularly. It foundered.

When the Illinois State Anti-Slavery Society met in Chicago on May 26, 1842, the nucleus of its members went on to form the Illinois branch of the Liberty Party. Owen Lovejoy, Elijah's brother, chaired the first meeting of the Liberty Party of Illinois.[144] The party was having trouble attracting a following and was concerned that the financial difficulties that Eastman was having meant that their voice was not being heard. The convention appointed a committee to report on whether an anti-slavery newspaper could be established in Chicago. The Chicago contingent stepped forward to rescue the effort to publish an abolitionist newspaper. Dr. Dyer was asked to take charge of a committee that included H.H. Kellogg, S. Stevens, L. Foote, C. De Wolf and S.D. Laughlin to report on their progress. The committee reported that it is "expedient to establish an Anti-Slavery press in Chicago" and urged the party faithful to raise money to purchase a good press and type. The "friends of the slave and the Liberty party" were requested to raise $1,000. Dr. Dyer devised a program that would guarantee financial support through the sale of shares at $5 each. He then set about to sell shares and took pledges. Armed with this financial support, Dr. Dyer then wrote Eastman asking him to move to Chicago to publish the paper.

Genius of Liberty was rechristened *Western Citizen*. However, it kept the same credo that Eastman had

Chicago April 20th 1842

My very dear Friend

In the last number of the "G.L." I observe you close its publication for Lowell & although I regret the suspension very much I still have some hope of success in the re-es- tablishment of the paper in this city; altho, all our plans have thus far failed.

Still we have a subscription (not one dollar of which will probably fail) of nearly four hundred dollars that we suppose may be made available for the establishment of a paper here. I do assure you that I have exerted myself thoroughly & fully in this matter and now, although there seems to be gloom and discourage- ment hanging over the matter, I am now ready as ever to prosecute this enterprize to completion. I wish you to come to Chicago prepared to stay two or three weeks and let us make a move in this matter — I know we can start something yet. I know farther that the paper once established we shall have friends, who are ready to give it a circulation —

There is enthusiasm in this matter and I have

Dr. Dyer wrote to Zabina Eastman inviting him to move from Lowell to Chicago, which was in need of an anti-slavery press. Eastman was publisher of *The Genius of Liberty*, successor of Lovejoy's *Alton Observer* and predecessor of the *Western Citizen*. (Chicago History Museum) no doubt of the success of the enterprise when once the paper is commenced.

We mean to procure the publication of the call for the State & Liberty conventions in the two papers of this City so as to give it a circulation as wide as possible.

I must see you & so do come to Chicago immediately. I am poor enough but I can do something & I can exert myself and will do so. I want you near me so that I can rely upon at least one who will be the same for a whole week at a time. These insinuations are confidential and you will please regard them as such; but they are not all I have to say. We want a practical printer for our file leader & then we can try to get onward.

I wish friend Fulton could live in these parts I admire him very much & do not believe he would need converting anew every new moon —

I am my dear Estman very sincerely and affectionately Your friend

Ch. V. Dyer

Zr Eastman Esqr
Lowell Ill.

Page two of Dr. Dyer's letter

already been using, borrowed from the Declaration of Independence, that all men are created equal.

In addition to championing the positions of the Liberty Party, *Western Citizen* regularly reported the proceedings of the Anti-Slavery Society. *Western Citizen* became the "organ of the Society." At its sixth annual meeting, held at the First Presbyterian Church in Chicago on June 7, 1843, the Society passed resolutions that included the following:

- *The Free States are not bound by that instrument [the Constitution] to deliver up fugitives from slavery.*
- *All laws enforcing and sustaining slavery [are declared] nugatory as contrary to divine law.*[145]

Among the readers of *Western Citizen* was a Springfield lawyer and aspiring politician – Abraham Lincoln. Eastman was told by William ("Billy") Herndon that Lincoln was "an attentive reader of your paper for years."[146]

The "Black Codes"

ONE TARGET THE Illinois Anti-Slavery Society went after was "The Black Codes." These were the laws passed by the Illinois Legislature limiting the rights of blacks. The Society adopted resolutions condemning the laws that had been passed in Illinois, saying, "the statute book of our own Illinois, is blotted with enactments, disgraceful to our boasted freedom and shameful to humanity." They decried the fact that the laws degraded the free colored man and continued to tolerate slavery. With regard to the pursuit of fugitive slaves by "slave-catchers," they deplored the fact that Illinois law gave slave-catchers a free hand:

The fierce and cruel man hunter pursues his victim through our state without molestation and free men and women are dragged in chains to the law of perpetual slavery and none dare interfere for their rescue.

The Black Codes started with the Act of the Indiana Territorial Legislature already referred to, *An Act Concerning the Introduction of Negroes and Mulattos into this Territory*, passed in 1807. This was the law that began the tolerance of slavery under the guise of "voluntary" indentured service.

But Illinois added to the statute book, devising a series of laws that reduced the rights of the free Negro. These provisions included:

- *A prohibition on any black or mulatto person settling or residing in the State without producing a certificate of freedom;*
- *A requirement that every black or mulatto register his name, his family and his evidence of freedom;*
- *A prohibition on hiring a free Negro who could not produce a certificate of freedom;*
- *A prohibition on bringing a slave into the State for the purpose of emancipating him, and a requirement to post a bond of $1,000 as a condition that any slave brought into the State not become a county charge;*
- *A provision voiding any contracts between a servant and master during the term of service;*
- *A provision allowing any servant being lazy, disorderly or refusing to work to be whipped upon an order of a justice; and*
- *A provision that if an indentured servant were found more than 10 miles from the tenement of his service without a pass he could be whipped not to exceed 35 lashes.*[147]

But this was not all. The Illinois legislature also passed a law denying the availability of the writ of *habeas corpus* to blacks, impairing their right to contest the legality of any attempt to treat them as slaves, fugitives, or voluntary indentured servants. Worse, there was a law that blacks could not testify against a white person in any court proceeding. A black was defined as anyone who had one quarter Negro blood. Finally, when Illinois set up a system of free tax-funded schools, it was limited to white children.[148]

The abolitionists recognized the inequity of all of this. They thought the double standard made the promise of democracy hypocritical. How could Illinois

WESTERN CITIZEN

THE SUPREMACY OF GOD AND THE EQUALITY OF MAN.

"We hold these truths to be self-evident: That all men are created equal, and endowed by their Creator with certain inalienable rights, among which are life, liberty, and the pursuit of happiness. — *Declaration of Independence*

VOL. V.---NO. I.   **CHICAGO, JULY 21, 1846.**   W

The credo of the *Western Citizen* appeared just below the masthead and it read as follows: The Supremacy of God and the Equality of Man "We hold these truths to be self-evident: That all men are created equal, and endowed by their Creator with certain inalienable rights, among which are life, liberty, and the pursuit of happiness. – *Declaration of Independence* (Chicago History Museum)

claim to be a "Free" State? *Western Citizen* reported the proceedings of the Society and published their resolutions, including their frequent bashing of the Black Codes. The paper regularly reported the outrages committed under these laws. For example, on December 29, 1846, the paper ran an expose on the injustice produced by Section 5 of the Code,[149] reporting that Lewis Mason had been jailed,

> *not for any crime, but because the section declares that "he shall be declared a runaway slave" not having in his possession a certificate of freedom.*

The Black Codes made free blacks second class citizens. Section 5 meant a free black had to live under the constant threat of being preyed upon by slave-owners' sympathizers with the horror of being cast again into involuntary servitude.

But the opponents to these laws were in the minority in the 1840s and 1850s. Illinois had plenty of citizens who were pro-slavery and had a rich history of attempts to undo the command of the Northwest Ordinance that the territory remain free.[150] The State's first Governor, Shadrach Bond, owned 13 slaves (or "indentured servants," to use the accepted terminology).[151] In 1824, thanks to the efforts of then Governor Cole and Attorney General Lockwood, the voters had narrowly defeated an attempt to officially convert Illinois into a Slave State.[152] The Illinois statute book was full of laws that accommodated slavery. For example, "slaves and colored servants" described a category of property to be assessed for taxation.[153]

By the 1840s, even among non-slave-owners, most citizens of Illinois, certainly the majority of voters, were worried about the specter of being overrun by fugitive slaves – that *unwelcome population* – in Justice Scates' words. This made opposition to the Black Codes a tough sell. Politicians, including Stephen Douglas played the race card. It was one thing to advocate freedom in the abstract. It was another for the citizens of Illinois to practice its teachings. The abolitionists made no progress in their quest to soften the impact of these laws. The Black Code laws were not repealed until after the Civil War when John Jones, a black who had lived in Chicago as a free man since 1845, went to Springfield with a petition with a long list of signatures asking that the laws be repealed in light of the fact that blacks were now free.[154]

A Slave Is Sold at Auction – in Chicago!

THAT A FREE Negro ran the risk of being accused of being a fugitive was not just a theoretical proposition. In 1842, Edwin Heathcock, a free Negro, was working as a laborer in a field next to the North Branch of the Chicago River. He got into a quarrel with a white workman. This led to his being arrested under the so-called "Black Laws" for being in Illinois without free papers.

Justice L.C. Kercheval committed him to jail. He was advertised for sale for a period of six weeks. The sale was to occur on Monday, November 14, 1843 at the northwest corner of Court House Square, at Randolph and LaSalle Streets.

Eastman and De Wolf were apoplectic about the prospect of a man being sold into slavery in "Free Illinois." They manned the press at *Western Citizen* and printed hundreds of circulars which they put all over town and especially around court house square. They wanted to give extraordinary publicity to the sale, to "bring home to the people of a free community the full nature of such a scandalous proceeding."[155] On the appointed day, a large crowd had gathered when Sheriff Lowe appeared with his charge. The sheriff asked for bids. The crowd was ominously silent. He asked again. Still no response. Sensing the mood of the crowd, he announced it was only by duty, not by choice, that he was conducting the sale. A few minutes passed. The sheriff then stated to the crowd, that if the Negro was not sold, he would have to reincarcerate him. Then a voice boomed out, "I bid 25 cents." It was Mahlon D. Ogden, brother of William B. Ogden,

who had been elected Chicago's first Mayor in 1837. The sheriff went through the ritual of asking for other bids. There were none. Ogden stepped forward, took a shiny quarter out of his pocket and presented it to the sheriff, who slipped away. Ogden then turned to Heathcock and said: "Edwin, I have bought you. You are my man – my slave. Now go where you please!"[156] The crowd roared their approval.

Illinois Hears about Slave-Catchers in Pennsylvania

Western *Citizen* REGULARLY ran stories about the plight of free Negroes who were preyed on by "slave-catchers." In one case, a man from Virginia swore out a warrant that the wife of Jabez Sowden had been his slave 12 years before. Sowden, a free Negro living in Philadelphia, was tricked into bringing his wife to a hotel where the slave-catchers locked her up. Sowden went to get help

Copyright secured by A. T. Andreas, 1884.

THE FIRST COURT-HOUSE.

At the northwest corner of Chicago's Court House Square, Sheriff Lowe auctioned a free Negro, Edwin Heathcock, to the highest bidder. M. D. Ogden offered 25 cents, won the auction, then set Heathcock free. (Chicago History Museum)

and, on his return, found the slave-catchers forcing his wife into a hack and driving away. Sowden followed the hack and screamed "murder!" which brought the police. The police stopped the hack and questioned the slave-catchers who said that they were in the charge of a constable. The police allowed them to proceed. Sowden followed and saw his wife loaded onto a train. He demanded to see a warrant and was shown instead a pistol and told he would be shot if he made any further protest or didn't leave. The train pulled out and he saw his wife no more. Sowden said he had been married seven years and had never heard his wife intimate that she had formerly been a slave. *Western Citizen* editorialized: "If this system of legalized kidnapping should be steadily persisted in, in the Free States, unless human nature shall alter, it will result in blood."[157]

The Slave-Catchers Come to Illinois

THERE WERE A number of people who were known as the operators of the Underground Railroad in Chicago. Besides Dr. Dyer, they were: Eastman, De Wolf, Carpenter, Pinkerton, Freer, Collins, Rev. L.F. Bascomb, Childs, H.L. Fulton , N. Rossiter and J.B. Bradwell.[158] Dr. Dyer's home was the central depot. Between 1839 and 1851 Dr. Dyer lived on Randolph between State and Dearborn Streets. From 1851 to 1857, he lived on the corner of Monroe and Dearborn.[159] Philo Carpenter and L.C.P. Freer lived close by. Passengers arrived at all times of the day or night. Of course, as these activities became known, the slave-catchers knew where to look for fugitives.

In 1846, slave-catchers from Kentucky came looking for a fugitive. Dr. Dyer was housing the young boy as

Dr. Dyer broke his cane when he hit a slave-catcher who confronted him with a bowie knife. A visitor from Virginia presented a new one, which Dyer used on "state occasions," to commemorate the event. (Chicago History Museum)

one of his "guests." One morning, he sent the lad on an errand to the market. The slave-catchers were waiting.

Someone came running to Dr. Dyer's home to tell him that the boy had been apprehended, that the slave-catchers had taken him to the Mansion House Hotel (the hotel built in 1831 on Lake Street just west of State Street) and summoned a blacksmith to fit him out in irons. Dr. Dyer stormed out of his house and headed to the Mansion House. People who saw him that morning knew that from his resolute expression that an encounter was about to take place that would result in the freeing of a slave or bloodshed – or both.

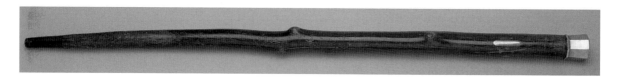

Dr. Dyer entered the hotel through the kitchen grabbing a butcher knife from the cook as he went through. He found the room where the captive was held, demanded entry and barged in. The captive was bound with rope. Dr. Dyer strode over to him, cut his bonds and pointed to the window. The fugitive fled.

The slave-catchers were stunned. They turned to wreak their vengeance on Dr. Dyer but he had "coolly walked out." They pursued him to the street outside. Screaming at him, one of the slave-catchers pulled a bowie knife and charged at the doctor. At that point, all that Dr. Dyer had to defend himself was his cane. He brought the cane down, bashing his attacker on the head and the man fell senseless. The cane broke into several pieces. The slave-catcher's confederates gathered up their fallen comrade, as Dr. Dyer faced them. They retreated as a small crowd gathered.

Hearing of this exploit, a visitor to Chicago from Virginia ordered a new hickory cane and sent it to the doctor with his compliments. Not to be outdone, the Negro citizens of Chicago borrowed the new cane, fitted it out with a gold inset and the inscription *Sic Semper Tyrannis* and presented it to him to commemorate the event and all that he had done. In his later years, the doctor enjoyed displaying the cane "on state occasions."[160]

De Tocqueville's Observations on Slavery and Racism

THE FIRST VOLUME of Alexander de Tocqueville's classic *Democracy in America* was published in 1835, right after he completed his grand tour of America in 1831. He visited the young democracy traveling from New York to the frontier at the Great Lakes, as well as seeing Boston, Philadelphia, Baltimore, Pittsburgh, Cincinnati, Nashville, Memphis, New Orleans and Washington, D.C. He unabashedly admired America's democracy and regarded the entrepreneurial spirit and self reliance of Americans –

"robust individualism" – to be key elements to its success. However, he also saw slavery and he listened to the excuses for why it was justified.

Of course, there were some who argued that slavery was biblically sanctioned. This was the sort of argument that had driven Elijah Lovejoy to distraction. The Anti-Slavery Societies would have none of it. Disputes over the biblical justifications for slavery led to major splits in churches throughout the United States. Even within congregations the differences could cause schisms. In Chicago, the Second Presbyterian Church was formed in 1842 because its members thought the abolitionist members of the First were too radical on the subject of slavery.[161]

But aside from the arguments falling back on the Bible, there were also arguments that Negroes were inferior, needed supervision, that benevolent slavery was good for them, etc. The insidious seeds of racism were sown a long time ago. De Tocqueville had a keen eye and saw the pervasiveness of race discrimination.

What is striking is how de Tocqueville heard all the justifications and saw through them. In his view, the attributes to which supporters of slavery pointed to prove racial superiority were the products of the Negro being brought up in a system of bondage. The tyranny of the Anglo-American majority virtually exterminated the Indian and enslaved the black:

Oppression has with one blow taken from the descendants of the Africans almost all the privileges of humanity.[162]

The slave had been deprived of homeland, family, religion, mores, language and ownership of his person. As a result, he lost all pride in himself and had no ambition to improve himself.

De Tocqueville thought that slavery was "the most dreadful of all the evils that threaten the future of the United States."[163] At the same time, De Tocqueville was far-sighted enough to see that the elimination of slavery was only part of the problem. The problem of racism was also a cancer on the young democracy:

In the portion of the Union where Negroes are no longer slaves, have they been brought closer to whites? Every man who has inhabited the United States will have noticed that a contrary effect has been produced.

Racial prejudice appears to me to be stronger in the states that have abolished slavery than in those where slavery still exists....[164]

When de Tocqueville speculated about whether the American Union would last, he recognized that racism was a problem separate and apart from slavery: "I perceive slavery receding; the prejudice to which it has given birth is unmoving."[165] De Tocqueville made the case for a more enlightened view of his fellow man. His thoughtful analysis was in harmony with the views of *Western Citizen* and the abolitionists in Chicago. But they were all voices crying in the wilderness. The weight of public opinion on the "fact" of racial inferiority, at the time, was undoubtedly against them, as is shown by the enactment and enforcement of the Black Codes. Even Lincoln, when baited by Douglas in their famous debates that the logic of his position meant that he favored intermarriage of blacks and whites, responded by explaining that his belief in freedom did not mean that he considered the Negro his equal in all respects:

He [Douglas] finds the Republicans insisting that the Declaration of Independence includes ALL men, black as well as white, and forthwith he boldly denies that includes Negroes at all, and proceeds to argue gravely that all who contend that it does, want to vote, eat, sleep and marry with Negroes. I protest against this counterfeit logic.... If I do not want a black woman for a slave, it does not follow that I want her for a wife.... In some respects she is not my equal, but in her natural right to eat the bread she earns with her own hand without asking leave of anyone else, she is my equal and the equal of all others.[166]

Lincoln and the Underground Railroad

IF THE ONLY evidence of Lincoln's involvement with fugitive slaves had been the cases identified above, one might have concluded that Lincoln was indifferent to the plight of fugitive slaves, but there is more to the story.

In 1837, as a Whig member of the Illinois General Assembly, he filed the protest described above that registered his disagreement with the resolutions approving the slave-holding States' position on slavery. He had said that slavery was founded on injustice and bad policy. At the same time he expressed skepticism over the efficacy of abolitionist societies.

In 1842, Eastman went to Springfield with Cassius Clay, a leading abolitionist from Kentucky, when the Liberty Party was considering Lincoln as a possible candidate to oppose Douglas for the Senate. The purpose of the visit was to determine whether Lincoln's position on slavery would satisfy the more radical members of the party. While Lincoln was on record as opposing slavery, he also was on record saying that Congress had "no power" to interfere with it in the slave-holding States. Eastman was trying to find out how far Lincoln's opposition to slavery went.

Eastman also visited with the agent for the Underground Railroad in Springfield who told him that he was a client of Lincoln's who had employed Lincoln "in all times of trouble." Apparently, Lincoln defended this person against, or helped him avoid, prosecution. Eastman's "agent" reported to the Liberty Party delegation that "Mr. Lincoln was all right on the Negro question; he gave money when necessary, to help the fugitives on the way to freedom."[167]

Lincoln's Early Encounters with Slavery

IN 1816, LINCOLN'S parents had moved from Virginia to Kentucky, where he had been born on February 12, 1809 in a log cabin. His mother, Nancy Hanks, died in 1818. His father, Thomas, then married Sarah, a widow with children of her own. The family lived in Indiana from 1816 until 1830.

Lincoln grew up fast and he was big – growing to a height of six feet four inches and weighing 200 pounds. From the time he was eight or nine his father hired him out as a day laborer and for odd jobs. As he later recalled it, he had an axe in his hand constantly until he was 23. He did not have a warm relationship with his father. He credited Sarah for being the one to encourage him to learn to read. His spare time was spent immersed in books.

In 1828, when he was 19 years old, he took his first trip away from his Indiana home. He built a raft, stocked it with surplus farm goods and headed down the rivers of Illinois to the Mississippi and then to New Orleans. He undoubtedly saw slaves and slave markets but made no note of it at the time.

On a later occasion, he did record his observations. He wrote a letter on September 27, 1841 to Mary Speed recounting a trip he took with his friend Joshua Speed from Springfield to St. Louis on the Steam Boat *Lebanon*. He observed a group of slaves being transported down river and was struck by their apparent good spirits despite being deprived of their families and the homes they had known:

By the way, a fine example was presented on board the boat for contemplating the effect of condition upon human happiness. A gentleman had purchased twelve Negroes in different parts of Kentucky and was taking them to a farm in the South. They were chained six and six together. A small iron clevis was around the left wrist of each, and this fastened to the main chain by a shorter one at a convenient distance from, the others,

so that the Negroes were strung together precisely like so many fish on a trot-line. In this condition they were being separated forever from scenes of their childhood, their friends, their fathers and mothers, and brothers and sisters, and many of them, from the wives and children, and going into perpetual slavery where the lash of the master is proverbially more ruthless and unrelenting than any other where; and yet amid all these distressing circumstances, as we would think them, they were the most cheerful and apparently happy creatures on board. One, whose offence for which he had been sold was an over-fondness for his wife, played fiddle almost continually; and others danced, sung, cracked jokes, played various games with cards from day to day. How true it is that "God tempers the wind to the shorn lamb," or in other words, that He renders the worst of human conditions tolerable, while He permits the best, to be nothing better than tolerable.[168]

This was probably a scene that many Americans encountered when they traveled by boat near the corridors of commerce with the South. The slave trade was carried on openly, and Lincoln at the age of 32 was not shocked by what he saw. The letter to Mary Speed suggests he was indifferent to the condition of the slaves.

However, 14 years later, in a letter to Joshua Speed in 1855, he recalled this trip and said the plight of the slaves tormented him:

In 1841 you and I had together a tedious low-water trip, on a Team Boat from Louisville to St. Louis. You may remember, as I well do, that from Louisville to the mouth of the Ohio there were, on board, ten or a dozen slaves, shackled together with irons. That sight was a continual torment to me; and I see something like it every time I touch the Ohio, or any other slave-border.[169]

Another benchmark in Lincoln's struggle with the prevalence of slavery occurred when he served in Congress. In 1849, he proposed to amend a resolution that would have required the committee on the District of Columbia to report a bill that would abolish slavery in the District prospectively and would encourage slave-holders presently in the District to emancipate their slaves by offering compensation, but only if the citizens of the District would approve the Bill in an election. The proposed Bill had several exceptions: military officers from slave-holding States would be allowed to bring slaves to attend on them while in the District on business and the Bill also would have required the return of fugitives who escaped into the District. It was a modest proposal that was never introduced. Lincoln was having a difficult time finding a way to translate his abhorrence of slavery into an effective policy.

The Disrupted Trial – An Armed Negro Riot?

THE CHICAGOANS WHO were agitating against slavery could not do much about slaves being transported from Kentucky to New Orleans. When fugitive slaves came their way, however, they could act and they did.

On Wednesday October 28, 1846, two blacks, accused of being runaway slaves from Missouri, were arrested by Deputy Sheriff Henry Rhines in Chicago and taken before Justice Lewis C. Kercheval who was asked to issue a writ for their extradition to Missouri.[170] News of the arrests spread quickly. Dr. Dyer "with a score of black friends of the prisoners" and, as one account goes, with "quite a number of 'respectable' people besides" interrupted this cozy proceeding and informed the judge that the case was to be contested.[171] James Collins – the friend of Dr. Dyer and the lawyer who had defended Owen Lovejoy – was sent for and a large crowd started to fill the justice's second floor office and spill out onto Clark Street. Collins was joined by De Wolf and the two attorneys examined the papers to see if they could find a defect in them. Soon Dr. Dyer's other abolitionist friends were at his side: Hamilton, Freer, John Daylin, and J.V. Smith. They all crowded into the courtroom.

Collins and De Wolf persuaded Justice Kercheval to quash the extradition writ. But the Justice ordered the fugitives "held for questioning." Collins and DeWolf were discouraged by the direction the hearing was taking based on the justice's pronouncements. Then, three hours into the hearing, Collins made one of his inspired objections that threw a monkey wrench into the proceedings. He objected that the slave-catcher's lawyers had not established that Missouri was a Slave State. The proposition seemed absurd. Everyone knew Missouri was a Slave State. But Justice Kercheval agreed that the proposition had to be proven properly. He told the slave-catcher's lawyers to offer the appropriate proof.

The Missouri statute book was called for. No copy was at hand. So, someone was dispatched to go to a neighboring law office and bring back a copy. Justice Kercheval declared a recess.

Meanwhile the crowd outside had grown in numbers and was getting noisier and more restless. Kercheval stepped outside to survey the crowd. Several of the Negro citizens tried to get into the courthouse but were denied entrance. Deputy Sheriff Henry Rhines went out to control the crowd. He was surrounded and swept away from the courthouse door. He yelled out that he was armed with a pistol and a Bowie knife and started to reach for the knife. No one backed off. Rhines thought better of it as the crowd pressed around him. He tried to get back to the doorway but made slow progress.

Meanwhile, inside the courtroom, during the lull, something extraordinary happened. How it happened is a matter that was later disputed. But the result was that the prisoners escaped!

While Kercheval and the deputy sheriff were gone, the two fugitives left the courtroom. How they managed to escape depends on whose version of the story is to be believed. The abolitionists were accused of overwhelming the slave-catcher and passing the two fugitives out the window. Some of the city's newspapers later called the whole affair "a Negro riot."

Dr. Dyer and company had a more benign story. They said that when Kercheval and Rhines left, the only ones left in the courtroom were Dr. Dyer, Collins,

Daylin, Smith, the two alleged fugitives, Gallagher (the slave-catcher) and Henry Brown (the slave-catcher's attorney). Brown sat at counsel table with his back to the door. Opposite him was Collins. Brown was engrossed reading the Missouri statute book which had been brought to the courtroom. Hamilton had left, come back and found the door to the courtroom locked. He knocked. Gallagher was closest to the door, got up, walked over and opened it slightly. The two fugitives meanwhile got up and walked over, pulled the door open and brushed past Gallagher despite his protests and fled down the stairs where the crowd swept them away.

When Justice Kercheval returned, he asked, "Where are the prisoners?" Dr. Dyer responded, "They have sunk into the bosom of the community."[172] Confusion reigned.

When Dr. Dyer, Freer and Collins left the courtroom and went outside, Rhines brandished his pistol and threatened to arrest Dr. Dyer. Rhines was convinced Dr. Dyer had engineered the escape. Dr. Dyer looked at him coldly and said "You are the only person deserving of arrest for displaying so much cutlery on the street!" With the crowd pressing around him, Rhines made a split-second decision not to pursue the issue. But his scowl made it clear he had marked an enemy he would dog again.

The First Public Meeting to Discuss "That Affair"

THE WHOLE EPISODE had the city in an uproar for several days. There were two public meetings that immediately followed. The first occurred the next night. It was a mass meeting of citizens. An announcement had been made that at the regular meeting of the Liberty Association, the circumstances of "that affair" (the escape of the fugitives) would be discussed. The Saloon Building was filled to overflowing. People who could not get in stood outside.

Dr. Dyer, J.V. Smith, Collins and Levi Spencer were all called on to speak.[173] The abolitionists were in complete control of this meeting.

Dr. Dyer spoke first. He read an article that appeared in *The Chicago Daily Journal* and excoriated the authors for misrepresenting what occurred. He said he knew that the "ostensible editors" of the paper had not written the article. Rather he said he recognized that some patrons under the control of a "political clique" prevailed upon them to publish it. *Western Citizen* reported that: "The Doctor went on in his peculiar style to give his opinion of its contemptible meanness and falsehood."[174] He lambasted Gallagher, the slave-catcher, Deputy Sheriff Rhines and the lawyers for the slave-catcher – all of whom were present! He described the prior days' proceedings as a triumph of liberty and asked one of the "redeemed fugitives" who was present to "jump up on the bench" and show himself. He did to a roar of applause. (The warrant had been quashed and apparently the proceeding had been abandoned.)

They sang a song.[175] Then Smith took the floor and scored the slave-catchers for being hypocrites because, on entering the meeting, Gallagher had said he, too, was an abolitionist. Smith went on to lambaste the Black Laws and applaud the failed effort to consign the two Negroes to slavery, saying that this episode was a "bright and beautiful spot on the page of humanity." After another song, Collins spoke and expounded on the legal argument he had made to oppose the extradition of the fugitives. He thought that the Illinois law that permitted hunting down Negroes was unconstitutional. Even if it were not, he said *it should not be followed*. In his view the great principles of law discussed by the highest authorities all "concurred in declaring that all laws which conflict with natural justice, or contravene divine law, are null and void."

Here was a call for civil disobedience. It was a position embraced by Dr. Dyer and his friends. It was the justification for operating the Underground Railroad. But defying the laws regarding fugitives just inflamed the slave-holders and their allies and gave them an excuse for lawlessness and mob action on their part.

Activists, Pacifists and the Quest for a Third Path

T HE CALL FOR civil disobedience revealed the break that had occurred between the *activist* abolitionists like Dr. Dyer and Collins and the *pacifist* abolitionists like Garrison.

Garrison was capable of very fiery rhetoric. From the very first issue of his paper, *The Liberator*, he spewed fire:

> *I will be as harsh as truth and as uncompromising as justice. On this subject I do not wish to think, or speak, or write, with moderation. No! No! Tell a man whose house is on fire to give a moderate alarm; tell him to moderately rescue his wife from the hands of ravishers; tell the mother to gradually extricate her babe from the fire into which it has fallen; but urge me not to use moderation.*[176]

As grand as that sounded, Garrison was reluctant to venture beyond fiery rhetoric. For many years he refused to become politically active. His view was that the nation had made a corrupt bargain when the Constitution was drafted. ("The compact which exists between the North and the South is a covenant with death and an agreement with hell."[177]) So, even though he was occasionally attacked by mobs, Garrison was content to write fiery editorials and give stem-winding speeches. He would have nothing to do with the Liberty and Free Soil Parties, the first of the political parties devoted to the election of candidates opposed to slavery.

At the other extreme was John Brown who stood up at the end of a memorial service to Elijah Lovejoy and proclaimed: "Here, before God, in the presence of these witnesses, from this time I consecrate my life to the destruction of slavery."[178] Brown believed slavery could not be abolished peacefully, could not be bothered with political efforts, fought and killed slave-owners in Kansas, planned an insurrection and,

ultimately, made war on the United States with his raid on Harper's Ferry in 1859. He hoped to provoke a revolution.

Where was Lincoln? Lincoln's reaction to the murder of Lovejoy was more muted. He accepted the Constitution with its inherent compromise on slavery. He despised the rule of the mob. He was fearful of giving rein to civil disobedience. When he spoke at the Young Men's Lyceum on January 27, 1838, he decried the "mobocratic spirit" abroad in the land with thinly veiled references to the McIntosh episode and the murder of Lovejoy:

> *When men take it in their heads today, to hang gamblers, or burn murderers, they should recollect, that, in the confusion usually attending such transactions, they will be as likely to hang or burn some one, who is neither a gambler or a murderer as one who is; and that, acting upon the example they set, the mob of tomorrow, may, and probably will, hang or burn some of them, by the very same mistake.... [W]henever the vicious portion of the population shall be permitted to gather in bands of hundreds and thousands, and burn churches, ravage and rob provision stores, throw printing presses into rivers, shoot editors, and hang and burn obnoxious persons at pleasure, and with impunity; depend on it, this Government cannot last.*[179]

Lincoln feared for the rule of law. Mobs and justice were incompatible. The Slave power could disregard the law, too. John C. Calhoun, the famous Southern Senator from South Carolina, had already tested the concept of nullification – the proposition that a State could nullify a law of Congress that it disagreed with – when South Carolina threatened to nullify the Tariffs of 1828 and 1832.[180] Secession would be its logical extension. Nullification and secession threatened to dismember the union. Lincoln was not comfortable with the fact that slavery was constitutionally sanctioned but, in the 1830s and 1840s, as an Illinois lawyer testing the waters for a possible run for national office as a Whig, like the rest of the northern Whigs, he did not see a path for altering the *status quo*.

The Second Public Meeting

A SECOND MEETING TO address the commotion caused by "that affair" was called by the Mayor, John P. Chapin. His call for a meeting suggested to *Western Citizen* that the City Council thought that the city was on the verge of being ransacked by a mob:

Fearful apprehensions, it appears, are entertained by our City Fathers that you will do something terrible, burn and sack the city, perhaps, as has been intimated by one of our dailies, and they wish to take measures to prevent your proceeding to such devastating lengths.[181]

The Mayor's call for a meeting asked citizens to attend "to consult upon such measures as may be deemed proper to prevent a recurrence of the disgraceful scenes enacted in our city on the 28th, by an armed Negro mob…." This meeting was held at the Court House and began with Alderman Curtis, the City Council member who had presented the resolution calling for the public meeting.[182] Curtis rose and began speaking about the importance of upholding the supremacy of the law, and preventing such occurrences as had taken place. He said the reputation of the city required that something be done.

At this point he was interrupted by a call that he "state the facts" in the case. This he "seemed little inclined to do." He said everyone knew that there had been a gross violation of law. More voices called out for him to state the facts of the case: "The facts, the facts, state the facts." He tried to go on but could not be heard over the calls for the facts. He then said that he was not present at the "riot" and could not state the facts further than what was generally known. He then said it was apparent that the majority of those present had come to make a disturbance and to defeat the object of the meeting. He said he would make a motion to adjourn so that the meeting could be moved to another place where they could proceed without interference. Dr. Dyer's friend, J. Y. Scammon, rose

to speak and was called out of order by Curtis. But Scammon pointed out the motion to adjourn was debatable and proceeded to explain why it was appropriate for the aldermen to get the facts as he and the Mayor had both been out of town. Curtis had lost control of the meeting he called.

Scammon then proceeded to present a series of resolutions which were immediately seconded. These were:

1. Resolved, *That we are unqualifiedly opposed to the existence of* Slavery *in all its forms, believing that every being who wears the image and likeness of his Maker should be free.*

2. Resolved, *That our sympathies are with the oppressed in all contests for freedom and we will do no act which tends to perpetuate Slavery, or deprive a human being of his liberty.*

3. Resolved, *That we are not less opposed to mobs and illegal violence, than we are to Slavery and under all circumstances not absolutely revolutionary in their character, we are in favor of the supremacy of the law and the maintenance of order.*

4. Resolved, *That while we will uphold the laws and public officers in enforcing them, we will never sanction their perversion to aid in kidnapping the oppressed, or in the illegal arrest and detention of the slave.*[183]

Scammon's motion was followed by remarks by Collins who recounted his version of "that affair," which was that there had been no mob action. He said the fugitives walked out with only a feeble attempt by the slave-catcher Gallagher to restrain them. He said the 2,000 people outside in the street were no more unruly than any election day gathering in Chicago.

There was a call for a vote on the resolutions and they all passed by a "thunder of yeas as we never heard before," according to *Western Citizen*. This was followed by three cheers each for the Mayor, Scammon and Collins.

The mob action story was also rebutted by a series of letters to the editor telling the "eye-witness accounts" of Freer, Collins, De Wolf and Hamilton. Consistent with what Collins said at the second meeting, their

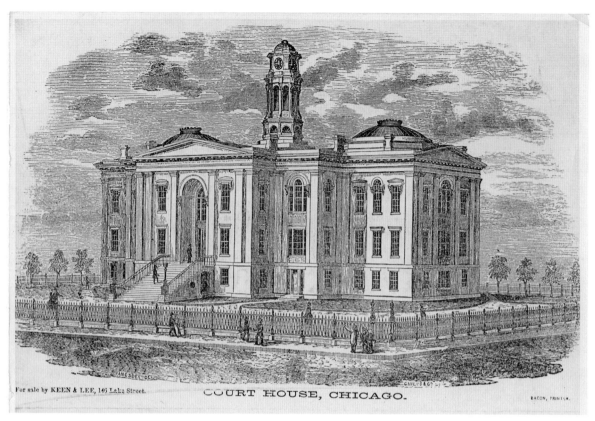

The Chicago Court House, where Y. A. Scammon presented key Resolutions against Slavery, which passed with "a thunder of yeas." (Chicago History Museum)

story was that the fugitives simply got up and walked out the door when it was opened. The only violence that occurred was the scuffle between the fugitives and the slave-catcher.[184]

Of course *Western Citizen* criticized its rival newspapers for siding with the slave-holding interests:

> [T]he *Journal* and the *Democrat* … [a]like anxious, it would seem, to show the slave-holders and their northern allies that they *are not to blame for the poor success of man-hunting in this quarter, they each characterize a peaceable assemblage of* two thousand *of our citizens, embracing those of all classes, occupations and professions, brought together by the noblest feeling of sympathy that can swell the heart of man, as* a "mob."[185]

The paper pointed out that the warrant for the two alleged fugitives was later quashed and therefore reasoned that they had been wrongly apprehended in the first place.

The Backlashes

THIS WAS CERTAINLY one of the high points in the travails of the abolitionists in Chicago. They succeeded in keeping two supposed runaway slaves free and they had the citizens behind them. But their activities did not go unnoticed.

This victory for the abolitionists produced several backlashes. The most immediate was that Deputy Sheriff Rhines went to Springfield and tried to get the "mobocrats" indicted. *Western Citizen* gleefully reported that this mission was unsuccessful: "The slave-hunters of this city, in their hot chase on the track of humanity have very unexpectedly run their snouts upon another snag."[186] Rhines swore out a complaint and went before the Grand Jury in Springfield but came back to Chicago empty-handed.

The more enduring backlash came from the clamor for a tougher fugitive slave law. The "poor success of man-hunting," the gloating of the abolitionists and unsubtle ads in *Western Citizen* for the Underground Railroad were just more pieces of evidence that the slaveholders would point to as they made their case for stronger laws to prevent the loss of their property. They asked Congress for a law with teeth in it. With the Fugitive Slave Act of 1850, they got it.

The losses to the South of slaves escaping to free territory in 1850 were estimated to number at least 300,000, worth $15 million at market prices. To support their demand for stronger legislation the Southerners cited these losses and estimates that even a small slave-holding State like Maryland was losing $100,000 worth of "property" every six months.[187]

A CARD.

To the friends of the underground Rail Road, in Jersey county, Illinois, the subscriber begs leave to say that he arrived in this place on the first inst., and that the U. R. R. is in excellent order. The station keepers and superintendents are all active and trust-worthy men, that any *chattels* intrusted to their care will be forwarded with great care, and *unparalleled speed*.

G. W. BURKE, Superintendent.
Chicago, June 3, 1844.

An advertisement promoting the Underground Railroad from the June 6, 1844 edition of *Western Citizen*. (Chicago History Museum)

Thornton's Case

IN 1849, THE Illinois Supreme Court decided *Thornton's Case*,[188] a case that adopted the very argument that Collins and the abolitionists had been making. It held unconstitutional the provision in the Illinois Black Laws that provided that a Negro found without a certificate of freedom was deemed a runaway and was to be arrested, held for his owner, or auctioned off.[189] Thornton had been arrested under the Illinois statute and brought a writ of *habeas corpus* which the court granted. The Court based its decision on the United States Supreme Court's decision in *Prigg v. Pennsylvania*,[190] where the Supreme Court threw out the Pennsylvania indictment of slave-catchers holding that "all state legislation, intended either to impede or assist the master in the recaption of his fugitive slave, was null and void, on the ground that the legislation of congress on the subject was exclusive."[191]

Here was the very proposition that Collins had been advocating. It nullified the law that had imprisoned Edwin Heathcock and Lewis Mason and that had provided the authority for the sheriff to auction them off. Free blacks could breath a little easier and slave-catching in Illinois became more difficult. But *Thornton's Case* also fueled the demands of the Slave States for a more rigorous fugitive slave law.

The Little Giant

STEPHEN A. DOUGLAS was the principal architect of the Compromise of 1850 which gave birth to the revised Fugitive Slave Act, an instantly highly controversial measure. This Act was intended to heal the divisions over slavery but it actually had the opposite unintended consequence – it propelled the country toward civil war. The visceral reaction in Chicago to this legislation was a harbinger of strife to come.

Douglas was born in Brandon, Vermont April 23, 1813. His father died shortly after he was born. His mother raised the family on a farm with her brother. When she remarried, the family went to live in upstate New York where Douglas attended Canandaigua Academy and read law, with a view to preparing for a career as a lawyer. But New York required three years of legal study to qualify for the bar. Lacking the funds to continue on in New York, in June of 1830, at the age of 20, with $300 in his pocket,[192] he headed west, via steamer, canal boat and stagecoach, seeking an opening in a law office in St. Louis. Finding no opportunities there he moved on to Illinois and, ultimately, to Jacksonville, Illinois in the central part of the State.

Fertile farm land and efficient transportation to the Great Lakes on the Illinois River made Jacksonville a hub for the development boom that occurred in central Illinois at the close of the Black Hawk Indian War in 1832. The area was a melting pot with some newcomers coming from southern and border States and others from New England.[193]

Douglas taught school for a year and, as was then permitted, was able to appear before the local justice of the peace who presided over less serious cases without being admitted to the bar. He used the year to improve his knowledge of the law and then appeared before Justice Lockwood of the Illinois Supreme Court to be examined for his license. (Lockwood was the jurist who had written the Court's opinion in *Phoebe v. Jay* six years earlier.)

Enamored of politics, Douglas was an ardent fan of Andrew Jackson. (Jacksonville had been named in honor of the hero of the Battle of New Orleans.) When he had been in school he gave speeches extolling Jackson's policies as President. Jackson had been elected for a second term in 1832. Upon arriving in Illinois, Douglas plunged into Democratic politics. At a meeting in Jacksonville, in March of 1834, he gave a rousing speech supporting Jackson's controversial "war" on the Second United States Bank – his withdrawal of government deposits and appointment of Roger B. Taney as Secretary of the Treasury. Although Illinois was considered Democratic and had voted for Jackson, many in Illinois were opposed to Jackson's policy for fear that without a national bank, internal improvements in Illinois – railroads and canals – could not be developed.[194] Jackson's withdrawal of government deposits caused the bank to curtail its lending and produced a panic as the money supply contracted.

On Saturdays nearly the entire population of the county came to the county seat to sell produce, trade horses, shop, and talk politics.[195] The Whigs had been lambasting Jackson and his policies effectively, and the Democrats determined that they had to meet this assault and state their position. A mass meeting was called to be held at the court house at which the Democrats would present their resolutions supporting Jackson. An enormous crowd gathered – so large, in fact, that the windows were removed from the court house so that people standing outside could hear the speeches. Douglas presented the Democrats' resolutions and read them to the crowd. Josiah Lamborn, a skillful lawyer, rose to speak for the Whigs. He accused Douglas of misstating the facts and referred to him caustically. When he had finished, Douglas took the floor. He spoke for more than an hour. He disproved Lamborn's charge and so overwhelmed him with facts and arguments that Lamborn stomped out of the assemblage while Douglas carried on in triumph. Douglas's speech defending Jackson so enthralled the audience that the crowd hoisted him up on their shoulders and carried him out of the hall. They dubbed him the "Little Giant," a nickname that stuck with him throughout his career.

This meeting set the stage for Douglas's entry into politics. At his urging, the Democrats staged similar meetings in neighboring counties. Douglas "volunteered" to carry the Democratic banner. He was a born talker. He loved the company of men, could debate all of the issues of the day, and drink whiskey with the best of them (almost a requisite for entering politics in that era). Douglas was short – five foot four – and stout, with a massive head, a full head of hair and penetrating eyes.[196] His intensity commanded attention. He was not subtle. He wanted to play a role in public life and everybody knew it. He honed his oratorical skills, which were formidable. He neglected his law practice and devoted himself to organizing the Democratic Party in his home county. He was attacked and defended by rival newspapers as the spokesman of Jacksonian policy. He soon became a well known political figure. He shrewdly persuaded his party to slate only one candidate per office, a measure of party discipline previously lacking. With his credentials as a lawyer and his ability to organize his party, a political career was the obvious path. He soon held a succession of governmental positions – state's attorney, state legislator, secretary of state – before being elected to the Illinois Supreme Court in 1841, seven years after being admitted to the practice of law.[197] He was 27 years old.

Douglas had run for Congress in 1838 and lost. He ran for the Senate in 1842 and lost. He was undeterred. With the establishment of a new Congressional district, he ran and won a seat in Congress in 1843. He set his course to follow Jackson's policies. Importantly, he led the campaign to expand the Union from coast to coast. He had come to the frontier, found opportunity and made his mark. He was optimistic about the future. The burgeoning west would soon displace the east in shaping America. He was going to play a part in shaping the destiny of the nation. He called for the annexation of Texas and the establishment of military outposts along the trails leading west. As chair of the House Committee on Territories, he called for the organization of a territorial government for the Territory of Nebraska. It was not long before he had enough support in the Illinois legislature to be elected to the U.S. Senate.[198] That would come in 1846 and

he would go on to become a leader of his party, a towering presence in the Senate and a Presidential hopeful who, on several occasions, was disappointed when his party turned to men of lesser ability to lead the ticket.

Douglas Makes his Mark in Congress

IN 1843, WHEN Douglas was elected to be a Congressman and first went to Washington, the senior statesman of the Whig party was John Quincy Adams who was known as "Old Man Eloquent," a name his colleagues in Congress gave him. The son of a President, Adams had held a long series of public posts. He had represented the United States in its foreign relations with the major powers of the day. He had served as Senator, Secretary of State and President. After being defeated in his run for re-election to the Presidency by Andrew Jackson, Massachusetts sent him back to Congress where he served for 17 years until the day he died.

Adams had been in Congress 12 years when Douglas arrived. Douglas must have struck Adams as a product of the untamed west – uncouth and unrefined. In fact, Adams kept a diary in which he penned a portrait of Douglas debating a point in his vigorous style. When Douglas responded to the Whigs' criticism of a report he drafted, Adams observed:

He now raved out his hour in abusive invective upon members who had pointed out its slanders and upon the Whig Party. His face was convulsed, his gesticulation frantic, and he lashed himself into such a heat that if his body had been made out of combustible matter, it would have burnt out. In the midst of his roaring, to save himself from choking, he stripped off and cast away his cravat, and unbuttoned his waistcoat, and had the air and aspect of a half-naked pugilist.[199]

Stephen Arnold Douglas, April 23, 1813–March 3, 1861.
(Chicago History Museum)

and give the slave power a greater say in the conduct of the nation. Douglas masterfully proved his point by citing a document written 30 years earlier – by none other than Adams when he was Secretary of State.

The Mexicans had attacked Americans east of the Rio Grande River. Douglas asserted that this was territory belonging to the United States and therefore justified the war. Adams and the Whigs took the position that the border of Texas was at the Nueces River and did not extend to the Rio Grande. Douglas posed a few questions that committed Adams to the position that the Nueces was the border. Then, Douglas reached into his desk and produced a document which he said would conclusively prove that the proper boundary was the Rio Grande:

Texas (before her revolution) was always understood to have been a portion of the old province of Louisiana, whilst Coahuila was one of the Spanish provinces of Mexico. By ascertaining the western boundary of Louisiana, therefore, prior to the transfer by France to Spain, we discovered the dividing line between Texas and Coahuila. I will not weary the patience of the House by an examination of the authorities in detail. I will content myself by referring the gentleman to a document in which he will find them all collected and analyzed in a masterly manner, by one whose learning and accuracy he will not question. I allude to a dispatch (perhaps I might with propriety call it a book from its great length) written by our Secretary of State in 1819 [Adams] to Don Onis, the Spanish Minister. The document is to be found in the State papers. He will there find a multitudinous collection of old maps and musty records, histories, and geographies – Spanish, English, and French – by which it is clearly established that the Rio del Norte was the western boundary of Louisiana, and so considered by Spain and France both, when they owned the opposite banks of that river. The venerable gentleman from Massachusetts in that famous dispatch reviews all the authorities on either side with a clearness and ability which defy refutation, and demonstrate the validity of our title by virtue of the purchase of Louisiana. He went further and expressed his own convictions, upon a full examination of the whole

This unfavorable impression was amplified by the fact that Adams and Douglas were on opposite sides of the aisle. They were natural adversaries and became more so as Douglas mastered the etiquette of Congressional debate, fine tuned his debating skills and became one of the leading spokesmen for his party's positions.

In one famous confrontation with Adams, in 1846, Douglas set out to defend the policies of President Polk who had asked for a Declaration of War on Mexico. Douglas supported the Mexican War and coveted adding the territories west of the Louisiana Purchase to the United States. Adams, representing the interests of the northeastern States, opposed the war and any acquisition of territory that would upset the balance of power *question, that our title as far as the Rio del Norte, was as clear as to the Island of New Orleans. That was the opinion of Mr. Adams in 1819. It was the opinion of Messrs. Monroe and Pinckney in 1805. It was the opinion of Jefferson and Madison – of all our Presidents and of all administrations from its acquisition in 1803 to its fatal relinquishment in 1819.[200]*

Adams was left with no ground to stand on. This episode surely caused him to revise his unflattering view of Douglas's ability to debate.

There were some who acknowledged that Douglas was a skilled debater, but thought he also could be evasive when it suited him. One was Harriet Beecher Stowe who expressed begrudging admiration at his ability to mesmerize a crowd. She sat in the Senate gallery during the debate over the Kansas-Nebraska Bill. She reported that Douglas was in constant animation, that he had a melodious voice and enunciated distinctly. "His forte in debating," she said, "is his power in mystifying the point." She explained that she meant that he would set up a "straw man" argument, demolish it and assume the posture that he had carried the day on the real issue.[201]

Debating was an important skill for a politician. However, there was more to Douglas. In addition to being a great orator, Douglas had other potent political skills. He mastered the art of being adroit

…in the undercover maneuvers of politics, the strategy and tactics of campaigns, the divisions of the spoils of office, the various ruses to embarrass or divide the opposition, the log-rolling essential to the passing of desired bills, and the selection of issues which would win votes.[202]

His political skills were on display when he shepherded the bills that made up the Compromise of 1850 through the Senate, after the old war horses, Henry Clay and Daniel Webster, had tried in vain to find a path that bridged the gap between the northerners and the southerners. Douglas was a consummate legislative infighter. He knew how to persevere to emerge victorious from a long legislative battle.

CHICAGO, ILL.   Douglas Monument, 35th Street near Lake.

The Stephen A. Douglas Monument commemorating the political life and leadership of "The Little Giant." (Private Collection)

Douglas's Effort to Finesse the Slavery Issue

D OUGLAS RECOGNIZED THE obvious, that slavery was an extremely divisive issue. The Senate had been unable to act on various measures to create new territories or admit new States because the Southerners feared that they would lose ground if more Free States were admitted to the

Union and various Northerners promoted measures such as the Wilmot Proviso, a provision aimed at making all new States and territories "Free." To bring the two sides together, Douglas would be the principal architect of the Compromise of 1850. This would embrace two compromises: The first was the doctrine of "Popular Sovereignty," the doctrine that the people of the Territories and New States should determine for themselves whether to be Slave or Free. This became the key to finessing the sectional divide that had stymied Congress in the admission of new States after the War with Mexico. His design for admitting new States was intended to remove an issue that was inflammatory and divisive from Congress and to permit Congress to get on with Douglas's agenda – the settlement of the west, the organization of the territories and the admission of new States. He was in the business of nation-building. He could see a Union comprised of States from the Atlantic to the Pacific. He also had a plan for tying these States together with railroads. The second compromise was the Fugitive Slave Act of 1850, which Douglas drafted. While Douglas thought these measures would reduce tensions and conflict between the sections, that is not what happened.

Mormons, Welcoming Free Blacks, Are Ejected from Missouri

BEFORE DOUGLAS REACHED the Senate, he had a brush with another prominent group in Illinois that favored abolition. His complicated relationship with the Mormons undoubtedly intensified his conviction that opponents to slavery were a menace to the public order.

Joseph Smith Jr. was the founder of The Church of Jesus Christ of Latter-Day Saints. Initial efforts to establish the church in New York, Pennsylvania and Ohio ran into local opposition. Smith had a

revelation that the church should be established on Indian lands near the Missouri River and his followers moved to Caldwell County in the northwest part of Missouri in 1833.

Smith advocated that black slaves be freed, educated and given equal rights. This, of course, got him into trouble in pro-slavery Missouri.

The Book of Mormon Another Testament of Jesus Christ is regarded as scripture by Mormons. It says of Jesus Christ: "He inviteth all to come unto him, and partake of his goodness, and he denieth none that come unto him, black or white, bond and free, male and female…."

In 1835, an article was published in a Missouri newspaper expressing the views of the Mormons regarding blacks. It invited "Free People of Color" to come to Missouri and join the church. The slaveholding Missourians regarded this as seditious. They accused the Mormons of scheming to bring free blacks to Missouri to encourage slaves to revolt.[203] The Missourians armed themselves to force the Mormons to leave Missouri. Hostilities escalated. The Mormons started to make preparations to defend themselves. The Governor of Missouri, Lilburn W. Boggs, a slaveholder, issued an order to the state militia that became known as the "Extermination Order:"

The Mormons must be treated as enemies and must be exterminated or driven from the state, if necessary, for the public good.[204]

The result was a massacre. Hundreds of Mormons, men and boys, were killed: "At Haun's Mill, a Mormon village in Northern Missouri, a mob of white Missourians had butchered 17 men and boys; cutting the throats of some, and killing some children in the arms of their mothers; then raping the mothers."[205]

News of the atrocity spread quickly. But President Van Buren did nothing, supposedly for fear of alienating his party.

The Mormons retreated to Quincy, where their Illinois neighbors took them in. Then they moved to a nearby swamp in Illinois. Here they founded Nauvoo. Over the next nine years, this settlement grew to a city of 20,000. But the tensions between the abolitionist Mormons and the slave-holding Missourians did not subside.

Dr. Dyer Prods the Mormons

D R. D YER WAS interested in building alliances with others who might help promote the abolitionists' cause. In 1842, Dr. Dyer wrote John C. Bennett, the Mayor of Nauvoo, to encourage the Mormons to speak out on the outrages of slavery and Missouri's unconscionable conduct in imprisoning the Quincy Three. At the time Bennett was a General in the Nauvoo militia, a right hand man to Joseph Smith and the person who persuaded the Illinois legislature to authorize the incorporation of Nauvoo (with the right to form a militia). Though Bennett would later be excommunicated and become one of those opposed to Smith and the Mormons, he was in good standing in 1842.[206]

Dr. Dyer sent Bennett a copy of *Genius of Liberty*, the abolitionist newspaper published by Eastman, in which Eastman described the arrest and conviction of the Quincy Three. Dr. Dyer asked Bennett, "What think you of the sentencing of three men from Quincy Mission Institute in this State, a short time since, to 12 years confinement in the penitentiary of Missouri, for no crime at all, or only such as God would regard as virtue? Please look into this matter, and see if you can not join with the benevolent and fearless, and call the attention of the nation or the State, to these outrages of Missouri." Dr. Dyer's letter did not make it clear whether he was just looking for sympathy or whether he wanted to prod the Mormons to take some (unspecified) direct action:

Well, can any Court, either State or national, rob me of liberty for twelve years, (even against their own State laws) for acting precisely in accordance with the letter and spirit of the Constitution of the United States, and the precepts of Jesus Christ? Is it to be

John C. Bennett, "a friend of Universal Liberty" and Mayor of Nauvoo, a town founded by the Mormons, who were against slavery. (LDS Church History Library)

submitted to tamely, that three men shall be immured in a dungeon for twelve years torn from their families and friends, and from society and usefulness, for barely teaching a fellow being how to go to a place where he may learn the sciences – have his own wages, aye, and his own person?[207]

Dr. Dyer may have gotten more than he bargained for. Bennett responded condemning slavery but linking the outrages of Missouri toward the Quincy Three with Missouri's assaults on Mormons. Then Bennett sent the correspondence to *Genius of Liberty* with directions that it be published to put the Mormons on record as being against slavery, against the imprisonment of the Quincy Three and against religious persecution. Bennett was far from subtle. He used bombastic language to declare his position. While he spoke of taking "every constitutional means to procure

Smith, Joseph

Joseph Smith, Jr. (December 23, 1805–June 27, 1844) translated the *Book of Mormon* and founded the Church of Jesus Christ of Latter-day Saints. (Chicago History Museum)

Joseph Smith read the correspondence and decided to reprint it in *Times and Seasons*, the newspaper he edited in Nauvoo that was the organ of the Mormons. Not only that, Smith added his own editorial comment in a letter to Bennett, joining in the condemnation of slavery:

Respected Brother:

I have just been perusing your correspondence with Doctor Dyer on the subject of American Slavery, and the students of the Quincy Mission Institute, and it makes my blood boil within me to reflect upon the injustice, cruelty, and oppression, of the rulers of the people – when will these things cease to be, and the Constitution and the Laws again bear rule? I fear for my beloved country – mob violence, injustice, and cruelty, appear to be the darling attributes of Missouri, and no man taketh it to heart!

Needless to say, while these statements were music to the abolitionists' ears, they aroused the Missourians who were fearful that the Mormons might start an insurrection in Missouri to free the Quincy Three. And this rhetoric made those sympathetic to the slaveholders in Illinois leery about what the Mormons and their militia might do.

a redress of grievances," he invoked militaristic imagery that suggested he might not be so confined:

I swore in my youth that my hands should never be bound, nor my feet fettered, nor my tongue palsied – I am a friend of liberty, UNIVERSAL LIBERTY, both civil and religious. I ever detested servile bondage. I wish to see the shackles fall from the feet of the oppressed, and the chains of slavery broken. I hate the oppressor's grasp, and the tyrant's rod; against them I set my brows like brass, and my face like steel; and my arm is nerved for conflict. Let the sons of thunder speak, achieve victories before the canon's mouth, and beard the lion in his den: 'til then the cry of the oppressed will not be heard....

Judge Douglas Presides over a Mormon Trial

ABOLITIONISM WAS ONLY one of the issues that caused friction between the Mormons and their neighbors. The new religion and its clannish adherents were viewed with suspicion. There were constant disputes between the "Saints" and the "Gentiles." In fact, when Douglas became a member of the Illinois Supreme Court, in an era when justices also served as trial judges, he was assigned to a circuit that included Nauvoo[208] and with it came the task of presiding over trials when Mormons were arrested and accused of crimes. These disputes were difficult to resolve because of the absence of conclusive proof on either side even on as simple an issue as ownership of a horse.

Douglas presided over one such trial when Smith was in the dock. On that occasion, a large crowd of people antagonistic to the Mormons and leery that Smith would get off lightly, gathered with the idea of imposing their own brand of justice. This mob erected a scaffold outside the court house and proceeded to barge in and disrupt the trial. Douglas called for order and directed the sheriff to eject the intruders. The sheriff made a futile attempt to turn them back and reported to Douglas that it was beyond his power to stop them. Douglas jumped up and pointed to the biggest man among the spectators, calling to him by name and saying he appointed him sheriff, commanded him to restore order and authorized him to deputize others as needed. Douglas chose well. This accidental sheriff rose to the occasion, loudly commanding order, knocking down the few who did not heed his order to leave the premises. Smith was saved.

The Mormons had previously been critical of Douglas's rulings, many of which had been adverse to their interests. This episode won him new respect from the Mormons. His credibility with the Mormons would serve Douglas well when the time came to mediate the next, potentially more lethal, war between the Mormons and their neighbors.

Smith ran for President in 1844. Following the position he took after commenting on the Dyer-Bennett correspondence, he unabashedly espoused an end to slavery. In fact, he devised a policy that might fund the freeing of slaves. He advocated selling public lands to purchase freedom and to give other land to freed slaves to help them obtain equality. Smith attacked Henry Clay for his role in authoring the Missouri Compromise, which Smith labeled a measure "derived for the benefit of slavery." (The Missouri Compromise brought Missouri into the Union as a Slave State in 1820.)

The Mormon Wars and the Murder of Joseph Smith, Jr.

THE FLASH POINT occurred on March 30, 1844, when Smith, who was then Mayor of Nauvoo, arrested a white man (a Missouri slave-owner) for whipping a black man in Nauvoo.[209] This enraged the Missouri slave-holders and their friends. They threatened to invade Nauvoo and take Smith back to be tried. At about the same time, Smith had ordered a newspaper, the *Expositor* that was critical of his leadership, declared a public nuisance and shut down. The ranks of those opposed to the Mormons swelled. The anti-Mormons gathered together threatening to invade Nauvoo, arrest Smith and drive the Mormons out of Nauvoo to the wilds of Iowa.

Smith called out the Nauvoo militia.

This backfired. The Governor of Illinois, Thomas Ford, ordered Smith arrested on a charge of *treason* because he had called out the militia without the written consent of the governor. Though he could have fled, Smith determined to surrender to save Nauvoo and its inhabitants from the likelihood of a repeat of the massacre that occurred in Missouri nine years earlier.

Smith had a premonition that he would not be coming back alive.

Indeed, he left Nauvoo on June 24, 1844 for Carthage and was murdered while awaiting trial there. The Illinois militia was stationed outside the jail in Carthage to supposedly protect Smith and the other Mormons with him. A mob, *with their faces painted black*, stormed the jail. They met no resistance. Smith was in an apartment on the second floor. On their first foray, Smith fired away with a pistol and repelled the mob. Two of his assailants were wounded. (Later, they reportedly died.) But the mob regrouped and attacked again. Smith had emptied the revolver. He had no more ammunition. As the mob entered his apartment, he backed up to the window and was fired upon, blasting him out the window. The mob killed his brother

Hyrum, as well. In the street below, the mob propped up Smith's bleeding body and pumped several more rounds into him. Then they fled.

Those who were arrested or charged with Smith's murder later got off.

Smith's death did not resolve the tensions. A war was about to break out between the Mormons and their enemies. Governor Ford of Illinois called out the militia, sending a regiment to put down the rebellion. The regiment consisting of 450 men was met by a force of over 4,000 well-armed Mormons. Undeterred, the commander of the militia proposed to attack. His orders were to arrest the 12 apostles. Douglas was there as a major in the militia and he asked if the attack could be postponed long enough to give him time to negotiate. The commander agreed and Douglas rode out alone, was stopped at the Mormon's lines and then let through. He met with Brigham Young and the apostles. They negotiated. The Mormons recognized that they could not live peaceably with their neighbors any longer in Nauvoo. When the negotiations were concluded, the Mormons agreed to leave Illinois. The Little Giant's intercession and diplomacy saved lives on both sides. The Mormons moved on and re-established themselves in Utah.

Smith's third-party presidential campaign in 1844 was an early sign of fissures in the then-prevailing two-party system. The issue that would break up the parties was the same one that would divide the country – slavery.[210] Smith's assassination was another testament to the incendiary nature of opposition to slavery. Douglas knew first hand what a powder keg the issue of slavery was. This experience undoubtedly fueled his search for compromises that could quell the tumult.

John Hossack

THROUGHOUT THE 1840s and 1850s there a steady stream of runaway slaves was brought to Chicago. Another conductor was John Hossack who had a farm 20 miles outside Chicago.

He helped a slave sent to him by Ichabod Codding in 1844 and then regularly transported slaves sent to him to Dr. Dyer. He would receive a telegram saying "Meet friends at depot," which was the signal that fugitive slaves would be sent his way. On one occasion, he had three fugitives in a wagon and drove past a gang of workmen who cried derisively, "The Niggers!" and ran menacingly at them only to be out run by the team of horses Hossack was driving. A shower of stones did little damage and the slaves were delivered safely to Dr. Dyer. Later, in 1859, because of his zeal to thwart the recapture of slaves, Hossack would be prosecuted and convicted of hindering federal officers carrying out their duties under the Fugitive Slave Act.[211]

Fugitive slaves being ushered through Chicago became a common sight. George Manierre's father came to Chicago in 1835. The son had this recollection:

Between 1846 and 1854 it was quite common for runaway slaves to pass through Chicago on their way to Canada. I remember my father taking a suit of his clothes and dressing a runaway slave in the rear kitchen of our house on Michigan Avenue and Jackson Boulevard.[212]

The Exclusion of Free Negroes from Illinois

ILLINOIS ENACTED A new constitution in 1848. This document was adopted in convention and submitted to the voters who ratified it on March 6, 1848. It excluded free Negroes from coming into the State. This was accomplished by directing the General Assembly to pass laws to prohibit: "free persons of color from immigrating to and settling in this state; and to effectually prevent owners of slaves from bringing them into this State for the purpose of setting them free."[213] Like the Black Codes, there was a strong current afoot in Illinois and other northern States that might best be called Negrophobia. While the citizens of these States opposed the institution of slavery, they were in no hurry to welcome individual blacks.

Illinois would probably just as soon forget about this chapter in its legal history. But, in 1850, there was no embarrassment about this measure. Douglas gave a speech on the Senate floor defending the right of States to enact such measures, which he said were justified as a matter of "police protection:"

> *Illinois has a provision in her Constitution making it the duty of the Legislature to provide efficient means for keeping all Negroes from coming into the state who were not natives of or residents in the state at the time of the adoption of the instrument..... These laws are passed among us as police regulations.... We border on Slave States on two sides [Missouri and Kentucky]. We do not wish to make our state an asylum for all the old, and decrepit, and broken down Negroes that may be sent to it. We desire every other state to take care of her own Negroes, whether free or slave, and we will take care of ours. That law was adopted for the purpose of preventing other states inundating and coloniz-ing Illinois with free Negroes. We do not believe it to be wise or politic to hold out inducements for that class of people to come and live among us.*[214]

Douglas explained that the free Negroes already in Illinois were "protected" in the enjoyment of their civil rights. But, in the same speech, he went on to explain that, in accordance with the Black Codes in Illinois, blacks were not allowed to vote, serve in the militia, serve on juries or to exercise other political rights. In his view, there was nothing remarkable that Negroes were not "placed upon an equality with the whites." Douglas thought the Illinois approach should serve as a model for other States to avoid colonies of Negroes "sent to us in order to get rid of the trouble of them at home." Moreover, the exclusion-of-Negroes provi-sion in the Illinois Constitution was not empty rhetoric according to the Little Giant. Douglas, in his speech in the Senate, boasted that Illinois actively enforced its policy of excluding free Negroes – keeping that "unwelcome population" out of Illinois.

Today, the exclusion-of-free Negroes provision in the Illinois Constitution of 1848 can only be viewed as a blot on the escutcheon of the "Free State" of Illinois. The abolitionists seethed that their State could enact such outrages. Obviously, in 1848, their views were in the minority. It would take quite a few more years to turn public sentiment around. (The provision was not removed until a new Illinois Constitution was passed in 1870.)[215]

The Prevalence of Racism

LINCOLN HAS OFTEN been criticized by some modern historians for not labeling the Civil War a war to end slavery and for not promoting emancipation earlier in his presidency. Those same criticisms were made in his own day when Lincoln was criticized for not embracing the cause of the abolitionists. This view fails to appreciate that the abolitionists were in the minority and their views were regarded as extremist and dangerous. In the 1850s, when Lincoln began exploring whether to run for the Senate, he had to chart a course that recognized the fact that a majority of Illinois voters, as reflected by the ratification vote on the 1848 Constitution, held Negroes to be inferior to whites, approved of measures such as the Black Codes, and favored excluding free Negroes from Illinois. Lincoln may have understood the attitudes of his fellow citizens better than most. As a trial lawyer, he traveled the circuit and represented people in lawsuits. He regularly picked juries from among the citizens of the various counties he practiced in. One of the skills of the trial lawyer is the ability to discern attitudes and detect biases of potential jurors, even when they do not openly admit to holding any prejudices. Sometimes jurors with prejudices can be excused. More often, the lawyer has to shape his arguments to fit within the moral code of the jurors. Lincoln was especially skilled in this regard.

Lincoln had to deal with the fact that the predomi-nant view of free Negroes was that they were a menace.

Just as slaveholders did not want territories or States on their borders that might become havens for runaway slaves, no "Free State's" citizens wanted to encourage settlement by free Negroes. When Prudence Crandall sought to establish a school "for young ladies and little misses of color," in Canterbury, Connecticut in 1833, with the support of William Lloyd Garrison, the town passed resolutions disapproving the idea and began a process of harassing the students by passing and enforcing loitering laws, among other measures. In a heated exchange of letters in the *Brooklyn Advertiser Press*, the general newspaper for Brooklyn, Connecticut, one of the organizers of the opposition to Crandall's school, candidly revealed the prevailing view of Northerners:

We are not merely opposed to the establishment of that school in Canterbury, we mean that there shall not be such a school set up anywhere in the state. The colored people can never rise from their menial condition in our country; they ought not to be permitted to rise. They are an inferior race of beings, and never can or ought to be recognized as the equals of whites. Africa is the place for them. I am in favor of colonization. Let the niggers and their descendants be sent back to their fatherland…. The sooner you abolitionists abandon your project the better for our country, the niggers and yourself.[216]

Thus, the predominant attitude in the north was not just that it was undesirable to educate or give *any* civil rights to free blacks, but also that abolitionists were a dangerous threat to the maintenance of order. Is it any wonder that Lincoln had to temper his anti-slavery advocacy?

The Union before 1850

THE SIZE AND shape of the Union was about to change radically in 1850. Adding States, however, presented the issue of whether the sphere of slavery would be expanded.

Seven of the original 13 States banished slavery in their constitutions shortly after the Revolution.[217] Of the 13 original States, six had laws upholding slavery: Georgia, North Carolina, South Carolina, Virginia, Maryland, and Delaware. The seven that were Free States were: New Hampshire, Massachusetts, Rhode Island, Connecticut, New York, New Jersey and Pennsylvania. Then Vermont came in Free, followed by Tennessee and Kentucky which came in as Slave States. There were then eight Free and eight Slave States. They were followed by: Ohio, in 1802, Free; Louisiana, in 1812, Slave; Indiana, in 1816, Free; Mississippi, in 1817, Slave; Illinois, in 1818, Free; and Alabama, in 1819, Slave.[218]

When Missouri sought admission, whether or not she would come in as a Slave or Free State was a contentious issue. The compromise fashioned by Henry Clay, in 1820, "the Missouri Compromise," was to admit Missouri as a Slave State and at the same time admit Maine as a Free State. This set a precedent of admitting one Free State to offset each new Slave State. The Compromise included an understanding that, in the future, slavery would be allowed south of the Mason-Dixon Line but not north of it.

The Mason-Dixon Line was the survey performed by Charles Mason and Jeremiah Dixon between 1763 and 1767 to delineate the boundary between Pennsylvania and Maryland.[219] (King Charles I gave Lord Baltimore the colony of Maryland in 1632. Fifty years later, in 1682, King Charles II gave William Penn what became Pennsylvania. But the grants had conflicting boundary descriptions requiring adjudication and, ultimately, the famous survey.) The boundary is essentially an east-west line, 15 miles South of Latitude 40° North (approximately 15 miles south of Philadelphia).

In 1820, the Missouri Compromise adopted the extension of this line, at 36°30', as a boundary to separate Free and Slave zones in the territory acquired in the Louisiana Purchase.[220] This solution would hold for 25 years. Then the question was: What to do about Texas?

Texas had successfully rebelled against Mexico in 1836. (After losing the Battle of the Alamo, a 13 day siege that ended March 6, 1836, the Texans went on to win the Texas Revolution when Sam Houston's army defeated Mexico in the Battle of San Jacinto.) Texas then campaigned to be admitted as a State. For nine years, the Texas question plagued Congress. Some were opposed to the admission of Texas because annexation presented the threat that slavery would be extended beyond the existing States. Others were opposed because of the likelihood that admitting Texas would precipitate a war with Mexico, because Mexico had never accepted Texas's independence. Politicians, who feared that opposition to the admission of Texas might cost them votes from pro-slavery constituencies in their parties, could claim their opposition was based on avoiding war, not limiting slavery. Both Henry Clay and Martin Van Buren tried to straddle the slavery issue in this way in 1844. It cost them. James Knox Polk was elected President to a term beginning in 1845. Slave holders wanted Texas to come into the union as a Slave State so as not to be a refuge or magnet for runaways.

Douglas championed the admission of Texas paired with the admission of Oregon. This would maintain the equilibrium of Free and Slave States. To permit the balancing to continue as the Union expanded, because there was more territory north of the line, he proposed that there could be as many as three States admitted in addition to Texas from the Territory of Texas in return for a prohibition on slavery in States formed north of 36°30' in the Louisiana Purchase. This became the approach that worked, though a substitute proposal was adopted that allowed as many as five States to be created. President Polk accepted the compromise and Texas joined the Union in 1845.

But this touched off a war with Mexico. When Texas was admitted as a State, Mexico broke off diplomatic relations with the United States. The United States had been warned that annexation would mean war. Despite its warning, Mexico did not attack until Zachary Taylor moved U.S. troops into a disputed area south of Corpus Christi that Texas had never claimed. (Polk had earlier tried to buy California and New Mexico. Some have speculated that he deliberately precipitated the war.) The war was opposed by some southerners (who thought it might lead to the admission of more Free States than Slave) and by Whigs, such as Lincoln, (who thought it would expand the domain of slavery). Whether the war was justified was the subject of the famous exchange in the House of Representatives between Douglas and John Quincy Adams.

The Mexican War was the event that precipitated Henry David Thoreau to write his essay *Civil Disobedience*, published in 1849, in which he expressed the view that he "would not go" if asked to be part of a militia to put down a slave rebellion or march on Mexico.[221] Nevertheless, as wars go, it was a sterling success. By the Treaty of Guadalupe-Hidalgo, signed February 2, 1848, the Republic of Mexico abandoned its claim to Texas and ceded to the United States most of what is now New Mexico, Arizona, California, Colorado, Utah and Nevada. The United States gained 200,000 square miles of territory. (The Gadsden Purchase of 1852 added another 45,000 square miles of territory to New Mexico and Arizona in a strip of land south of the Gila River.)

The question of whether the sphere of slavery should grow with the expansion of the Union exploded as an issue after the Mexican War. Should slavery be allowed or banned in new territories? The issue stymied Congress, which was unable to pass any legislation as to how the territories were to be governed or how they should go about becoming States. When gold was discovered at Sutter's Mill in Coloma, California in 1848, people began streaming west into that territory. A major population shift was occurring and Illinois was the scene of wagon trains being organized for the trek west to join the Gold Rush of 1849. The people swept up in the gold rush became the "forty-niners." Over night San Francisco grew from a town of 800 to a city of 100,000. Californians met in convention and formed their own government with a State constitution that proclaimed California a Free State. Then they pressed for admission to the Union. The issue of statehood for Texas could no longer be neglected.

Douglas was particularly concerned that if Congress did not act, California might decide to be independent. He was especially leery of allowing "petty rival republics" to spring up.[222] But accommodating the divergent positions on slavery seemed impossible. Northern and Southern Senators were both intransigent, unable to agree on the scope of slavery in the territories and new States. Douglas set out to find a solution that would bring the intransigents to some middle path so the Union could expand by admitting new States. The task was Herculean.

The Deadlock Prior to the Compromise of 1850

HOW SHOULD CONGRESS address slavery in establishing territorial governments and admitting States? There were three basic positions on the issue.[223] The first was that of the Northerners who sought passage of the "Wilmot Proviso." They wanted Congress to prohibit slavery in any territory acquired from Mexico in the War. This was the position of the abolitionists, the "free soil" democrats, and many Whigs. The purpose of the Proviso was to contain slavery in the original Slave States where it already existed.

The Wilmot Proviso, and its variants, inflamed the Southerners. Led by John C. Calhoun, who had threatened secession as a way to veto challenges to slavery ever since the Missouri Compromise, they saw this as a first step in a process that would reduce their political strength and their ability to maintain slavery.

The second position was Calhoun's counter to the Wilmot Proviso. He argued that the territories were owned in common by all the States and that Congress *did not have the power* to exclude slavery. In his view it would violate the Constitution if slave-holders could not take their "property" with them when they moved into the territories. This would discriminate against citizens of States where slavery was allowed and destroy the equality of the States. If the Slave States were not treated fairly he threatened that they would secede. The threat of secession had been made before but

there were now more southern States embracing this extreme position.[224]

Douglas opposed the Wilmot Proviso. He was for expanding the Union and if the Wilmot Proviso were adopted no southern State would ever vote for the admission of a State from territory ceded by Mexico. He championed the third position, "Popular Sovereignty." The idea was that Congress should not dictate to the territories or the States whether to embrace slavery or not. Rather, the people in each territory should decide the issue for themselves and govern themselves accordingly. This position ultimately prevailed and it spelled the end of the Missouri Compromise.

These issues were not argued just in Washington. Every State legislature debated whether their delegation should support the Wilmot Proviso or one of the alternatives.

Dr. Dyer Pushes the Liberty Party Forward

DR. DYER WAS in the forefront of the Liberty Party's effort to expand its base. The Liberty Party, started in 1840, had fielded candidates with little success. Dr. Dyer and Lovejoy attended the October, 1843 convention of the National Liberty Party in Buffalo, New York where Dr. Dyer was elected a vice president of the convention and Lovejoy was one of the secretaries. The convention nominated James G. Birney for President and Thomas Morris for Vice President.

In Illinois, the party nominated Eells for Governor in 1846. They then began the arduous task of party building. They tried to organize committees in as many Illinois counties as possible and slate local candidates. The State had a recognizable schism. The north was considered abolitionist territory while the south (which Douglas called "little Egypt") had southern sympathies and supported slaveholding. Dr. Dyer was chair of the Cook County delegation. While there

As Chairman of the Cook County delegation and Vice President of the 1843 Convention, Dr. Dyer was asked to lead a committee calling members of the Liberty Party to the "Northwestern Liberty Party Convention" in 1846. (Chicago History Museum)

were parts of Illinois that would not come on board, there was also an effort to coordinate with the organizations in the other States.

In May of 1846, Dr. Dyer led a committee that issued a call to the members of the Liberty Party from other States to attend a "Northwestern Liberty Party Convention" to be held June 24, 1846 in Chicago.

The Convention was held and 6,000 people attended.[225] Dr. Dyer called the meeting to order and asked the delegates of each State to report on the status of their efforts to abolish slavery, to repeal the Black Codes, to elect abolitionist candidates and to spread the message of the Party. Lovejoy, Codding, L.C.P. Freer and John Cross were among the Illinoisans participating. One issue that the delegates had on their agenda was the pressing need to publish more newspapers promoting their cause and to combat the restraints on free speech the existing papers were encountering. One delegate, Beckley of Michigan, summed up

the attitude of those attending: "We must labor on, through the press, by public lectures, and disseminate the truth in every possible way. We must give the car of liberty greater impetus than ever, and we shall be able publicly to triumph in the downfall of that institution which is a disgrace to our country."[226] Beckley noted that there were then 30 anti-slavery newspapers issuing 66,000 copies published every week and that articles from them were being republished in other papers, even some in the South.

The Convention established various working committees. One was the Committee on Establishing an Anti-Slavery Paper in Washington, D.C. This committee accomplished its objective by turning to Dr. Dyer who founded *National Era*, a newspaper that played a significant role in the debate over slavery.

Before adopting a raft of anti-slavery resolutions, the Convention heard from a former slave and was entertained by George C. Clark, who sang liberty songs. A few notables who could not attend wrote letters. Salmon P. Chase's letter addressed to Dr. Dyer was read to the Convention.

The effort to build a broader base was succeeding, though slowly. The Liberty Party candidate for governor in 1846 polled 5,147 votes, an increase of 1,600 over the Presidential vote in Illinois for the Liberty Party candidate in 1844.[227] Owen Lovejoy ran unsuccessfully for Congress under the Liberty banner in 1846 and 1848. The time was ripe for a new political party.

Wilmot's Proviso Unravels the Existing Political Fabric

FOR A MEASURE that never passed in Congress, the Wilmot Proviso had a profound effect on the future of the nation. Introduced in 1846 by David Wilmot of Pennsylvania, the bill proposed to prohibit slavery in any territory acquired from Mexico. This concisely stated proposition exposed the fault lines in the existing political parties. As the northern States took up the measure resolving to instruct their representatives to vote for the Proviso, the political dividing line became north versus south, and it fractured both the Whig and Democratic parties which, up until then, had straddled the sectional difference. The divisions gave new life to the effort to launch third parties and ultimately led to the successful fusion of political interests of the northerners in the new Republican Party.

In Massachusetts, when the Whig convention in that State balked at adopting the Wilmot Proviso, Henry Wilson led a walk-out of Whigs who were dubbed the "Conscience Whigs." In New York, former President Martin Van Buren defied President Polk and led the Democrats to embrace the measure. President Polk retaliated by terminating all of the patronage positions that Van Buren had held sway over. Van Buren and his followers became "Barnburners," having cut themselves off from the spoils of their own party. (The Democrats who stayed with Polk were "Hunkerers," having hunkered down to hold on to their positions.)

The Free Soil Party

THE VAN BUREN Democrats issued a call for a convention in Buffalo in 1848 that gave birth to the Free Soil Party. Journeying from Chicago, Dr. Dyer, Lovejoy, and Collins were joined by C.D. Wells, John Cross, Isaac Newton (I.N.) Arnold and C. Sedgwick. The anti-slavery men who had been the backbone of the Liberty Party in Illinois joined the disaffected factions from the Whigs, Democrats and other dispirited Liberty men.[228] The Free Soil platform adopted at this convention centered on the Wilmot principle: prohibit the extension of slavery. The platform also advocated abolishing slavery where Congress had the power to do so (Washington, D.C.). To broaden the appeal of the party, the Free Soilers also favored internal improvements, a homestead law and a tariff.

In the 1848 election, the new Free Soil Party slated Martin Van Buren as its candidate, the regular Democrats slated Lewis Cass (a Democrat with Southern leanings) and the Whigs ran with Zachary Taylor who won.

Dr. Dyer Runs for Governor as the Free Soil Candidate

IN ILLINOIS THE Constitution called for a new election for Governor in 1848 even though the incumbent Augustus C. French had only served two years of the term to which he was elected in 1846. French ran for re-election in 1848. The Free Soil Party slated Charles Volney Dyer to run against him for Governor.[229] French won handily, receiving 67,453 votes to Dr. Dyer's 3,834 in the field of four candidates.[230] Support for the Free Soil Party in Illinois was slim.[231] However, the Free Soilers enjoyed some successes nationally, electing nine Representatives and two Senators to Congress. Dr. Dyer, a genuinely modest man, was philosophic when it came to running for public office. He said, "I did not ask a single man to vote for me and none did."

The Wilmot Proviso in Illinois

NOWHERE WAS THE debate over the Wilmot Proviso more heated than in Illinois. The Illinois legislature *instructed* its Senators "to use all honorable means in their power to procure the enactment of such laws by Congress … as shall contain express declaration, that there shall be neither slavery, nor involuntary servitude in said Territories."[232] (Because United States Senators were then elected by their respective State legislatures, legislatures would occasionally give explicit instructions to their Senators who naturally felt obliged to follow them.)

The instructions by the Illinois legislature on the Wilmot Proviso were passed in part in an attempt to unseat Senator Douglas, who had said he would resign if so instructed. Douglas then thought better of his ultimatum. If he resigned, he would just be giving his seat to a "Free Soil" democrat, given the way the most recent elections had gone in Illinois. He decided instead to proclaim to his colleagues in the Senate that he was casting his vote for the Proviso as instructed but was actually opposed to it as a matter of policy. The Wilmot Proviso died with the admission of California. But Douglas's falling out with the voters of Illinois over the issue was the first sign that his efforts to fashion compromises on the issue of slavery could backfire on him at home. He would soon have to hurry home to patch things up.

Famine and Immigration

IN 1848 THERE was a terrible famine in Ireland and Scotland. On February 23, 1847, *Western Citizen* published an appeal over the signatures of Dr. Dyer, Eastman, Wheeler, DeWolf and (George) Anderson asking citizens to come to the City Saloon on Thursday the 25th with "donations of provisions to the starving poor in Ireland and Scotland."[233] This cataclysm would actually have a direct effect on the political landscape because the famine would bring a new wave of immigration to the United States and to the north in particular, changing the demographics and bringing future citizens whose economic interests made them naturally opposed to slavery.

Slavery in the Nation's Capitol

ONE UNRESOLVED ISSUE that was on the nation's agenda was the fact that slavery thrived in the nation's capitol. In fact, Lincoln probably witnessed first hand how slave-catchers worked. When he was serving his term as a Congressman, in 1849, he boarded at Mrs. Ann Sprigg's boardinghouse. Slave hunters forced their way in to her boardinghouse and arrested a black waiter who had been working to purchase his freedom.[234] Certainly when Lincoln was a Congressman living in Washington he encountered slavery daily. Within seven blocks from the capitol was a warehouse operated by the country's largest slave traders. Lincoln referred to this as "a sort of Negro livery-stable," where slaves were collected and dispatched to be sold in the South.[235]

For Northerners, it was intolerable that the nation's capital should be polluted with the business of the slave trade.

PART II

1850–1860:

Restraining Slavery Becomes the Issue

The Compromise of 1850

THE COMPROMISE OF 1850 consisted of six separate pieces of legislation:

1. *The admission of California with her Free Constitution.*
2. *The establishment of a territorial government for Utah, leaving to the people the right to regulate their domestic institutions (i.e., slavery).*
3. *The establishment of a territorial government for New Mexico with the same provision.*
4. *The adjustment of the boundary dispute between Texas and New Mexico.*
5. *The abolition of the slave trade in the District of Columbia.*
6. *The Fugitive Slave Bill.*

The debate over these measures in 1850 dragged on in the Senate for eight months.[236] The stalemate that persisted put the rest of the nation's business on hold. There were extreme positions on both sides. Seward, the advocate of the abolitionist cause, argued that California must come in Free, that the territories must be Free, that slavery must be abolished in the District of Columbia, and that no Fugitive Slave Act should be passed. In response to the Southerners' Constitutional arguments supporting their pro-slavery views, Seward, in a stirring speech on March 11, 1850, argued forcefully that there was no reason to compromise: "There is a *higher law* than the Constitution."[237] This electrified the abolitionists following the debates.

When Seward later became a candidate for the Republican nomination in 1860, he repeated this along with his other famous remark that the country faced an "irresistible conflict" because of slavery. Herndon noted that, in 1860, Lincoln wrote on a copy of the *Missouri Democrat* reporting on one of Seward's speeches where he said this, "I agree with Seward in his 'Irrepressible Conflict,' but I do not endorse his 'Higher Law' doctrine."[238]

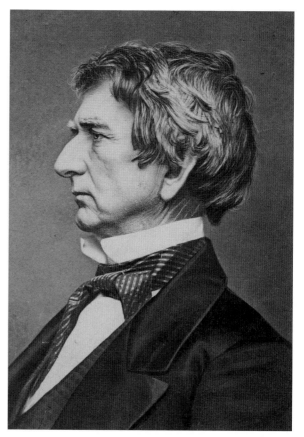

William H. Seward (May 16, 1801–October 10, 1872) was Secretary of State in the Lincoln administration. (Chicago History Museum)

In the beginning of this watershed year, the three towering figures of the Senate over the last quarter century – Daniel Webster, Henry Clay and John Calhoun – all tried to guide the destiny of these provisions. Calhoun died on March 7, 1850.[239] On July 22, 1850, Webster resigned, after President Taylor died, to become a cabinet member in the administration of Millard Fillmore.[240] Clay had tried to sponsor an "Omnibus Bill" that would force the measures through by tying them together.[241] But the omnibus approach was defeated. Clay absented himself. Douglas, who had been Chair of the Committee on Territories and the original author of the bills concerning new States and Territories, picked up the cudgel and worked tirelessly to make the effort succeed.

He succeeded by deftly presenting his bills in proper strategic sequence and cobbling together the votes needed.[242] His main stratagem was to promote popular sovereignty as the way to avoid resolving whether Congress should decide whether Territories and new States would be Slave or Free. Rather than confront directly the Calhoun argument that the Constitution did not give Congress the power to legislate on the question of slavery, Douglas argued that "Popular Sovereignty" fit exactly with the Constitution's scheme: "Every people ought to possess the right of forming and regulating their own internal concerns and domestic institutions."[243] In other words, the existing States all decided the issue for themselves. Therefore it would be unjust to deprive the territories and new States of that prerogative. He then sought to mediate between the extremists on the opposing sides. He told the Northerners that Popular Sovereignty would achieve what they wanted because slavery could not flourish in the new territories as a matter of climate and geography: Where is there "territory so adapted to slavery that new Slave States might be formed from it? There is none – none at all."[244] (This argument presumed that the only economically viable reason for owning slaves was to grow cotton.) He told the slave-holders that they were protected because of the exceptions that the Free States already recognized – registered indentures and the right of transit. A continued balancing of Free and Slave Sates was "unrealistic."[245] And he was willing to beef up the old fugitive slave law with a new one to curb the runaway slave problem. He thought Popular Sovereignty would take the slavery issue out of Congress where it had held up the admission of new States and prevented acting on important projects for developing the west, such as building railroads connecting the various regions together. Let each State decide for itself whether to be Slave or Free. And finally, he agreed to support the Fugitive Slave Act to meet the demands of Southerners to stop the problem of runaway slaves and to curtail the activities of abolitionists.

Douglas's position triumphed in the Compromise of 1850. The Senate passed each of the measures. Douglas then turned his energies to influencing the House. With the help of John McClerand and the rest of the Illinois delegation, he was able to help steer the bills through the House. President Fillmore signed them.[246]

This saga had consumed everyone in Washington. When the measures were passed, on Saturday, September 7, 1850, a spontaneous celebration began. Washington, D.C. went wild. There was a 100 gun salute, rockets and fireworks. The Marine Band played and marched around the city in the evening to serenade the leading figures of Congress who had worked so hard for passage. Douglas, Cass, Webster and the others came out in turn and made impromptu remarks to the crowd following the Band. Douglas's popularity was at an all time high – in Washington.

Things were different in Chicago. The debates were followed closely in every State, and the Compromise ignited opposition. Nowhere was that opposition more vociferous than in Chicago, the city to which Douglas had recently moved his residence. There was a storm of protest. Though he was exhausted from the long legislative battles, Douglas headed back home to Chicago to see what he could do to quiet down the clamor for his resignation and the threatened defiance to the Fugitive Slave Act.

Douglas and Slavery

PRIVATELY, DOUGLAS SAID slavery was "a curse beyond computation to both black and white."[247] But that sentiment never intruded into his public actions.

What motivated Douglas? Clearly he was a champion of his party. Douglas wanted the Democratic Party to represent the interests of all sections of the country. He embodied the melded interests of the various regions. He was born and raised in New England and he lived in a western State where he dealt regularly with the issues of the new States and Territories. He was a popular politician, a leader of his party and it was natural for him to have presidential aspirations.

He also could claim southern ties. He had remained a bachelor until the age of 33 when he married a southern planter's daughter, Martha Martin, to whom he had been introduced by a fellow member of Congress from North Carolina. But this connection introduced another factor. Not only was Martha the daughter of a wealthy planter, her father offered to give the newlyweds a plantation in Mississippi with 100 slaves as a wedding present. Recognizing that this might become a political liability, Douglas politely declined. The gift was bestowed on his wife. When his father-in-law died, the publication of his will disclosed that Douglas had been named a manager of the plantation and derived an income from it. So Douglas's detractors criticized him as a hypocrite because of his own connection to slave-holding.

Whatever sympathy he had for slave-holders, Douglas's principal motivation for compromising on slavery was undoubtedly his vision of an American Empire. He wanted the territory between the Mississippi and the Pacific to be filled with American States. Foreign powers should be excluded. This was the command of the Monroe Doctrine of 1823. Independent republics should be discouraged. His goal was to create an American Empire from sea to sea. A railroad to the Pacific was in his sights. He had seen how Illinois had grown as the Illinois legislature authorized railroads to expand from 2,524 miles of track prior to 1835 to over 3,400 after that year.[248]

It was equally important not to provoke the political leaders of the Slave States who had, from time to time, threatened to secede. It would be a mistake to make a legislative misstep that called their bluff. So, to preserve the Union and his party and to pursue his goal of an American Empire stretching from sea to sea, he accepted the status quo. He accepted slavery.

Slavery had existed since before the birth of the Republic and it was sanctioned by the Constitution. Douglas did not think slavery could be maintained in the new territories because the climate did not support it. He thought it was just a matter of time before slavery died out. To accommodate the interests of the Slave States to preserve the Union, he was willing to hold off prohibiting slavery in new Territories and States. He thought the issue distracted Congress from his goal of expanding the Union. This was the genius of "Popular Sovereignty."

Popular Sovereignty would remove a contentious issue from the debates in Congress:

Let us banish the agitation from these halls. Let us remove the causes which produced it; let us settle the Territories we have acquired, in a manner to satisfy the honor and respect the feelings of every portion of the Union…. Bring these Territories into this Union as States upon an equal footing with the original States. Let the people of such States settle the question of slavery within their limits, as they would settle the question of banking or any other domestic institution, according to their own will.[249]

Popular Sovereignty was the keystone to the Compromise of 1850. Admitting California as a State, setting up the territorial governments for Utah and New Mexico, and resolving the Texas boundary question were all neatly resolved by the Compromise. Those provisions worked out well, but the Fugitive Slave Act was another matter.

The Fugitive Slave Act

WHEN THE FUGITIVE Slave Act was passed, the stakes became higher for those who would help runaway slaves. The measure was designed to break the back of the Underground Railroad. Slave owners could pursue their runaway slaves in Free States, federal marshals were commanded to apprehend runaways, the marshals could organize posses. A supposed fugitive did not have a right to a jury trial. Nor could he or she testify. There were no safeguards against perjury or fraud.[250] Federal commissioners (appointed by judges of the federal circuit courts) would hear the cases. The commissioners were paid $5 if the supposed fugitive was allowed to go free and $10 if he or she was found to be a fugitive and turned over to the claimant.

The Act unleashed a reign of terror on free blacks. Many fled to Canada. Roving bands of slave-catchers harassed free blacks in all the major cities. The Act also commanded every citizen to assist, if asked, in the arrest of supposed fugitives. There were fines if one did not. The Act produced an unintended consequence. Rather than quell the furor over slavery, it actually aided the Abolitionist cause. As fugitives were pursued, each instance brought more Northerners face-to-face with slavery and the harsh realities of what slavery meant. The divisions between north and south were being forced to the forefront. "Eighteen fifty was the year in which the congressional compromise over slavery, ushering in a strict new fugitive slave law, instilled in Northerners a deep hostility to the federal government, which now seemed clearly allied to the pro-slavery cause."[251]

Dr. Dyer and Friends Defy the New Fugitive Slave Act

THE NEWS THAT the Fugitive Slave Law had been passed reached Chicago on September 18, 1850.[252] *The Chicago Democrat* and *The Chicago Tribune* attacked the law and provoked a series of mass meetings.[253] First the Negroes in Chicago convened in the African Methodist Episcopal Church on Wells Street[254] and immediately passed a resolution condemning the passage of the Act. They resolved not to flee to Canada but to remain and defend themselves. They set up "vigilance committees" to watch out for slave-catchers.[255]

For those who were less sure of their status, the friends of freedom chartered enough railroad cars to transport them to Canada. Mary Jones, the wife of John Jones, recalled that the people who did this were: Dr. Dyer, Eastman, Jones, Freer, De Wolf, Henry Bradford, Louis Isabell and H.O. Wagner.[256]

Then, on October 21, 1850, the City Council (then called the Common Council) passed a resolution calling the Fugitive Slave Act "a cruel and unjust law [that] ought not to be respected by an intelligent community."[257] The City took the stance that "the city police would not be required to aid in the recovery of slaves." This was followed by a mass meeting of citizens on the 22nd at which similar resolutions were passed condemning the Fugitive Slave Act and resolving not to obey its commands.[258]

What happened next remains one of the most extraordinary episodes in the career of Stephen A. Douglas. Douglas stepped into the maelstrom to defend his handiwork and to turn the tide of public opinion. And he succeeded!

On October 23, 1850, Douglas addressed one of the largest mass meetings the City had ever seen. Four thousand people attended. He spoke for three and a half hours, setting forth a detailed defense of the Compromise and of the Fugitive Slave Act. He mildly protested the resolution's labeling of anyone who would vote for the Fugitive Slave Act as "ranking with the traitors Benedict Arnold and Judas Iscariot." He went on to mock the City Council's act of nullification reminding everyone that it was for the Supreme Court to declare whether a law passed by Congress was unconstitutional. He said the City Council had surpassed South Carolina, referring to the episode where South Carolina earlier tried to nullify a law of Congress through an act of its legislature and a convention. Then he tackled the officious parts of the Fugitive Slave Act that had been the focus of the City Council's wrath.

He argued that: (1) the Fugitive Slave Act was just an amendment to the predecessor law of 1793, (2) the Act did not suspend the writ of *habeas corpus*, (3) there was no denial of the right to trial by jury, and (4) the real objection the Chicagoans had was not to the law but to the Constitution itself.

Douglas's pitch that the new Fugitive Slave Law was not different from the prior law was disingenuous. While it is true that the prior law called for the return of fugitive slaves, its enforcement mechanism had been weak. The United States Supreme Court, in *Prigg v. Pennsylvania*,[259] in 1842, held that State officials were not compelled to enforce the law. Its enforcement became practically a dead letter following that decision because there were not enough federal officers available to enforce it. The new law had teeth in it because it created a whole new enforcement mechanism.

Douglas also made a skillful argument about *habeas corpus*. He explained that the writ could still issue but that its office would be to determine by what authority a person was held in custody. He maintained that "[u]pon the return of the writ of *habeas corpus*, the claimant will be required to exhibit to the court his authority for conveying the servant back; and if he produces a 'certificate' from the commissioner or judge in due form of law, the court will decide it has no power" to free the fugitive and that if no authority were shown, the alleged fugitive would be released. In any proceeding the certificate from a commissioner would be conclusive evidence that the suspected fugitive could be held.

As to the jury point, he argued that any jury trial had to take place in the State from which a fugitive fled, the State whose laws were alleged to have been violated. This was a great example of Douglas's skills as an orator, "mystifying" the point as Harriet Beecher Stowe had said. Did anyone seriously believe that a fugitive slave could successfully demand a jury trial in a Slave State to contest his or her captivity after being dragged back there?

Then Douglas boldly confronted what the Chicagoans were really upset about:

> *You would not care a farthing about the new law … if there was a hole big enough for the fugitive to slip through and escape.* Habeas corpus – *trials by jury – records from other states – pains and penalties – the whole catalog of objections, would be all moonshine, if the Negro was not required to go back to his master.*[260]

Douglas then asked if this was not the gist of their objections. Several in the audience said it was. He then read from the Constitution the "shall be delivered up" clause:

> *No Person held to service or Labour in one State, under the Laws thereof, escaping into another, shall, in Consequence of any Law or Regulation therein, be*

discharged from such Service or Labour, but shall be delivered up *on Claim of the Party to whom such Service or Labour may be due.*

This was followed by a civics lesson in which he excoriated his listeners reminding them that it was his duty as a Senator and theirs as citizens to uphold the Constitution. In summation, he said, "We must stand by the Constitution of the Union, with all its compromises, or we must abolish it, and resolve each state back into its original elements. It is therefore a question of union or disunion."[261]

Someone in the crowd then asked whether the clause in the Constitution providing for the surrender of fugitive slaves was not in violation of the law of God. And Douglas had an answer to that argument as well. He began by saying the general proposition "that there is a law paramount to all human enactments – the law of the Supreme Ruler of the Universe I trust that no civilized or Christian people is prepared to question, much less deny. We should all recognize, revere and respect divine law."

While conceding that, he pointed out that the divine law did not prescribe the form of government under which we live or furnish us with a code of international law or a system of jurisprudence. The law of God, "as revealed to us, is intended to operate on our consciences, and insure the performance of our duties as individuals and Christians." Imperfect as our laws may be, it is the better course to follow them:

> *If the Constitution of the United States is to be repudiated upon the ground that it is repugnant to the divine law, where are the friends of freedom and Christianity to look for another and a better? Who is to be the prophet to reveal the will of God, and establish a theocracy for us?…*
>
> *For my part, I am prepared to maintain and preserve inviolate the Constitution as it is, with all its compromises; to stand or fall by the American Union, clinging with tenacity of life to all its glorious memories of the past, and precious hopes for the future.*[262]

Douglas then presented his own resolutions to the meeting and they passed. These included the following:

Resolved, *That so long as the Constitution of the United States provides that all persons held to service or labor in one state, escaping to another state, "SHALL BE DELIVERED UP on the claim of the party to whom the service or labor may be due," and so long as members of Congress are required to take an oath to support the Constitution, it is their solemn and religious duty to pass all laws necessary to carry that provision of the Constitution into effect.*[263]

The next day the City Council repealed its resolution. Douglas published his remarks in pamphlet form, a common practice of aspiring politicians in that day. Shortly after his remarks were published, the legislature of Illinois rescinded its resolutions that instructed the senators from Illinois to vote for the Wilmot proviso measures. Moreover, the legislature passed a resolution endorsing the doctrine of popular sovereignty.[264] These actions were a testament to Douglas's powers of persuasion and also to his ability to command party loyalty. For the time being, Douglas could dismiss the Chicago abolitionists and their cause as a nuisance that was getting in the way of the nation's business. But not for long.

Escaping Via the Coal Hole

DESPITE ENHANCED PENALTIES, in the 10 years after the 1850 passage of the Fugitive Slave Act, the Underground Railroad flourished and the activities of its operators intensified.

In 1854, Eastman defiantly reported in his new newspaper, *The Free West*, that passengers on the "Chicago route" of the underground railroad "come and go in a continuous stream."[265] Dr. Dyer now had a regular arrangement with the steam ship operators plying the waters from the harbor of Chicago. Captain Walker, who commanded the *S.S. Great Western*, and Captain Blake, who commanded the *S.S. Illinois*, willingly helped Dr. Dyer and the other Chicagoans running the Underground Railroad. They worked out a simple routine: The fugitives would be disguised as firemen and put to work in the coal hole. Of course, they worked feverishly, recognizing that this was their ticket to Canada. The voyages were not without occasional irony. In the saloons of these steamers might be found a southern slave-owner with his family enjoying a summer cruise. Below in the hold, might be runaway slaves from their own plantation.[266] Even though the slave-catchers had information that this was a well-used route, they never figured out how to disrupt it.

Another person that Dr. Dyer and company enlisted was Sylvester Lind.[267] At midnight one night, Carpenter went to Lind's house and told him he had four gentlemen in his barn in need of passage to Canada. Lind owned some lumber mills in northern Wisconsin and had boats regularly going back and forth. He enthusiastically joined in the enterprise. Because they knew that Deputy Sheriff Rhines might try to intercept them, Lind agreed to drive his carriage down to his boat to scout the route in advance of Carpenter who would bring the passengers in his closed carriage. Once on board, the fugitives were en route to the Death's Door passage to Canada:

In reaching the lumber region these boats had to pass through a narrow channel called "Death's Door" near which was an island where all lake steamers took on wood. It was customary for slaves to be left at this island until a boat came along which could take them down through the St. Claire River. The channel was so narrow in some places that the slaves could easily jump from the boat onto the Canada side before Detroit was reached.[268]

There were also more episodes in the courtroom. Dr. Dyer was noted for his sharpness in defending and aiding fugitives. He could make a "telling speech in court. And many a poor slave owes his freedom to Dr. Dyer's quick wits."[269] In one case, a female fugitive slave who was waiting while other cases were heard asked the judge if she could wash her face and hands. The judge ushered her in to the wash room at the back of the courtroom. Later, when she had not reappeared, it was discovered that she had fled out the window, climbed a 10 foot fence and was no where to be found.[270]

Dr. Dyer Gets Even with the "Officious" Henry Rhines

I N THE AFTERMATH of the Fugitive Slave Act of 1850, the Underground Railroad was running at full steam in Chicago. Its adversaries also stepped up their efforts. Deputy Sheriff Rhines, described in a contemporary account as "an officious Irish constable," was a particular menace to Dr. Dyer.[271] He came from Kentucky and his sympathies were not with the abolitionists. He had a special mission "to preserve the integrity of the union…. He made the doctor the particular object of his attention."[272] He would barge in with a search warrant (issued by the always dependable Justice Kerchival) at all hours. But all his efforts bore no fruit. Somehow, the sought-after fugitives vanished into thin air.

There was another side to Deputy Sheriff Rhines. He was also known for his seductive ways. Though he was a staunch protector of the purity of the Irish blood, on one occasion a woman "from the south" staying at Dr. Dyer's attracted Rhines's special attention. Rhines was often seen trying to court her. Despite the efforts of her friends to keep him away, it was later reported that "at last, as such things will happen sometimes, the dark woman of the south had a baby." Here was Dr. Dyer's opportunity! The doctor "rewarded the constable for his zeal in her behalf by naming the baby Henry Rhines."[273]

Uncle Tom's Cabin

T HE MYTHOLOGY – THAT Southern slave owners were benign masters, that slaves were treated benevolently and better off in bondage – was unraveling. The publication of *Uncle Tom's Cabin* galvanized public opinion in the north to the opposite belief as the compelling story reached an ever wider public.

The story was first published serially in 40 installments starting June 5, 1851 in *National Era*. This newspaper was started to promote the views of the Liberty Party. When the party met in its national convention in 1846, they were joined by Salmon P. Chase who embraced the Liberty Party at that convention, giving a new level of credibility to the splinter party movement. The Liberty Party men wanted to publish an abolitionist newspaper that would spread their message nationally. So to get the newspaper started to whom did they turn? To Charles Volney Dyer, naturally. Dr. Dyer was asked to chair the committee to start the newspaper. Dr. Dyer relished the opportunity to take the abolitionist cause to another level and he succeeded in establishing a newspaper that gave the abolitionists the platform they sought to debate slavery on the national stage. The *National Era* began life in Washington, D.C. on January 7, 1847.[274] *National Era* was one of the newspapers that Lincoln read regularly.[275] It had another Chicago connection besides Dr. Dyer. *Western Citizen* announced December 1, 1846, that Chicago's Dr. Gammiel Bailey would go to Washington, D.C. to publish the newspaper.[276] With *Uncle Tom's Cabin*, they struck gold.

Uncle Tom's Cabin was a fictional story that telescoped together all of the evils and perils of slavery into one verisimilitudinous saga that captured the public's imagination: the financial predicament of a well-meaning master (Arthur Shelby) forces him to forfeit a valued slave (Uncle Tom) to a creditor. The slave's family is torn apart when he is sold "down river." To get out of debt he cannot repay, the impecunious master also agrees to deed over a young slave, a boy four or five

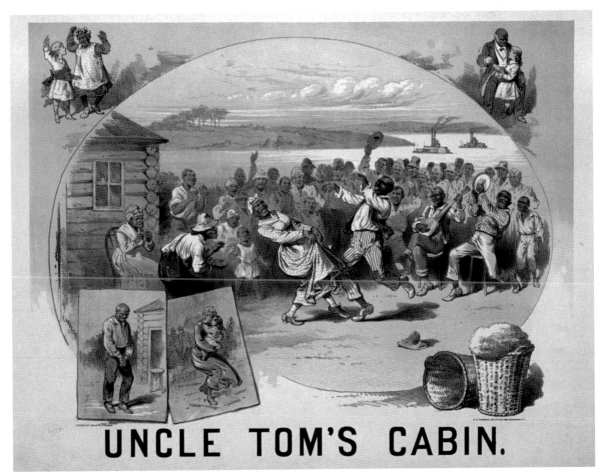

UNCLE TOM'S CABIN.

Published in Boston in 1852, Harriet Beecher Stowe's anti-slavery novel was the best-selling novel of the 19th Century, and among all books sold in that Century, it was second only to the Bible. (Library of Congress)

years old (Harry). The boy's mother (Eliza) overhears the bargaining and flees that night with her child. She is pursued. This leads to a harrowing chase, with the mother and her babe escaping only by crossing the partially frozen Ohio River by jumping from ice floe to ice floe.

Meanwhile, the slave being sold down river (Uncle Tom) saves a young girl (Little Eva) from drowning when she accidentally falls into the river from the deck of a paddle wheeler. His heroic act is repaid when her father (Augustine St. Clare) purchases the slave (Uncle Tom) and brings him to New Orleans. The little girl's health deteriorates, she knows she is going to die and she extracts a promise from her father to give the slave his freedom. But fate intervenes and the father is

stabbed to death when he tries to stop a brawl. Instead the slave owner's heartless wife (Marie St. Clare) sells the slave – this time to a cruel master (the odious Simon Legree). This cruel master runs a cotton plantation where he works his slaves to death. If they do not jump when he says jump, he whips them senseless. Of course, for good measure, he preys on young female slaves, rapes them, and has his dogs ready to tear them to bits if they flee.

When two female slaves escape, Legree demands to know where they are. Tom refuses to tell and Legree beats him to death just as the first owner's son (George Shelby) arrives with cash in hand to purchase Uncle Tom's freedom. But he is too late. The hero (Uncle Tom) dies.

The parallel story tells of the journey of three slaves (Eliza and Harry reunited with the father) as they make their way to Canada. They are chased by a gang of slave-catchers (led by Loker), confronted in a shoot-out where the lead slave-catcher is wounded, aided by sympathetic Quakers, helped to reach Lake Erie, and, ultimately, given safe passage to Canada. It is, of course, the saga of a slave's journey on the Underground Railroad to freedom.

Harriet Beecher Stowe crafted her story based on a number of real events. The mother crossing the frozen river retold an episode of a slave who escaped across the Ohio River at Ripley, Ohio and on to Canada.[277] She probably also had collected some stories of slaves escaping on the Underground Railroad from her brother, Edward Beecher, who was an abolitionist in Illinois. Edward was a Presbyterian minister who became the first president of Illinois College at Jacksonville in 1830. Edward had gone to Alton, Illinois to stand with Elijah Lovejoy when Lovejoy's last press was delivered and was there when Lovejoy was being threatened by a mob, though he was not present when Lovejoy was shot.

When it was published in book form the first printing of 5,000 copies sold out in two days. In its first year *Uncle Tom's Cabin* sold 300,000 copies in the United States. The extraordinary impact of *Uncle Tom's* Cabin was recognized by Abraham Lincoln. Stowe went to the White House in 1862 and met President Lincoln. Lincoln greeted her with the following remark: "So, you're the little woman who made this great war."[278]

While her book was later criticized by some for perpetuating a racial stereotype because of Uncle Tom's submissiveness, Stowe presented Uncle Tom as the embodiment of the Christian ideal – he endured humiliation and punishment without fighting back and forgave his tormentors.[279] This magnified the veniality, ruthlessness and cruelty of Legree, the embodiment of everything wrong with slavery. Even among northerners who were not prepared to view the Negro as an equal, the destruction of the slave's family and the brutal treatment of slaves underscored the injustice of the slave system – and the cruelty wrought by enforcement of the Fugitive Slave Act.

Before the publication of *Uncle Tom's Cabin*, the abolitionists battled a head wind trying to proselytize for their cause. After its publication the wind was at their back.

Religion and Slavery

ELIJAH LOVEJOY BELIEVED slavery was a sin. He began as an adherent of colonization but soon gravitated to immediatism. He had been influenced by David Nelson. Both were Presbyterian ministers. But the Presbyterian Church did not speak with one voice on the issue of slavery.[280]

Lovejoy tried on several occasions to get citizens' groups and church leaders to adopt a set of resolutions condemning slavery. He was optimistic that he might succeed when he went to a general assembly of Presbyterian ministers held in Pittsburgh in 1836.[281] He wanted the church to throw its authority behind the anti-slavery movement. He presented his resolutions staking out the anti-slavery position. The question was referred to a committee. The committee advised against taking any position because the slavery issue would divide the church. Lovejoy joined in a "minority report."[282]

Lovejoy's support from fellow ministers in Illinois was undercut when Rev. Joel Parker, another Presbyterian minister, later president of Union Theological Seminary from 1840 to 1842, came to Alton. Parker professed to be anti-slavery, but he condemned abolitionists for agitating the community. Worse, he distributed copies of a pamphlet authored by Rev. James Smylie of Mississippi. Smylie took the position that while slavery had some bad aspects, it was sanctioned by the Bible and accepted by the Prophets.[283]

The state of disagreement among Presbyterian ministers and other theologians would seem to validate the Honey Pickren axiom: "You can pull whatever you want from the Bible and put your own spin on it."[284] The churches of that era were as divided on the issue of slavery as was the rest of the country. For example, the Second Presbyterian Church was organized on June 1, 1842 by dissidents from the First who did not want to endorse the anti-slavery crusade actively.[285]

Dissatisfaction with the traditional churches spurred interest in new approaches. Dr. Dyer led a group of similarly disaffected parishioners from various churches to join the Swedenborg Society which held meetings in the Saloon Building. The teachings of Emanuel Swedenborg (1688–1772) undoubtedly struck a chord with Dr. Dyer. Instead of predestination, Swedenborg taught that "all people who live good lives, no matter what their religion, have a place in heaven."

In those days, the residents of Chicago kept goats, and the goats had a way of showing up in unexpected places. One day Dr. Dyer was seen driving the goats away from the entrance to the Saloon Building before a meeting of the Society. An acquaintance happened upon him and remarked: "You have goats in your congregation." "No sir," replied the doctor, "ours is the only congregation in town which turns them out."[286]

Illinois had its share of ministers and churches committed to the anti-slavery cause. The efforts of David Nelson, Elijah and Owen Lovejoy, Joseph Smith, and Edward Beecher have already been mentioned. Another Illinois church that signed on to the cause was the Methodist Church. At their annual convention in September of 1854 they resolved "that our opposition to Slavery in all its forms was never more decided and uncompromising than at present."[287]

Yet, like Reverend Smiley, there were many who pointed to the Bible and accepted slavery. The Episcopal bishop refused to ordain Owen Lovejoy unless he agreed not to "agitate" on the anti-slavery issue.[288] (Lovejoy became a Presbyterian minister.) Where a Christian's duty lay was a question that could be answered in a host of ways – some answers being the polar opposite of others. Recognizing that the argument against slavery would probably not be won by pointing to the Bible, the abolitionists turned to another weapon – the personal testimony of former slaves. One answer to the Biblical justification rationale was the testimony of former slaves describing how they were treated by the Bible-wielding slave-owners. What better way to show the horrors of slavery?

Frederick Augustus Washington Baily was fathered by an unknown white man and born to a slave woman in 1818. He escaped slavery in 1838 by fleeing Baltimore by train, ship then another train, arriving in New York within 24 hours of his escape. He moved to New Bedford, Massachusetts, changed his name, married and became a great orator, denouncing slavery and arguing for the rights of women. (Library of Congress)

Frederick Douglass

FREDERICK DOUGLASS WAS an electrifying orator who could speak from personal experience about slavery because he was formerly a slave. An address he gave in 1841 exemplifies the power of his personal testimony:

My friends, I have come to tell you something about slavery – what I know of it, as I have felt it. When I came North, I was astonished to find that the abolitionists knew so much about it, that they were acquainted with its deadly effects as well as if they had lived in its midst. But though they can give you its history – though they can depict its horrors, they cannot speak as I can from experience; they cannot refer you to a back covered with scars, as I can: for I have felt these wounds; I have suffered under the lash without the power of resisting. Yes my blood has sprung out as the lash embedded itself in my flesh. And yet my master has the reputation of being a pious man and a good Christian. He was a class leader in the Methodist church. I have seen this pious class leader cross and tie the hands of one of his young female slaves, and lash her on the bare skin and justify the deed by the quotation from the Bible, "he who knoweth his master's will and doeth it not, shall be beaten with many stripes."[289]

The abolitionists recognized that the personal testimony of Frederick Douglass made Biblical aphorisms hollow by comparison. Douglass would become a regular visitor to Illinois, drawing large crowds wherever he spoke.

The Election of 1852

WITH THE PUBLICATION of *Uncle Tom's Cabin*, the abolitionists had new credibility. Their efforts to publish newspapers to spread their message had finally begun to pay off. Their audience was growing. The new attitudes, however, did not intrude into the election of 1852.

In 1852, both national political parties, the Democrats and the Whigs adopted platforms that approved of the Compromise of 1850 and expressly endorsed the Fugitive Slave Law. The Democrats nominated Franklin Pierce (the "dark horse") for President.[290] The Whigs nominated Winfield Scott. Pierce won.

In August, the National Free Soil Democratic Convention held at Pittsburgh nominated John P. Hale. That party's platform was written by Chase. It was uncompromising on the slavery issue: Nobody was bound to observe the Fugitive Slave Law because it violated the Constitution, Christianity, and the Common

Law. It should be repealed immediately.[291] The Hale ticket made a poor showing and the Free Soil Party was on its last legs. But the position it had taken on the Fugitive Slave Law reverberated with voters in the northern States and anticipated the sectional divide that would soon kill of the Whig Party and hopelessly split the Democrats.

In Illinois, the Liberty men and Free Soilers "stood by their colors" and voted for Hale.[292] But, recognizing that the State was "despotically democratic," and that they held the balance of power, many diverted their congressional votes to vote for Whigs they knew were opposed to Douglas's doctrines. This effort succeeded in gaining several seats for the Whigs in Congress. In the State legislature they also held the balance of power. Lincoln was a candidate for the Senate, but, rather than vote for Lincoln (which might have been interpreted as a Whig victory), the Liberty men and Free Soilers voted for "anti-Nebraska" Democrat Lyman Trumbull, who became Illinois's second senator. In recounting this later, Eastman observed that it was fortuitous that Lincoln did not get elected to the Senate in 1854.[293] Douglas's term would expire in 1858 and Lincoln was "opportunely in reserve to be put into the field in this contest."[294] And the political landscape would look different in 1858.

Uncle Tom's Cabin, the increased visibility of roving bands of slave-catchers, patrols of vigilance committees, arrests of supposed fugitives and summary hearings, and the testimony of former slaves changed the north's tolerance for slavery. The population was growing, fed by a new wave of immigration from Europe led by refugees from the Irish potato famine. Immigration had been steady at about 10,000 per year up through the 1820s. Then it began to surge. In the period 1845 – 1850, some 1,700,000 immigrants came to America.[295] "Free labor" was the code word for the new immigrants who did not want to see jobs building railroads and canals given to slave labor. The ranks of those doubting the efficacy of the Fugitive Slave Law were growing. The climate for enforcing the law in Chicago was more and more inhospitable to the slave-catchers.

Building Out Chicago

IN 1845 CHICAGO had no gas lights or electric lights. There were no tall buildings. There was no water or sewer system. Mail service was irregular. According to George Manierre, Jackson Boulevard, where his father had his residence, was considered "out of town." Manierre recalled the rustic aspect of the city in those years:

All those who kept cows at that time had them driven out by boys to near Twelfth Street, where there was wild prairie grass, and at night they were driven back to their respective homes. All the land west of Chicago … was wild land … roamed over by wild Indians and buffalo in countless numbers.[296]

In 1848 the Illinois and Michigan Canal was completed to Lockport and a breakwater on Lake Michigan. The first train came in 1849.

Dr. Dyer was active in promoting city improvements. He was an incorporator of the North Chicago Street Railway Company. In 1852 he was a Drainage Commissioner for Cook County.[297] In 1853, he suggested a system of tunnels to facilitate travel because of the log jam that was caused by the bridges being opened to accommodate boats. From 6:00 A.M. to 7:00 P.M., 24,000 people and 6,000 teams crossed the Clark St bridge. It was open for three hours to accommodate passing boats.[298] In 1854, the City Council voted to build a tunnel under the river. The City was investing in municipal improvements and the boundaries were expanding.

In 1855, the Board or Sewage Commissioners authorized a sewage disposal system that required the streets to be raised eight feet. Property owners protested. First floors would become basements. The Tremont Hotel "appeared to be situated in a deep ditch."[299] George M. Pullman, a young engineer offered to raise the hotel using the method he had successfully used to raise houses along the Erie Canal. "Using 5,000 jackscrews and scores of men, who gave each screw a half turn on signal," the hotel was lifted to street level, a feat hailed around the world.

There were many stories about Dr. Dyer, his irrepressible good nature and quick wit. He had a glass eye which gave him a somewhat comical look. One story that was told about him was that he went in to see the city collector, a man named Boyden, who was grousing about his failing eyesight and the necessity of wearing glasses. Dr. Dyer disengaged his glass eye and said, "Why confound you Boyden, I'll make you a present of an eye that will never go back on you. Now, give me yours in exchange." Boyden declined the offer but stopped grousing.[300]

Then there is the story about Dr. Dyer living "beyond the grave:"

The old cemetery was in those days located in what is now Lincoln Park. Beyond that was only a scattering settlement. Here, to this locality, about the year 1840, Mr. Dyer moved, from a former residence in the city. One day, in the street, a friend accosted him with the remark, "Hello, Dyer, I don't see you very often. Where do you live now?" "O, I am very comfortably situated," replied Mr. Dyer without relaxing a muscle of his features, "I have a home beyond the grave." His friend saw the point, circulated the story, and Dyer was long known as the sojourner on earth who had "a home beyond the grave."[301]

This story referred to the house Dr. Dyer actually built in 1855 and moved to in 1857 which the *Chicago Daily Democrat* commented on as being a "fine residence near the toll gate on the lake shore plank road." In 1857, the address was "Green Bay Road." But Green Bay Road was later renamed Clark Street, because it was the extension of Clark Street, and the home was probably at what is now Wrightwood and Clark Streets. According to the *Democrat*, the house, with a "fine brick barn" was near E. Peck's. The paper described both as "princely mansions among the oaks just beyond the suburbs of the city."[302]

The Free West

EASTMAN HAD BEEN publishing *Western Citizen* from 1842 until 1853. Hard economic times for farmers, divisions in the Liberty Party and competition from other newspapers were undercutting the financial viability of *Western Citizen*. Eastman announced that he would stop publishing it and give the subscription list over to *The Free West*, a new newspaper to be published in Chicago, continuing to promote abolition but aimed at attracting a broader readership. Though promoted by the Free Soilers, the new paper claimed not to be affiliated with any particular party. While *The Free West* searched for a new editor, Eastman agreed to carry it on. The motto of the new paper, taken from the Northwest Ordinance, was: "Neither slavery nor involuntary servitude shall exist in this said territory."[303]

Prior to the enactment of the Fugitive Slave Act, abolitionists had been viewed as pariahs – agitators – whose views were a threat to law and order and the preservation of the Union. With the passage of the Fugitive Slave Act and the publication of *Uncle Tom's Cabin*, that changed. While the abolitionist were not about to become a majority political party over night, abolitionist speakers were now welcomed and Illinois began to see a parade of the leading abolitionist speakers of the day. With great fanfare, *The Free West* announced the arrival of these speakers, previewed their appearances, published their schedules and reported on their remarks after they spoke, sometimes reprinting their speeches in full. For example, in the fall of 1854, Frederick Douglass was scheduled to speak in Joliet, Princeton and Ottawa in the span of October 24–26. Salmon P. Chase, the abolitionist senator from Ohio, came to Chicago to speak on October 12, 1854 and went on to give speeches in Belvedere, Aurora, Joliet, Springfield, Jacksonville and Granville. J.R. Giddings, abolitionist Congressman from Ohio, spoke in Dearborn Park on September 20, 1854; the paper reported that 3,000 people attended. During September, Giddings was scheduled to speak in 11

Lovejoy Monument, Alton, Ill.

The Lovejoy Monument[305] erected to honor Elijah Lovejoy, editor of the *Alton Observer* newspaper. Lovejoy was assassinated in 1837 while defending his printing press against a pro-slavery mob in Alton, Illinois.
(Private Collection)

Illinois cities and then 14 more in October.[304] Ichabod Codding, the Congregational minister, abolitionist, and mainstay of the Illinois Liberty Party (and later one of the founders of the Republican Party in Illinois), spoke in 32 different Illinois cities between September 29 and November 6, 1854. Cassius M. Clay, the abolitionist from Kentucky, had spoken earlier on June 29, July 5 and 6, 1854.

The Princeton meeting was also the Free Democratic State Convention. In addition to Frederick Douglass, Owen Lovejoy spoke and Dr. Dyer was asked to head up another committee – this time to erect a monument to Elijah Lovejoy. The monument was planned in the 1850s but not erected until 1890 and dedicated November 7, 1897.

The Free West reported every advance in the abolitionist cause. On December 8, 1853, *The Free West* reported that the play of *Uncle Tom's Cabin* at the National Theater in New York had been drawing full houses since last summer and would continue to be produced through July 18, 1854. Eastman's comment: "[M]ore than one and 20 representations of this drama have done a good deal of good in awakening sympathy for slaves, in removing prejudices against Abolitionists, and especially in arousing hatred towards the Fugitive Slave Act...."[306]

Nebraska Becomes the Dominant Issue

The *Free West* also stood ready to report every looming setback. The paper reported on the progress of the Kansas-Nebraska Bill and the threatened extension of slavery into territories just to the west. The Bill that Douglas drafted would create two territories – Nebraska and Kansas – and allow them to determine for themselves whether to be Slave or Free when they sought admission as States. Douglas viewed this as the natural extension of the policy of Popular Sovereignty.

The Free West was naturally opposed to Senator Douglas who was the author and chief sponsor of the Kansas-Nebraska Bill. *The Free West* viewed it differently from Douglas because to allow the citizens of Kansas and Nebraska to vote on whether to come in as a Free or Slave State meant that the Missouri Compromise, which had established the line at 36°30' above which there was to be no slavery, had to be abandoned. In the paper, the Senator was referred to as "Arnold Douglas," which was short-hand for Benedict Arnold.

In fact, all the newspapers of the day followed the Nebraska issue. As the debates in Congress unfolded, the speeches were reported in great detail. Bashing Douglas was a regular theme for *The Free West*. One can imagine the great joy Eastman had when, on October 26, 1854, he reported that it could now be proved that Douglas owned slaves, a fact revealed when his father-in-law died and his estate was probated.[307] Actually, Douglas's wife was the owner of the plantation in Mississippi with over 100 slaves. In Eastman's view, that was a legal fiction:

Douglas derives rents and profits from both Mississippi plantations and annually pockets the surplus labor of 160 or more slaves. – He visits his plantations frequently and gives his Negroes a grand barbeque once a year, inspects his crop of picaninies of African, American and Senatorial paternity, gives instructions to his overseers, and receipts for the cash extracted from the sweat and toil of his human chattels....

Douglas does not technically own the Mississippi Slaves, but he owns their usufruct, as a lawyer would term it, which means the right of enjoying a thing which belongs to another and of deriving all the profit or benefit it may produce.[308]

The question of whether slavery could be extended to the territories was about to rip the nation in two. The existing political parties would be split north and south. The attacks on Douglas now became more virulent. One attack was that as a slave owner, Douglas's slaves would be more valuable if the domain of slavery were extended. Another was that if the Mormons wanted to bring Utah in as a polygamous State, they could do so under Popular Sovereignty. Therefore, Douglas favored polygamy.

Douglas was not about to be cowed by the abolitionist newspapers. He had his vision for expanding the nation by settling the territories to the west and building a transcontinental railroad. He was unbowed by attacks that showed he had a financial connection to slavery.

The Nebraska Act

IN 1854 THE divisions between north and south were exacerbated and the country took a step closer to the "irrepressible conflict" that was to come.

There were four attempts to organize the Nebraska Territory (all of what is now Kansas and Nebraska). The first three failed because of Southern opposition to the continued observation of the Missouri Compromise which, if followed, would have required the entire territory to enter as Free. Senator David R. Atchinson, a pro-slavery Senator from Missouri, explained that his State was surrounded on three sides by Free soil. He objected to any legislation organizing the Nebraska Territory that did not remove the prohibition on slavery. Atchinson declared that he would see the Nebraska Territory "sink in Hell" before he would permit it to become Free soil.[309]

Douglas, as chair of the Committee on Territories, put together a bill that divided the territory in two and finessed the Free or Slave question by providing that the status of each territory on applying for Statehood would be determined by the vote of the citizens, *i.e.*, popular sovereignty. Bending to the Southerners' position, the Bill expressly repealed the Missouri Compromise.

This set off a fire storm. Douglas's first taste of the depth of feeling that his new compromise measure would unleash came when, after he introduced the Bill on January 4, 1854, he agreed to a brief postponement in the consideration of the Bill. This interlude gave the abolitionists in the Congress time to sound the alarm. They did so with an article in *National Era* signed by Senators Chase, Sumner and Seward. Douglas was stunned by their action and the personal attacks aimed at him. He took the floor of the Senate to protest:

> ... *I proposed on Tuesday last, that the Senate should proceed to the consideration of the bill to organize the Territories of Nebraska and Kansas....*
>
> *The Senator from Ohio (Mr. Chase) ... asked for a postponement ... and the Senator from Massachusetts (Mr. Sumner) suggested that the postponement should be for one week for that purpose. These suggestions seeming to be reasonable ... I yielded to their request....*
>
> *Sir, little did I suppose, at the time that I granted that act of courtesy to those two senators, that they had drafted and published to the world a document, over their own signatures, in which they arraigned me as having been guilty of a criminal betrayal of my trust, as having been guilty of an act of bad faith, and as having been engaged in an atrocious plot against the cause of free government.... I have since discovered that on that very morning the* National Era, *the abolition organ in this city, contained an address, signed by certain abolition confederates, to the people, in which the bill is grossly misrepresented, in which the action of the committee is grossly perverted, in which our motives are arraigned and our characters calumniated.*[310]

Senator Chase tried to speak but Douglas refused to yield and carried on for over two hours defending the Bill and bashing his opponents.

Douglas took the position that the Nebraska Act was merely an extension of the policy already adopted in the Compromise of 1850. It extended popular sovereignty – the right given Utah and New Mexico – to the citizens of the Kansas and Nebraska Territories: "These measures are established and rest upon the great principle of self-government – that the people should be allowed to decide the question of their domestic institutions for themselves, subject only to such limitations as are imposed by the Constitution of the United States, instead of having them determined by an arbitrary or geographical line."[311] In fact, giving his argument an extra twist, Douglas argued, it would *discriminate against* the residents of the new territories not to give them the same rights as were granted the residents of Utah and New Mexico. The Missouri Compromise had already been "superseded by the Compromise measure of 1850 and has become and ought to be declared inoperative."[312]

The debate was acrimonious. It continued for three months. The burning issue at the center of the debate was: what was the status of the Missouri Compromise of 1820? The Southern Senators argued that Congress did not have either the *power* to introduce or to exclude slavery in any territory or State. Slavery was sanctioned by the Constitution, a consistent position of the Southerners, first articulated by Calhoun, that had prevented agreement on legislation organizing the territories. The anti-slavery Northerners, led by Chase, Seward and Sumner, argued that the Missouri Compromise was a *compact* between North and South that resolved the slavery issue by establishing a line north of which slavery would not be permitted.

Douglas took the position that the Missouri Compromise was just another piece of legislation, that it did not set a precedent that applied to the western territories and that, in any event, it had been superseded by the Compromise of 1850 that embraced popular sovereignty. In response to those Northerners who argued that they had relied on the "compact" when they allowed Missouri and Arkansas to come in as Slave States, Douglas pointed out that New York and others voted against the admission of Missouri even after the compromise had been agreed to. In other words, they had reneged and could not claim they were part of a compact.

There was a long line of Senators who wanted to engage in the debate. The speeches in the Senate went on for days on end. Finally, on March 3, 1854, the Senate reached the end of the line. The speeches went on until midnight. Then Douglas took the floor in the candle-lit chamber for the final remarks. Even though it was after midnight when he rose to speak, the galleries were packed and the aisles and corridors filled to capacity. He spoke until daylight restating all the arguments for the Bill and minimizing the significance of the abandonment of the Missouri Compromise, saying it had been superseded by the Compromise of 1850. He explained the work of the committee that drafted the Bill, as follows:

> We were aware that from 1820 to 1850 the abolition doctrine of congressional interference with slavery in the territories and new states had so far prevailed as to keep up an incessant slavery agitation in Congress and throughout the country, whenever any new territory was to be acquired or organized. We were also aware that,

in 1850, the right of the people to decide this question for themselves, subject only to the Constitution, was substituted for the doctrine of Congressional intervention. The first question, therefore, which the committee were called upon to decide, and indeed the only question of any material importance, in framing this bill, was this: Shall we adhere to and carry out the principles recognized by the Compromise of 1850, or shall we go back to the old exploded doctrine of congressional interference, as established in 1820 in a large portion of the country....[313]

Characterizing the Missouri Compromise as "congressional interference" and anointing the doctrine of popular sovereignty as the hallmark of democracy, Douglas proceeded to embellish all of his arguments that had made it possible for the Senators to agree on the Compromise of 1850, urging them to view the Nebraska Act as a benign extension of an established policy.

Continuing in his marathon speech, Douglas argued that the Compromise of 1850 established a new policy that the nation had accepted. For proof, Douglas cited his own speech in Chicago, on October 23, 1850, and the subsequent action of the City Council and the Illinois House endorsing the principles of the Compromise. He pointed out that the Illinois House had rescinded its earlier resolution that called for the Illinois Senators to vote for the Wilmot Proviso. In fact, he read the resolution that the Illinois House passed as evidence that the country had abandoned the Missouri Compromise:

> Resolved, *That our liberty and independence are based upon the right of the people to form for themselves such a government as they may choose; that this great privilege – the birthright of free men, the gift of heaven, secured to us by the blood of our ancestors – ought to be extended to future generations; and no limitations ought to be applied to this power, in the organization of any territory of the United States, of either a territorial government or a State Constitution:* Provided, *the government so established shall be republican, and in conformity with the Constitution.*[314]

The *Washington Union* reported that it was the greatest speech of Douglas's life. It was indeed a triumph. Douglas won the day in the Senate. The Kansas-Nebraska Bill was adopted and signed by President Franklin Pierce May 30, 1854.

But, try as he might to neutralize the opposition and build support for his latest compromise, this time Douglas would not have the success he had when he garnered support for the Compromise of 1850. This time the opposition was better organized and cut deeper into his traditional base of support. "Anti-Nebraska" clubs sprang up everywhere. Douglas was burned in effigy. Nowhere was this opposition hotter than in Chicago. Once again Douglas headed home to try to undo the damage.

The Chicago Tribune

THERE WERE A number of newspapers that were highly partisan and catered to a small but devoted audience. *Free West* was one of these and, like *Western Citizen*, it faced the prospect of failing unless it grew. The solution was to merge with another fledgling newspaper. In 1855 *Free West* would do so and from then on was published under the name of its merger partner – *The Chicago Tribune*.[315]

The *Tribune* had been started by K.C. Forrest and John E. Wheeler in 1847.[316] They were friends of Dr. Dyer's and joined with Dr. and Mrs. Dyer and Mr. and Mrs. J.Y. Scammon in establishing the Society of New Jerusalem, the Swedenborgian Church which started life using the Saloon Building at Wabash and Adams and later moved to 18th Street near Prairie Ave. Under Forrest and Wheeler, the paper objected to the Black Laws and the Fugitive Slave Law. However, under successor owners it was also anti-Irish and anti-Catholic, tenets of the Know-Nothing Party. Its "stiff-necked policies" was causing it to lose readers.

In 1855, Joseph Medill, then 32 years old, and Dr. Charles H. Ray, then 34 years old, took over the paper and sought to attract a broader audience. They were definitely anti-slavery describing President Pierce as "a poor, weak, vacillating tool of slave power."[317] Abraham Lincoln was among the aspiring politicians who stopped by to meet the new editors. According to Medill they had a lively chat, Lincoln paid four dollars in advance for a six months subscription and told Medill that he "didn't like the paper before you boys took hold of it. It was too much of a Know-Nothing sheet."[318]

The *Tribune* would be closely identified with the Republican Party. In fact, Dr. Ray and Lincoln attended the meeting of newspaper editors in Decatur that led to the formation of the Republican Party in Illinois.

Douglas Gets Mobbed in Chicago

WHEN THE NEBRASKA Act passed, there were protests all across the north. Douglas quipped that he could make his way from Boston to Chicago by the light of burning effigies of himself. That was not too far off the mark. The depth of feeling was extraordinary. In Chicago, it was particularly intense. To have cited the action of the Illinois House and the response he got in Chicago in 1850 as evidence that the people endorsed the repeal of the Missouri Compromise, as Douglas did in his speech in the Senate arguing for the passage of the Kansas-Nebraska Bill, was an outrage. It was not just Chicago's abolitionists who were aroused. The newspapers in Chicago were already beating the drum. They did not want Douglas to claim Chicago was with him this time as he did after his earlier speech on the Compromise of 1850 and the Fugitive Slave Law. The *Tribune* sounded the alarm:

If he tries to get up what he calls a "vindication" of his crimes; if he collects around him a crowd of Irish rowdies and attempts to send forth their approbation as "the voice of the people of Chicago" it will not be our fault if he arouses a lion he cannot tame.[319]

The Free West (in its last year as an independent paper) reported that: "Mr. Douglas came quietly to Chicago from the theater of his victories over freedom in the Senate, not as the conquering hero returns to his home – but as one guilty of a crime."[320] He had been warned by friends not to come to Chicago. Douglas was not one to back down from a fight. He came to town and after a week of testing the waters, he announced that he would appear to defend the Nebraska Act. The meeting was set for North Market Square. The meeting was to be held outside because it was "one of the hottest nights Chicago had ever experienced."[321] There were signs of trouble brewing early on. Flags in the harbor were lowered to half-mast at one o'clock in the afternoon and the bells of the city tolled for an hour. Eight to ten thousand people assembled. It was not a friendly crowd. The Mayor presided and introduced Douglas.

The *Chicago Journal* reported what happened next:

Mr. Douglas arose and observed that he had come to explain the objects and provisions of the Nebraska Bill. This announcement was followed by a storm of hisses, groans, cheers, etc. He then said that he would answer all questions that were put to him in a respectful manner. – He had come to lay before the people the grand principles of the Nebraska Bill. – They did not understand the Bill and but few of them had ever read it. This remark brought forth such a tornado of discordant noises, that it was some minutes before he could proceed. He proceeded. The whole of the city press have united in condemning me but none of them have published my bill in order that it might vindicate itself. You see they have done me great injustice. You have been told that the bill was a measure to extend slavery into territory then free. (Yells, groans, hisses, etc. for some minutes.)
***
I will expose the slanders heaped upon me. The principle of the bill is to allow the people the privilege of regulating their own institutions in their own manner. This is the great principle that our Revolutionary fathers struggled for. (Laughter.) This is the great principle upon which the glorious Declaration of Independence is founded. (A voice – "all men are created free and

equal.") Gentlemen, if you will be quiet I will go on, but it is impossible for me to proceed with so much interruption. (Renewed interruption.)
***
I repeat you don't understand the measure. The State of New York has the same right to have slavery as Kansas or Nebraska. The State of Illinois wants slavery herself. (Tremendous uproar.)
***
You say that it was wrong to repeal the Missouri Compromise. (Cries of YES for some minutes.)

Will any man rise and tell me that he was in favor of that Compromise? (Cries of YES and renewed disturbance.) I will proceed to show that none of you were ever in favor of the Missouri Compromise. (NO, NO.)

Douglas kept on trying to make his speech and the crowd kept on shouting him down. This went on for two hours. He realized it was a standoff when he said:

I am talking about the Nebraska Bill and I intend to talk about it. If you think to put a stop to the free discussion of this measure, you are dealing with the wrong person. I shall stay here and talk as long as it suits my convenience. (Chorus: We won't go home until morning, til morning….)[322]

But the crowd persisted and, after a while, Douglas changed his tune. At midnight, Douglas looked at his watch, shook his fist at the crowd and shouted: "It is now Sunday morning – I'll go to church and you may go to Hell!"[323] Douglas retreated, guarded by friends who escorted him through the unruly crowd to the Tremont House.

Before coming to Chicago, Douglas had given a speech on July 4th in Independence Square in Philadelphia. There, he confronted the tenets of the Know-Nothing Party, the splinter party that was hostile to Catholics and foreigners and operated under a cloak of secrecy. Douglas drew on the location to recall that Philadelphia was where the Constitution was drafted with its principles of civil and religious freedom. He then bashed the Know-Nothings for standing against these principles. It was a partisan speech pointing out that his party, the Democracy, as they liked to refer to themselves, was open to all (though he surely meant all *white men*).

Douglas attributed the mobbing in Chicago to retaliation by the Know-Nothings.[324] He decoded the *Tribune's* reference to "Irish rowdies" to be a signal that he was supported by Irish Catholics and a secret call for the Know-Nothings to do battle with the Douglas supporters. There may be an element of truth to this observation. However, the Anti-Nebraska attitude was the dominant reason for the crowd's reaction. Given Douglas's use of his prior Chicago triumph in 1850 to validate his thesis for discarding the Missouri Compromise in 1854, the vast majority of Chicagoans who turned out for his speech wanted to make sure that he did not score another victory at their expense. It is inconceivable that the abolitionists would have stood still and let Douglas claim Chicago was behind him on the Nebraska Act.

Douglas was not one to back off. Though shouted down in Chicago by a menacing crowd, he took his defense of the Nebraska Act on the road. Over the next few weeks, he proceeded to give his stump speech in Galena, Freeport, Waukegan, Woodstock and other cities.[325] Douglas still had a firm grip on the Democratic Party in Illinois, but fissures were starting to appear.

Birth of the Republican Party

D R. DYER, LOVEJOY and the other abolitionists had been in the vanguard of those willing to abandon the existing two party system to confront slavery. Prior to 1852 the splinter parties they championed – the Liberty Party, The Free Soil Party, the Free Democrats – never commanded much of a following. But after 1854, all of that changed. Across the country a phenomenon was occurring which came to be called "fusion." The Democrats lost members who became "Free Democrats," reflecting their disagreement over the Nebraska Act's repeal of the Missouri Compromise.

The Whig Party disappeared entirely. Its anti-slavery members gravitated to the Anti-Nebraska parties. All of these splinter parties would soon *fuse* together to form the Republican Party. There were several false starts in Illinois before the party got organized and before Lincoln agreed to join it and become its leading spokesman in Illinois.

Alvan Earle Bovay, of Ripon, Wisconsin, predicted to his friend Horace Greeley that Winfield Scott would lose the election of 1852 and that the Whig Party would collapse. He suggested that the anti-slavery parties be brought together under one banner. He asked Greeley what would be a suitable name or the new party. Greeley suggested "The Republican Party."[326] Bovay went ahead and called a meeting in Ripon, Wisconsin in March of 1854. Fifty-four voters attended. The local Free Soil and Whig committees were dissolved and a new political organization was formed. Wisconsin thus claims to be the birthplace of the Republican Party and claims Bovay as the founder of the party.

Michigan also claims Republican paternity based on a meeting held July 6, 1854 in Jackson, Michigan in response to a call signed by 10,000 voters. Similar meetings were taking place in other States. In each case, the anti-slavery forces joined together to form a new party and adopted the name "Republican."[327] The first national convention of the party would occur on February 22, 1856 in Pittsburgh.

The organizers of the effort in Illinois called for a meeting in Springfield on October 5, 1854. The appeal was printed in *The Free West* on September 7, 1854:

> *A Convention of all citizens of … Illinois who are opposed to the repeal of the Missouri Compromise and to further extension and consolidation of the slave power … will be held on the 5th day of October, A.D., 1854 at 2 o'clock, at Springfield, for the organization of a party which shall put the Government upon a Republican track….*[328]

However, Abraham Lincoln was scheduled to speak in Springfield at that exact time, so the meeting was postponed until that evening.[329] The organizers wanted Lincoln to participate. They were going to be disappointed.

The Daily Register, Springfield's daily newspaper that championed Douglas and bashed his enemies, reported that this attempt to form a tentacle of the nascent Republican Party in Illinois was unsuccessful. Under a headline of "The Black Republican Fizzle," the *Register* mocked the convention reporting that it was attended by only 26 men and a boy, that the "one-idea tribe" adopted "the entire 'Black Republican' platform, without changing a comma," and that "after letting off some extra abolition steam, adjourned." The *Register's* caustic verdict on the initial attempt to form a Republican Party in Illinois: "Thus fizzled out this long trumpeted abolition affair."[330]

The newspaper correctly identified the dilemma that the organizers of the Republican Party faced. If they adopted the abolitionists' preferred platform, they would lose the "national men" of the Whig Party. This gave pause to the Whigs in Illinois, Lincoln included. Lincoln did not attend this first meeting intended to launch the Republican effort in Illinois.

The Convention had been a two day affair. Owen Lovejoy, Ichabod Codding, H.K. Jones and Erastus Wright were among its leaders.[331] It adopted resolutions and appointed various committees, naming Lincoln to one. Lincoln never participated, causing some to say that this committee never formally organized and faded out of existence. However, Paul Selby, who later chronicled the birth of the Republican Party, credited the Springfield meeting in October of 1854 as the starting point of the party in Illinois.[332]

Illinois needed to get organized. *National Era* had issued a call for united action by 1856.[333] The splintered parties in Illinois made this especially difficult. Selby, the publisher of the *Morgan Journal* would be instrumental in restarting the Illinois effort.

Lincoln Re-enters Politics

THE PIERCE VICTORY over Scott in 1852 left the Whig Party in a shambles. Lincoln later said that it was a time when he was starting to lose interest in politics.[334] The prospects for a politician of the Whig or Free Soil stripe were bleak in Illinois. One reason was that, when he had been in Congress, Lincoln, joining with John Quincy Adams and the other Whigs, had opposed the Mexican War, a stance unpopular at home. As a Congressman, Lincoln introduced resolutions demanding that President Polk identify the "spot" where the Mexican troops fired on U.S. soldiers. These resolutions posed a question to the President. They were crafted much the way a lawyer would draft an interrogatory, a written question to an adversary. Lincoln was hoping his question would force an admission that fit with the boundary argument that Adams and the other Whigs had been making. The effort was unsuccessful. (Douglas would later cleverly remind voters of Lincoln's opposition to the Mexican War by referring to his ideas as "spotty.") So, in the wake of Scott's loss in 1852, Lincoln's future as a politician looked bleak. The Democrats, led by Douglas, were in full control in Illinois – until the Nebraska Act changed the equation.

Up until 1854, Lincoln's pursuit of a political career could only be called moderately successful. In 1837 Lincoln had persuaded his fellow representatives in the Illinois House to move the capital to Springfield. He promptly moved there himself and established a law office. From there he ventured forth on the circuit and gained a reputation as a skilled trial lawyer. In fact, he became one of the most sought-after trial attorneys of his day.[335] Riding the circuit gave Lincoln an opportunity to further his political ambitions by forging friendships across a wide swath of State.

From the Illinois House Lincoln went to the United States Congress where he served one term. Nevertheless, he was recognized as one of the leaders of the Whig Party in Illinois. It was Lincoln who introduced Millard Fillmore when the former President came to Illinois in 1854 and Fillmore was already the Whig candidate for the 1856 election. (Fillmore had become President when President Zachary Taylor died in office, and he served from July 10, 1850 to March 3, 1853. Later, when the Whig Party collapsed, Fillmore joined the Know-Nothings and ran on the American Party ticket. Lincoln steered clear of that party.)

The Nebraska Act with its explicit repeal of the Missouri Compromise rekindled Lincoln's ambition to hold public office. In 1854 he launched a campaign to serve again in the Illinois House. But his real goal was to hold national office, to serve as a Senator from Illinois. While Lincoln later claimed that the repeal of the Missouri Compromise "aroused him" to re-enter politics, Herndon, his law partner and, after Lincoln's death, his biographer, thought there was another factor deserving of equal weight – ambition – not just Lincoln's, but also his wife's.[336] In any event, the repeal of the Missouri Compromise was an opportunity to be seized.

Lincoln was candid about his ambition. When he first ran for public office, seeking a seat in the Illinois General Assembly in 1836, he wrote an open letter to the People of Sangamo County, explaining his motivation:

Every man is said to have his peculiar ambition. Whether it be true or not, I can say for one that I have no other so great as that of being truly esteemed of my fellow men, by rendering myself worthy of their esteem.[337]

While Lincoln was not a member of a church and historians have speculated about the extent of his religious belief, mining his references to God in his speeches and writings, this self-professed motivation echoes the beliefs of the Swedenborgians to which Dr. Dyer was attracted, the idea that one's immortality is derived from leading a good life.

In 1854, the election for the Senate seat was four years away. But challenging Douglas now would position Lincoln to be the challenger and, to the extent he was successful in galvanizing opposition to Douglas and his policies, would help elect opponents to Douglas

to the Illinois General Assembly, the body that would elect the State's next Senator.

Lincoln Prepares to Do Battle

IN THE WATERSHED year of 1854, Lincoln, at the age of 46, was a seasoned politician. He had spoken to the voters and written many editorials during his campaigns for the Illinois House and the U.S. Congress. He was good at public speaking, having honed his skill by telling stories or reciting Shakespeare to childhood friends over the years, arguing cases to juries and appeals to appellate courts. Now, as he moved to the national stage, he brought a unique combination of qualities that made him a fitting rival to Douglas.

First and foremost was Lincoln's ability to construct tightly reasoned legal arguments. Despite no formal schooling and no apprenticeship, Lincoln taught himself what he needed to know to succeed as a lawyer. He had borrowed law books from John Logan, who would later be his first law partner, and devoured them. As he considered how to address the Nebraska Act, he drew on the roots of the young nation's democracy: the Declaration of Independence, the Constitution and the Northwest Ordinance. He had studied the speeches of Clay and Webster and the arguments they and others had made that led to the Missouri Compromise. Now he prepared the way a lawyer would for a Supreme Court argument. He pored over Douglas's speeches. He spent countless hours in the State Library digging into the history of the Constitution and the debates in Congress over the Missouri Compromise. He constructed a penetrating analysis of the origins and development of the country's policy on slavery.[338]

Lincoln's legal training taught him to streamline his arguments. He stripped them of extraneous issues. Lincoln followed a simple rule: "In law it is good policy to never *plead* what you *need* not, lest you oblige yourself to *prove* what you *can* not. Reflect on this well before you proceed."[339] Thus, he focused on the repeal of the Missouri Compromise which threatened to permit the extension of slavery to new territories and States. He avoided other issues over which opponents to the extension of slavery might be divided.

Lincoln's process caused him to focus intently on how to frame the issue. Like a military commander, Lincoln intuitively knew that choosing the ground on which to fight can often decide the outcome of the battle. Here, his years of experience as a lawyer who tried cases and argued appeals paid off. Herndon explained that Lincoln would often concede major points in an opponent's case, with a casual, "I reckon that's so...." But these concessions were carefully thought out. Lincoln would figure out exactly where to draw the line, focus all of his resources on that point and marshal the facts and arguments that demonstrated the case had to be decided his way.

Second, Lincoln was skilled in the art of persuasion. He knew that it was easier to persuade people to accept his reasoning if he did not first denounce them or ideas that might be opposed to his. In a speech he gave in 1842, Lincoln revealed his understanding of this art: "If you would win a man to your cause, *first* convince him that you are his sincere friend." He explained that this opened up the road to his reason. If instead, you "assumed to dictate to his judgment, or to command his action, or to mark him as one to be shunned and despised ... he will retreat within himself, close all the avenues to his head and his heart, and tho' your cause be naked truth itself ... you shall be no more be able to pierce him, than to penetrate the hard shell of a tortoise with a rye straw."[340]

A third quality was Lincoln's penchant for plain speaking. He used imagery familiar to his listeners. This is exemplified by one of his first attacks on Douglas's new compromise, the editorial he wrote for the *Illinois Journal*. Borrowing from a technique that he had honed as a trial lawyer when he needed to persuade a jury to see matters his way, he crafted an anecdote that mocked Douglas's explanation for repealing the Missouri Compromise:

Abraham Lincoln has a fine meadow, containing beautiful springs of water, and well fenced, which

John Calhoun[341] *had agreed with Abraham (originally owning the land in common) should be his, and the agreement had been consummated in the most solemn manner....*

John Calhoun then looks with a longing eye on Lincoln's meadow, and goes to it and throws down the fences, and exposes it to the ravishes of his starving and famished cattle.

"You rascal," says Lincoln, "what have you done? What do you do this for?"

"Oh," replies Calhoun, "everything is right. I have taken down your fence but nothing more. It is my true intent and meaning not to drive my cattle into your meadow, not to exclude them therefrom, but to leave them perfectly free to form their own notions of the feed, and to direct their movements in their own way."

Now would not the man who committed this outrage be deemed both a knave and a fool — a knave in removing the restrictive fence, which he had solemnly pledged himself to sustain; and a fool in supposing that there could be one man found in the country to believe that he had not pulled down the fence for the purpose of opening the meadow to his cattle?[342]

Lincoln designed his analogies using homespun examples like the fence between two pastures. He chose instrumentalities well known to his audience and avoided rhetorical flourishes with allusions to Greek, Roman or other classical figures. Everyone could grasp that the repeal of the Missouri Compromise was just like tearing down the fence between two neighbors. After first trying out his "tear down the fence" metaphor in an editorial, Lincoln deployed it with great effect in some of his speeches attacking the repeal of the Missouri Compromise.

A fourth quality was Lincoln's ear for compelling rhetoric. Lincoln was particular about his choice of words. He paid attention not only to their meaning, but also to their sound. Herndon, his young law partner, was often annoyed when Lincoln would flop down on the couch in their office and read aloud from a newspaper article or a speech that had been printed. Lincoln told Herndon that he liked hearing the words in addition to seeing them. He said he could "catch the idea by two senses, for when I read aloud I *hear* what is read and I see it; and hence two senses get it and I remember it better."[343] Reversing the process, Lincoln's speeches were interspersed with many passages that were lyrical.

Finally, a fifth quality was charisma. Lincoln's audiences found him spell-binding. Speeches in Lincoln's day were expository essays delivered over several hours. He mastered this style of oratory, delivering his message building his thesis from a small foundation, stone by stone. Lincoln would organize his ideas by developing an outline and by writing down snippets to include in his speeches. He would underline words he wanted to emphasize. These scraps of paper would then go into his portable filing system – his stove-pipe hat. Lincoln did not usually read his speeches. Unless he read his remarks, listeners thought they were extemporaneous. But he rehearsed what he was going to say, making the same speech several times as he took it from one county or city to the next. The force of his logic mixed with his choice of imagery and examples built up to a crescendo that drew his listeners to embrace the conclusion he was advocating. Initially, Lincoln drew a crowd because he was taking on Douglas. Before long, the crowds came to recognize that Lincoln was one of the most effective speakers of his day in his own right.

After meticulously preparing for battle, it was time to get on the stump.

Douglas and Lincoln Meet at the State Fair in Springfield

P RIOR TO THE State Fair which would run for a week in Springfield in October, Lincoln made speeches where he tested his ideas – one at Carollton on August 28, 1854, and another at Jacksonville on September 2. In both he argued for restoration of the Missouri Compromise.

Lincoln then went on to Bloomington where he was called on to speak in reply to Douglas who gave his standard defense of the Nebraska Act. Both men were honing their stump speeches. These speeches were warm-ups. They would again face each other, and larger crowds, in Springfield and then in Peoria.

The State Fair in Springfield opened on October 3, 1854 and Douglas was scheduled to speak the first day. Seats had been set up for 5,000 in a grove. But it rained, forcing everyone inside the Hall of Representatives which could accommodate less than half that number. Douglas gave his argument defending the Nebraska Act with all its embellishments. Douglas gave one of his sterling performances, stirring up the crowd in a three hour long harangue. He was enthusiastically received by the crowd with many roars of approval and cheers. The editor of the *Illinois State Register*, a Douglas partisan, thought his speech in defense of the Nebraska Act was "unanswerable."[344]

Lincoln spoke the next day. He too spoke in the Hall of Representatives to virtually the same crowd and he too spent three hours laying out his carefully reasoned arguments. He invited Douglas to attend so that he could reply (and to assure a big turnout). Albert Beveridge, author of one of the most comprehensive biographies of Lincoln, called it Lincoln's "first great speech." Herndon called it Lincoln's "profoundest" speech and reported that the crowd responded with tremendous enthusiasm.[345]

Of course, the Douglas partisans thought he had carried the day. The *Daily Register* reported that Judge Douglas, at first pass, "gored and tossed him upon the horns of a dilemma, while the thunders of the applauding multitude shook the State house from turret top to foundation stone." Douglas refuted Lincoln point by point so thoroughly that "the people could not be restrained…. We have seen many an outburst of approbation from political gatherings, but never, such a deep, heartfelt and heart-reaching concurrence in the sentiments of a public speaker."[346]

What the *Daily Register* missed was that a great rivalry had been born and that these two skilled debaters would attract tremendous crowds as they parried each other's blows over the next several years. Lincoln would become one of the leading spokesmen for the Anti-Nebraskans.

Though Lincoln usually provided copies of the text of his speeches to the *Illinois State Journal* or the other local papers when he spoke, he only provided an outline of the Springfield speech. However, Lincoln later wrote out the "Peoria Speech," so the argument he constructed was preserved.[347]

The Peoria Speech – previewed in Springfield – is a thorough exposition of Lincoln's argument for restoring the Missouri Compromise and sets out Lincoln's position on slavery, a carefully chosen condemnation of slavery *but without a call for its abolition.*

The "Peoria Speech"

L INCOLN'S SPEECH ON the Nebraska Act given in Peoria on October 16, 1854, was a remarkable display of all of the qualities that made him an outstanding orator. It was a clear articulation of his opposition to the extension of slavery, the issue he would pound home over the next five years and that would propel him to the forefront in the contest for the Presidency.

By pre-arrangement this was another joint appearance with "Judge Douglas," to use the honorific that Lincoln used when he referred to his adversary. The Judge carried on for over three hours. It was 5:00 o'clock when Douglas finished his remarks. He was loudly cheered. Lincoln thought the audience needed a break, so he invited everyone to get a bite of supper and come back at 6:30 or 7:00 to hear what he had to say because he intended to speak for an equal amount of time. This was agreed to.

When the crowd reassembled, Lincoln began by directing them to the narrow issue he would focus on: the repeal of the Missouri Compromise which threatened to extend the domain of slavery. He discarded other topics, staying away from other burning issues of the day such as homesteading, prohibition, the tariff, and the caning of Senator Sumner by Congressman

PHOTO FROM AMBROTYPE TAKEN AT URBANA ILL'S IN THE FALL OF 1857.

Copyright by W. H. SOMERS, 1885.

BEATRICE. *Campbell,* NEBRASKA.

A brilliant orator, Lincoln was guided by a simple principle: "I do not propose to question the patriotism of any man … but rather to strictly confine myself to the naked merits of the question." (Chicago History Museum)

Preston Brooks from South Carolina. He did not dwell on the events in "Bloody Kansas."

He signaled his single purpose with a simple beginning:

The repeal of the Missouri Compromise, and the propriety of its restoration, constitute the subject of what I am about to say.

***

And, as this subject is no other, than part and parcel of the larger general question of domestic-slavery, I wish to MAKE and KEEP the distinction between

the EXISTING institution [of slavery] and the EXTENSION of it, so broad, and so clear, that no honest man can misunderstand me, and no dishonest one, successfully misrepresent me.[348]

Unlike most political orations of the day, Lincoln avoided vituperation and abuse in his speeches.[349] Senator Chase and many newspapers had attacked Douglas saying the legislation Douglas authored was the product of a *conspiracy* hatched by the Slave States. Lincoln would have none of that. He made this point by saying, "I do not propose to question the patriotism, or to assail the motives of any man, or class of men; but rather to strictly confine myself to the naked merits of the question."[350]

In the same vein, he did not portray slave-owners as demented or depraved. He expressed sympathy for their plight:

When the southern people tell us they are no more responsible for the origin of slavery, than we; I acknowledge the fact. When it is said that the institution exists; and that it is very difficult to get rid of it, in any satisfactory way, I can understand and appreciate the saying. I surely will not blame them for not doing what I should not know how to do myself. If all earthly power were given me, I should not know what to do as to the existing institution.[351]

Lincoln's argument – that slavery should not be extended, that it was incompatible with the purposes for which the nation was founded, and that the Missouri Compromise should be restored – was carefully constructed. He traced the development of Illinois from Territory to State and reminded everyone of the significance of the Northwest Ordinance as the blueprint for the development of the Territory and its transformation into a State. Not only did he exalt the Northwest Ordinance but he extolled its author, Thomas Jefferson ("the most distinguished politician of our history"[352]).

Of course, Douglas argued that the Declaration's "All men are created equal" did not include blacks. How else could one explain that so many of the Founders were slave-holders and that their States

embraced slavery? Douglas surely delighted in posing this quandary for Lincoln. But Lincoln had an answer. He conceded that Jefferson had been a slave-holder but pointed to the fact that Jefferson was also the architect of the Northwest Ordinance where he explicitly banished slavery from that territory. From this, Lincoln reasoned that the Founding Fathers, and Jefferson in particular, envisioned containing slavery and preventing its extension. These arguments rested on a thorough analysis of the Declaration of Independence, what Jefferson intended by declaring all men equal and how that foundation stone fit with what Congress did when it enacted the Missouri Compromise. Yes, Lincoln conceded, the Founders did not touch slavery. Slavery was tolerated by the Founders in the formation of the union out of *necessity*, because it was already there.

Lincoln traced the events leading up to the Compromise of 1850. He pointed out how the Wilmot Proviso was constantly injected into legislative initiatives as Congress struggled to deal with the proposed admission of California as a State and the organization of the territories acquired from Mexico by the Treaty ending the War and the Gadsden Purchase. (Lincoln was able to boast that he had voted for the Wilmot Proviso forty times during his brief stint as a Congressman.[353]) He then outlined the elements of the Nebraska Act with its explicit repeal of the Missouri Compromise. With this background he restated the issue he would address in the plainest of terms: "whether the repeal of the Missouri Compromise is right or wrong."

Douglas had cleverly argued that Congress had "in principle" repudiated the Missouri Compromise. To answer this, Lincoln had to explain that he and the other proponents of the Wilmot Proviso voted *against* extension of the Missouri Compromise line across the territory acquired from Mexico in the War. He explained that this vote did not repudiate the Missouri Compromise, rather, he and his fellow Whigs wanted no slavery in the new territory and the extension of the Missouri Compromise line would have opened half to slavery. He pointed out that the Missouri Compromise applied to *the Louisiana Territory*. It was legislation allowing slavery in Missouri but prohibiting slavery in the remainder of the Louisiana Purchase north of

36°30'N latitude (the southern boundary of Missouri). There was nothing in the Compromise suggesting that it had any application to territory not yet owned.

To rebut Douglas's assertion that the Compromise of 1850 established a new principle, Lincoln closely analyzed what the bargain was. Yes, Utah and New Mexico came in as Territories with popular sovereignty, but in return for California coming into the union as a Free State, the slave trade removed from the District of Columbia and an adjustment of Texas's border (which Lincoln characterized as a slight reduction in the domain of slavery). In contrast, opening up Kansas and Nebraska was not accompanied with any counterbalancing concessions. And, if Popular Sovereignty were a new universal principle, why did Congress not ask the citizens of the District of Columbia to decide for themselves whether to have slavery?

In the same vein, Lincoln took Douglas to task for claiming the resolutions of the Illinois legislature approving the Compromise of 1850 signaled a desire to repeal the Missouri Compromise.

Lincoln then addressed whether the repeal "is intrinsically right." His answer was straightforward: "I insist that it is not." The Missouri Compromise was the result of a hard fought bargain between the advocates and opponents of Slavery. ("After an angry and dangerous controversy, the parties made friends by dividing the bone of contention.") To renege on that bargain was "as if two starving men had divided their only loaf; the one had hastily swallowed his half, and then grabbed the other half just as he was putting it in his mouth!"

Douglas had argued that the climate in Kansas and Nebraska would prevent slavery from becoming established there. Lincoln pointed out that there were already five States, all north of the Missouri Compromise line that had slavery: Delaware, Maryland, Virginia, Kentucky and Missouri, and also the District of Columbia. The census of 1850 showed that there were 867,276 slaves there – "more than one-fourth of all the slaves in the nation." The history of slavery's expansion within Missouri also undercut the suggestion that slavery could not go north or flourish outside the cotton belt.

Douglas had made a subtle argument that there would be no law on the books *allowing* slaves to be brought in to the Kansas and Nebraska territories. Lincoln explained that if there were a positive law *prohibiting* slavery it would take a much bolder man to venture in. In fact this was exactly the experience of Illinois and Missouri where the one State had a positive law prohibiting slavery and the other did not:

> *We have some experience of this practical difference. In spite of the Ordinance of '87, a few Negroes were brought into Illinois, and held in a state of quasi-slavery; not enough, however to carry a vote of the people in favor of the institution when they came to form a constitution. But in the adjoining Missouri country, where there was no ordinance of '87 – was no restriction – they were carried ten times, nay a hundred times, as fast, and actually made a Slave State. This is fact – naked fact.*[354]

Douglas had made another argument that could have called forth a scholarly legalistic analysis construing the Constitution's Equal Protection Clause. Douglas had argued that Southerners should have the same right as Northerners to take their property wherever they chose. Lincoln dealt with this with one of his well designed analogies:

> *Equal justice to the south, it is said, requires us to consent to the extending of slavery to new countries. That is to say, inasmuch as you do not object to my taking my hog to Nebraska, therefore I should not object to you taking your slave. Now, I admit this is perfectly logical if there is no difference between hogs and Negroes.*[355]

The hog/Negro comparison gave Lincoln the opportunity to probe the validity of the assertion that Negroes were just *property*. Lincoln pointed out that Southerners did not always deny the humanity of slaves. They had joined with the north in 1820 to vote to end the importation of slaves from Africa, declaring the African slave trade piracy and agreeing that violators could be put to death. Lincoln gave the hog/Negro analogy an extra twist:

The practice [the slave trade] was no more than bring-ing wild Negroes from Africa, to sell to such as would buy them. But you never thought of hanging men for catching and selling wild horses, wild buffaloes or wild bears.[356]

Lincoln pointed to other instances showing *Southerners* recognized the humanity of slaves. He asked why it is that the Southerner shirks from the company of slave-dealers? And, if slaves were just *property* how did one account for the free Negro population:

[T]here are in the United States and territories, includ-ing the District of Columbia, 433,643 free blacks. At $500 per head they are worth over two hundred mil-lions of dollars. How comes this vast amount of prop-erty to be running about without owners? We do not see free horses or free cattle running at large. How is this? All these free blacks are the descendants of slaves, or have been slaves themselves, and they would be slaves now. But for SOMETHING which has operated on their white owners, inducing them, at vast pecuniary sacrifices, to liberate them. What is that something? Is there any mistaking it? In all these cases it is your sense of justice, and human sympathy, continually tell-ing you, that the poor Negro has some natural right to himself – that those who deny it, and make mere mer-chandise of him, deserve kickings, contempt and death.

Recognizing the extent of prejudice against blacks that many Illinois voters had at this time, Lincoln put forth the proposition that slaves are not just property but humans with certain basic rights by suggesting that even Southerners recognized this. The elegance of this argument was that Lincoln was not himself the spon-sor of an idea that many of his listeners considered anathema; instead, he was simply conveying the fact of *others'* sentiments. The indirect argument he crafted avoided embracing the abolitionist viewpoint. At the same time, by portraying Southerners as the ones who were motivated to free some of their slaves because they recognized the humanity of the slave, Lincoln laid the groundwork for his condemnation of slavery as tyr-anny and a corrosive force.

The most appealing argument that Douglas had made was that Popular Sovereignty was the embodi-ment of "the sacred right of self-government," Douglas's "great principle." Lincoln addressed this argument head on. He agreed that "the doctrine of self-government is right – absolutely and eternally right…." But he said whether it applies depends on "whether a Negro is or is not a man." If he is not, those who are may do with him as they please. If he is, then slavery is the "total destruction of self-government."

Lincoln had built a formidable case based on his analysis of the Declaration, the Northwest Ordinance and the intentions of the Founders, showing that slav-ery was incompatible with the principles upon which the nation was founded. The nation was founded on the principle of self-government. If a Negro is just property, then the extension of slavery is of no moment. But, if he is a man, then the extension of slavery destroys the principle of self-government. He distilled this down to a simple proposition:

What I do say is this, no man is good enough to gov-ern another man, without that other's consent. I say this is the leading principle – the sheet anchor of American republicanism.

This fundamental principle was exactly what was said in the Declaration that "[G]overnments are insti-tuted among men, DERIVING THEIR JUST POWERS FROM THE CONSENT OF THE GOVERNED."

Taken to its logical conclusion, the right of self-government, as Douglas employed it, would mean that every man could decide for himself whether to hold slaves – not just in Slave States or new Territories but everywhere. And if Nebraska can decide for itself, does that not take away from the principle of self-govern-ment and negate what the Founders did when they passed the Northwest Ordinance? Whether slavery goes into Nebraska is not the exclusive concern of the people who live there. "The whole nation is interested that the best use be made of the Territories." This led Lincoln to explain why it was in the interests of citizens in the other Free States to oppose slavery in Nebraska. First was the obligation to return runaway slaves. If the domain of slavery were expanded the Free States would be burdened with more instances where they would be called on to honor and enforce the Fugitive Slave Act. Lincoln termed the obligation to catch and return runaway slaves a "dirty, disagreeable job."

Then there was the control of the government. Every State had two senators. Presidential electors were based on the number of Senators and Representatives. But the Slave States enjoyed more Representatives because of the three fifths clause which counted three people for every five slaves. While the slaves do not vote, they "swell the influence of the white people's vote." Lincoln pointed out that South Carolina has six representatives, the same as Maine. But, Maine has all of 581,813 white people whereas South Carolina has just 274,567. This is because South Carolina has 384,984 slaves. So allowing slavery into Nebraska would give a voting advantage to the advocates of slavery.

Lincoln's Peoria speech laid out the case for restoring the Missouri Compromise. By taking on Douglas and calling the Nebraska Act (with its repeal of the Missouri Compromise) wrong, Lincoln focused the nation's attention on the danger of allowing the domain of slavery to expand. He would address this issue again and again over the next several years, making a number of other memorable speeches – his House Divided Speech, the Lincoln-Douglas debates, and his Cooper Union Speech.

Hating Slavery but Not Calling for Its Abolition

IN ALL OF his speeches, Lincoln's condemnation of slavery was unequivocal. In the Peoria Speech, he said: "I hate it because of the monstrous injustice of slavery itself. I hate it because it deprives our republican example of its just influence in the world – enables the enemies of free institutions, with plausibility, to taunt us as hypocrites – causes the real friends of freedom to doubt our sincerity...."

He objected to the Nebraska Act "because it assumes that there CAN be MORAL RIGHT in the enslaving of one man by another."

This was exactly what the abolitionists had been saying. How then could Lincoln not follow this condemnation to its logical conclusion? Why did he not embrace the abolitionist cause? In fact, Lincoln made a point of distinguishing his policy from the cause of the abolitionists. He would stand *with* the abolitionists in restoring the Missouri Compromise but he would stand *against* them in their call for the repeal of the Fugitive Slave Act. The Constitution tolerated slavery as a matter of necessity. It was already here. The Founders demonstrated a desire to limit it by a series of measures such as the Northwest Ordinance. But they also sanctioned the return of fugitive slaves. It was part of the original bargain and must be honored to keep the union together. Not only did Lincoln not advocate disobedience of the Fugitive Slave Act, he did not advocate its repeal.

Lincoln's First Run for the Senate in 1855

LINCOLN SPOKE AT North Market Hall in Chicago, October 27, 1854 criticizing the Nebraska Act[357] and again on July 19, 1856 in Dearborn Park on the same subject. The attack on the Nebraska Act (which repealed the Missouri Compromise) by Lincoln and his fellow Republicans started to pay off. "Anti-Nebraska" clubs were formed. Only four of 42 Democrats who voted for the Nebraska Act retained their seats in the next election.[358]

In Illinois the Democratic Party was starting to show fissures. Lincoln had run for a seat in the Illinois General Assembly as a Whig and won. The General Assembly would elect the next senator and the incumbent, James Shields, a Douglas Democrat, could not count on the support of the anti-Nebraska Democrats.[359] Lincoln sought the seat hoping to win votes from anti-

Nebraska Democrats in addition to the Whigs. When the General Assembly convened on February 8, 1855, the anti-Nebraska Democrats had their own candidate, Congressman Lyman Trumbull. Needing 51 votes to be elected, on the first ballot, Lincoln won 45 votes to Shields's 41 and Trumbull's five. The balloting went on for hours. Lincoln got up to 47 votes, but the five anti-Nebraska Democrats refused to vote for Lincoln because they had been elected as Democrats. The plan of the Douglas Democrats was to switch to Governor Joel Matteson calculating that he might attract enough votes from the anti-Nebraska Democrats to get the needed majority. Lincoln, realizing that the Douglas Democrats would win unless the Whigs supported Trumbull, instructed his Whig supporters to vote for Trumbull on the next ballot. On the tenth ballot Lyman Trumbull was elected.[360]

In the gallery, Mary Todd Lincoln had watched the whole process. She had sat with Julia Jayne Trumbull who had been a bridesmaid in her wedding. Convinced that Trumbull and his supporters had acted dishonorably, she never spoke to Mrs. Trumbull again. Also incurring her wrath was Norman Judd, one of the five anti-Nebraska Democrats who held out and refused to vote for Lincoln. Though Judd later led the anti-Nebraska Democrats to "fuse" with the Whigs to form the Republican Party, became chairman of the Illinois Republican Party and was key to Lincoln's winning the nomination for President, Mary not only never forgave him, she actively campaigned against him when he was being considered for a seat in the cabinet.[361]

Unlike his wife, Lincoln did not bear a grudge. He went to Trumbull's victory party and congratulated him and told one of his correspondents that he took pleasure in having defeated Governor Matteson and the other Douglas Democrats who were "worse whipped than I was."[362] Trumbull and Judd would not forget Lincoln's magnanimity. Both would provide crucial support to Lincoln in the future.

Bloody Kansas and Beecher's Bibles

WHEN DOUGLAS FORGED the compromise that gave birth to the Nebraska Act and the doctrine of Popular Sovereignty, he not only sought to remove the "agitation" roiling Congress over the slavery issue but hoped to quiet the nation with a policy that he viewed as the essence of democracy. Lincoln, of course, observed that this doctrine did nothing of the kind. The events in Kansas proved Lincoln right.

"Bloody Kansas," was the direct result of the enactment of the Nebraska Act. If the people of Kansas were going to decide for themselves whether to be Slave or Free, then, once the territory was open for settlement, the proponents of slavery and the champions of freedom were both going to descend upon Kansas and try to vote their system in. "Squatter sovereignty," the term Lincoln used, meant the residents of a territory could make their own laws. Lincoln ridiculed the policy by providing his own definition: "If any one man chooses to enslave another, no third person shall be allowed to object."[363] and, as the term "squatter" implied, many did not wait until the territory was officially opened for settlement.

Kansas was in a state of turmoil. Rumors spread through the south that 20,000 Northerners were invading Kansas. Missouri's fiery Senator, David Atchison, proclaimed them to be "Negro thieves" and told Missourians to defend their institution "with the bayonet and blood." Dr. John Stringfellow, editor of the *Squatter Sovereign*, told a crowd in St. Joseph, Missouri:

I tell you to mark every scoundrel among you that is the least tainted with free soilism, or abolitionism, and exterminate him ... I advise you one and all to enter every election district in Kansas ... and vote at the point of a Bowie knife or revolver![364]

Many Southerners saw it as an all or nothing proposition. If Kansas became a Slave State, abolitionism would be defeated, slavery could be extended, and the South's power in Congress secured. If the North gained Kansas, the South's power would be diminished and the value of slaves depreciated.[365] There were skirmishes and violence at every turn. Free-Staters and pro-slavers alike were attacked by mobs and occasionally killed.

Missourians rushed into Kansas to settle and take over towns in order to prepare for any referendum. From the east, abolitionists also mobilized. A group of 60 or more men from New Haven, Connecticut organized the Connecticut-Kansas Company. Henry Ward Beecher, the abolitionist preacher from Brooklyn and brother of Harriet Beecher Stowe, the author of *Uncle Tom's Cabin*, pledged to give them 25 rifles. The *New York Tribune*, on February 8, 1856, reported that to raise money for the company, Beecher preached that abolitionists must take up arms to defeat the slave-holders in Kansas, extolling the Sharp's Rifle, a significant advancement in the development of firearms in the 1850s, as a "moral agency" superior to the Bible when it came to persuading slave-holders:

> He [Henry W. Beecher] believed that the Sharp's Rifle was a truly moral agency, and that there was more moral power in one of those instruments, so far as the slave-holders of Kansas were concerned, than in a hundred Bibles. You might just as well. . . read the Bible to Buffaloes as to those fellows who follow Atchison and Stringfellow; but they have a supreme respect for the logic that is embodied in Sharp's rifle.

The cases in which the rifles were shipped were labeled as "Books" and "Bibles," to hide the identity of the contents from the pro-slavery men and to keep the recipients from having any difficulties with the authorities who had forbidden the shipping of arms to the bloody region.[366] Sharp's rifles became known as "Beecher's Bibles."

A Second Effort to Form an Illinois Republican Party Succeeds

HERNDON HAD URGED Lincoln to absent himself from the 1854 attempt to form a Republican Party in Springfield. Herndon was afraid that Owen Lovejoy and the other abolitionists might put pressure on Lincoln to take up their cause and Herndon knew that if Lincoln were going to succeed in politics, he could not be too closely identified with the extremists.[367] The 1854 convention adopted a mild platform, disapproving the extension of slavery but not calling for its abolition. But the convention did not result in the formation of a party with all the trappings of a political organization. The Convention did not even adopt the label of Republican Party.

In February of 1856, Paul Selby, the editor of the *Morgan Journal*, the Jacksonville newspaper, called for a meeting of anti-Nebraska editors to promote a State-wide Republican Party. The editors met in Decatur and Abraham Lincoln, who was now ready to join the Republican effort, came from Springfield to join them, the only non-editor to attend this plotting session. Lincoln said he was now ready to "buckle on his armor for the approaching contest with the Pierce party."[368] A resolutions committee was formed that included Lincoln, Dr. Charles Ray from the *Chicago Tribune* and George Schneider from the German newspaper *Illinois Staats-Zeitung*.[369] The resolutions they adopted declared that they had no intention of interfering with slavery where it already existed in the States but that they demanded restoration of the Missouri Compromise. They also disavowed the Know-Nothing movement saying: "In regard to office, we hold merit, not birth place to be the test.... We should welcome the exiles and emigrants from the Old World, to homes of enterprise and of freedom of the New."[370] The editors then issued a call for a State–wide convention to be held in

In May of 1856, Lincoln and his supporters met at Major's Hall in Bloomington, Illinois to formalize the organization of the Illinois Republican Party. (Chicago History Museum)

Bloomington on May 29. This became the first State-wide convention attended by 270 delegates covering every county in the State.[371]

The resolutions which would be the starting point of a platform were important because the new Republicans wanted to attract not just former Whigs but also the Democrats who were breaking with Douglas over the Nebraska Act. Lyman Trumbull, Norman Judd, John M. Palmer, John McClernand, among others, had made it clear they opposed the Nebraska Act.[372] The new party hoped that the anti-Nebraska issue would cement the former antagonists.

Lincoln's "Lost Speech"

THE FORMER WHIGS, now led by Lincoln, Anti-Nebraska Democrats, and anti-slavery veterans converged on Bloomington on May 29, 1856 to organize the Illinois Republican Party formally. Orville H. Browning and David Davis, two of Lincoln's staunchest supporters, joined Lovejoy, Codding, and the others for a meeting comprised of 270 delegates. They met in Major's Hall above Humphrey's Cheap Store. They approved a slate of candidates and adopted the following resolution:

Resolved, *That we hold in accordance with the opinions and practices of all the great statesmen of all parties for the first sixty years of the administration of the government, that under the Constitution, Congress possesses full power to prohibit slavery in the Territories;*

and that while we will maintain all constitutional rights of the South, we also hold that justice, humanity, the principles of freedom, as expressed in our Declaration of Independence and our National Constitution, and the purity and perpetuity of our government require that that power should be exerted, to prevent the extension of slavery into Territories heretofore free.

There were several speeches and the delegates called for Lincoln. Lincoln spoke for 90 minutes. He realized this was the moment to solidify the fusion of the new participants in a party devoted to stopping the spread of slavery. He had clearly thought through the positions that all the delegates could join. While he spoke extemporaneously, the speech was an exposition of those ideas. Although there were reporters there, including Medill from the *Chicago Tribune*, they were so mesmerized by Lincoln's speech that they forgot to take notes. Because there is no contemporaneous record of what he said, the Bloomington speech is known as "Lincoln's Lost Speech." It was clearly an electrifying oration. Medill's recollection, later given to Ida Tarbell, a Lincoln biographer, was:

> *There stood Lincoln in the forefront … hurling thunderbolts at the foes of freedom, while the great convention roared its endorsement! I never witnessed such a scene before or since. As he described the aims and aggressions of the unappeasable slave-holders and the servility of their Northern allies … and the grasping after the rich prairies of Kansas and Nebraska to blight them with slavery and to deprive free labor of this rich inheritance, and exhorted the friends of freedom to resist them to the death – the convention went fairly wild.*[373]

While Lincoln's words are lost, there is a general consensus that the ideas he presented were as follows:

1. *That there were pressing reasons for the formation of the Republican Party.*
2. *That the Republican movement was very important to the future of the nation.*
3. *All Free Soil people needed to rally against slavery and the existing political evils.*
4. *The nation must be preserved in the purity of its principles as well as the integrity of its territorial parts, and the Republicans were the ones to do it.*[374]

Dr. Dyer and the Abolitionists "Fuse" to Become Republicans

WITH THE REPUBLICAN Party established in Illinois at the Bloomington Convention, the Republicans could now get down to the business of party building. The Nebraska controversy had given them an opportunity both in Illinois and nationally. While the abolitionists were being told to play a less visible role so as to bring the Democrats into the party, nevertheless they were a mainstay of the new party. Lovejoy and Dr. Dyer and their friends made significant contributions to help build the party. Even before the Bloomington Convention, Freer, DeWolf and Eastman had been delegates to a Republican meeting convened in the Second Congressional District in Aurora in September of 1854.[375] Just before the Bloomington Convention there had been a meeting to plan the national Republican Convention. Delegates met in Pittsburgh from February 20–23, 1856 to plan for a national convention to be held in Philadelphia in June. Lovejoy attended the meeting.[376] Lovejoy gave an impassioned speech on the subject of Kansas: "Who would not lose his life in such a cause? In defense of Kansas I will offer myself as a captain, and if not wanted in that capacity, I will shoulder a gun and go as a private."[377] All the abolitionists in Illinois would enthusiastically become Republicans. They sensed that the Nebraska issue was bringing a sea change. Dr. Dyer would be a delegate to the Republican State Conventions in both 1858 and 1860, two crucial conventions in the trajectory of Abraham Lincoln.

Foiling the Recapture of Fugitives

THE ABOLITIONISTS WELCOMED the advent of the Republican Party and the prospect that it would bring more people to the cause of abolishing slavery. While Lincoln and the Republicans might stop short of defiance of the Fugitive Slave Act, the abolitionists were not about to pull in their horns. They were always searching for creative ways to disrupt the recapture of a slave when slave-catchers came to town to enforce a warrant issued under the Fugitive Slave Act. The warrant gave the slave-catchers the legal power to arrest a Negro. The abolitionists came up with an ingenious strategy to bollix up the efforts of the slave-catchers: hold the slave-catchers responsible for any misconduct they might engage in under state law. Arrest them for kidnapping, disturbing the peace or whatever else fit the circumstances.

An early test of this tactic came in 1854, when Dr. Dyer's friend Calvin DeWolf, then a Justice of the Peace, presided over a trial where three Missouri slave-catchers, George and John Buchanan and William Grant, were accused of assault with a deadly weapon upon a colored man named Turner.[378] This nicely disrupted the efforts of the slave-catchers and sent a message to those who had dispatched them.

When DeWolf attended the meeting Dr. Dyer called to protest the death of Elijah Lovejoy in 1838, he was 23 years old. He had come from Ohio where he attended the Grand River Institute and became proficient in mathematics, Latin and surveying. He taught school for two years and then embarked on the study of law.[379] He practiced law for 11 years and was active in politics. Then, in 1854 he ran for and was elected a justice of the peace. He was a well known abolitionist, having been a founder of the anti-slavery society and having helped bring Zebina Eastman to Chicago to start *Western Citizen*. As a justice of the peace, his sympathies were clearly not with the slave-catchers.

The next time the "arrest them first" tactic was tried, things did not go so smoothly. During the attempt to

Calvin DeWolf, a Justice of the Peace, was among the first to preside over a trial resulting from the clever use of the "arrest them (slave-catchers) first" tactic.
(Chicago History Museum)

introduce slavery into the Nebraska Territory, a slave named Eliza, who had escaped from her owner, F. Nuckolls of Nebraska, made her way to Chicago. She had been pursued, and on September 1, 1858 was seized by Nuckolls. But, turning the tables on the slave-catcher, the locals arrested Nuckolls and brought him before Judge DeWolf on a charge of riotous conduct. Nuckolls was locked up for only a few hours. But it was enough time to get Eliza sent on her way by the ever-efficient Underground Railroad to Canada.

Nuckolls complained bitterly about the loss of his property and the "misconduct" of Judge DeWolf and his co-conspirators. Nuckolls succeeded in getting DeWolf and three others indicted "for aiding a Negro slave to escape from her master."[380]

This, of course, became a new cause célèbre in Chicago. DeWolf sought to quash the federal indictment with another creative legal argument: the woman could not be taken because she was not lawfully a slave in Nebraska. Why? *Because Nebraska was only a Territory*. The motion to quash was never heard. The case languished and then, in 1861, after Lincoln had been elected President, the case was dismissed by the United States District Attorney, E.C. Larned, on the authority of the President.

There were other episodes like this. One occurred earlier in Pennsylvania when Deputy Marshall Wynkoop and three of his deputies in the Eastern District of Pennsylvania were arrested for riotous or illegal conduct and an attempt upon the life of "Bill," a supposed fugitive slave.[381] Bill was shot in the head. Eastman reported the exchange of wires between the Marshall and the Secretary of the Interior. The Marshall asked for authority to retain counsel and incur the necessary expenses to defend the suit. The Secretary wired back saying he should "lose no time in consulting the District Attorney, and taking any measures for the defense that he might deem necessary, and assuring him that the Department and the whole Government are determined, at all hazards, and at any cost, to carry out the provisions of the Fugitive Slave Law."[382] To most Northerners, this response was just another piece of evidence that the federal government was in the hands of the slave power.

That Pennsylvania case gave rise to further proof to the abolitionist press that the federal government was pervasively controlled by those committed to the cause of slavery. Justice Grier, of the United States Supreme Court, in his role as a circuit judge, had issued the original warrant for the arrest of the fugitive. When the Marshall and his deputies who shot the supposed fugitive were arrested by the Pennsylvania authorities, Justice Grier threatened to indict them. This provoked the Pennsylvanian on whose affidavit the State warrant was issued to write an open letter to the justice pointing out the inappropriateness of his threat and poking fun at the logic of his position: "We are left to infer that no degree of violence or brutality in catching Negroes is culpable or illegal. You seem to have forgotten that

the Negro is not charged with a crime. He is merely charged with owing service. He is an unfortunate debtor. Can it be that you supposed a sheriff, in serving process in an action of debt, may take an armed posse and deliberate with his associates on the propriety of shooting the defendant if they cannot otherwise take him?"[383]

Every episode of this sort just gave the abolitionist newspapers a field day. Eastman and the other abolitionist editors were building the case to sway public opinion in the North in favor of the abolitionist view that the Fugitive Slave Law should not be enforced – that it should be resisted at every turn.

John Brown's Raids in Kansas

EVER SINCE THE death of Lovejoy, John Brown had been an active abolitionist. From his home in North Elba in upstate New York, he frequently came to Chicago and, when he did so, he stayed with John and Mary Richardson Jones. The Joneses were leaders of the free black community and played a prominent role in Chicago's Underground Railroad. Brown fit in with the abolitionist community in Chicago, befriending Dr. Dyer and Alan Pinkerton and others conducting the activities of the Underground Railroad in Chicago. (Pinkerton was a detective in Chicago, started a detective agency that investigated train robberies that was later known as the Pinkerton National Detective Agency, and, during the Civil War, served in the Lincoln Administration by heading up the Intelligence Service, forerunner of the Secret Service.)

John Brown had an apocalyptic view of how slavery would be brought to an end. His views were more extreme than those of his Chicago hosts. He spoke of fomenting a slave revolt and taking other aggressive action to confront the slave power.[384] He confided to some his plan to wage pre-emptive war on the United States by attacking the United States arsenal at Harpers Ferry, Virginia (now West Virginia),

John Brown, leader of anti-slavery guerilla attacks in Kansas and the raid on the arsenal at Harper's Ferry where he was wounded, arrested and hanged for treason in 1859.[386] (Chicago History Museum)

where he would seize guns to arm slaves whom he would free from a nearby plantation first. This would spark a slave insurrection.

Mary Jones first met John Brown when Frederick Douglass brought him by and asked her to put him up for the night. They stayed up all night talking. Mary Jones told her husband she thought that Brown "was a little off" on the slavery question because of his desire to precipitate Armageddon. At one point John Jones said to Brown that he would lose his life if he carried out his plan. Brown snapped his finger and said, "What do I care for my life, if I can do what I want to do – if I can free these Negroes?"[385]

In 1854, when conflict erupted in Kansas, three of Brown's sons headed to Kansas intending to stand

with the anti-slavery settlers. In the summer of 1855, John Brown headed to Kansas with another son and a son-in-law, traveling through Chicago to join his sons in Kansas.[387] They were well armed. Though Brown professed to be a devout Christian, he was about to go on a murderous rampage, killing defenseless pro-slavery men. What led to this murderous spree? Partly Brown's actions reflected the lawlessness and violence that prevailed in Kansas. He was giving the Southerners a taste of their own medicine. But the political developments concerning Kansas may also have provoked him.

On March 30, 1855, an election was held to elect the Territorial legislature. On election day, pro-slavery Missourians poured over the border and stuffed the ballot boxes. According to the census, there were 2,950 legal voters in Kansas, but 6,307 ballots had been cast.[388] They established a pro-slavery legislature, which set about drafting a constitution that included an article sanctifying slavery:

> *The right of property is before and higher than any constitutional sanction, and the right of the owner of a slave to such slave and its increase is the same and as inviolable as the right of the owner of all property whatever.*[389]

The proposed constitution also prohibited the legislature from passing any laws for the emancipation of slaves.

The opponents of slavery held a rival convention in Topeka on September 19, 1855 and drafted their own constitution that banned slavery. They set up a rival government in Topeka.

Then, President Franklin Pierce declared the Topeka government to be in rebellion against the legitimate government of the Territory. The leaders of the Topeka convention were indicted and a posse formed to assist the United States Marshall in serving subpoenas from a Grand Jury investigating the rebels' conduct. This led to the "sack of Lawrence" when the posse, made up of pro-slavery men from Missouri, invaded Lawrence, the center of the Free State movement, found it deserted, and proceeded to destroy several houses and a hotel and to pillage the town. Reporting on these forays from the scene, the *Chicago Tribune's* James Redpath called the Missourians "Border Ruffians" and the name stuck.[390]

This occurred on May 21, 1856. As soon as they heard the news, Brown and his sons rode over to Lawrence to aid in its defense. But they arrived after all the damage had been done and the perpetrators were gone.[391]

Then Brown learned about the caning of Massachusetts Senator Charles Sumner. On May 19 and 20, Senator Sumner, a staunch abolitionist, delivered a speech in the Senate that he had prepared titled "The Crime against Kansas." In it he attacked South Carolina's Senator Butler saying he was infatuated with the "harlot Slavery." On May 22, Congressman Brooks, of South Carolina, went to the Senate Chamber, found Sumner working at his desk, and proceeded to beat him senseless with his gold-tipped cane to vindicate the South's honor.

These events and continuing local acts of violence against Free State men added up in Brown's mind. Brown and his band set out to settle the score. At 10 o'clock at night on May 24, they went to the home of James Doyle, near Pottawatomie Creek in Osawatomie, Kansas. They knocked on the door, rousing the family, pretending to need directions. When the door was opened, Brown's men barged in and took Doyle and his two oldest sons captive, announcing that they were with the Northern Army. They led them down the road and then attacked them with *swords and knives*, hacking them to death.[392]

A half mile down the road, the ruse was repeated and Allen Wilkinson was led into the dark and his doom. Their final victim was William Sherman, who was staying at the home of James Harris.[393] He met the same fate.

Brown was never brought to justice for these murders. He and his followers hid out for a while. Then they participated in the ongoing skirmishes between Free State men and pro-slavery forces, and raided pro-slavery farms for provisions. In September of 1856, the new governor of Kansas, John Geary, issued several proclamations ordering both sides to disarm and disband. He offered clemency to the combatants on both sides which brought the open warfare to a close.[394]

In June of 1857 Brown headed east intending to raise money for his grand scheme. He was under indictment for the Pottawatomie killings and pursued by a contingent of U.S. troops. He made it to Tabor, Iowa, an outpost of the Underground Railroad run by Quakers.[395] He stayed a week and then went on to Chicago and then east where he spoke to anti-slavery sympathizers and raised money, supposedly to assist in the settlement of Kansas by those opposed to slavery. His true intent was to take the war to the South.

He learned that a United States Marshall was on his way east to arrest him, which caused him to go back into hiding. In June he was back in Chicago, and then on his way to Tabor where supplies and arms he had gathered were waiting.[396] From there, Brown went back to Kansas to find recruits for the army he needed for his planned invasion of Harpers Ferry, Virginia.[397] He assembled a band, provided them with the materiel stashed at Tabor and sent some of them off to Chambersburg, Virginia, the staging area for his planned attack. When he went east, he had professed to be soliciting funds for his endeavors in Kansas. Brown would be back and forth through Chicago several more times over the next year looking for money, recruits, and supplies.[398] The Chicago abolitionists were eager to help him – up to a point.

1856 – The Republican Party's First Presidential Election

T HE EVENTS IN Kansas so dominated the national debate that the anti-slavery voices finally were able to coalesce into a political party and make slavery an issue. Illinois was just one of the many States where Republican parties sprung up. The national Republican Party adopted a platform that demanded that Kansas be admitted as a Free State. It condemned the repeal of the Missouri Compromise in the Nebraska Act and opposed Popular Sovereignty. Their candidate was John Charles Frémont and their slogan was: "Free speech, free press, free soil, free men, Frémont and victory!"

Frémont was the Senator from California who had won fame as the leader of an expedition exploring the west on the eve of the War with Mexico. The election of 1856 was a three way affair with James Buchanan heading the Democratic ticket and Millard Fillmore running on the American Party ticket (the party of the "Know Nothings"). Buchanan won with 1,836,072 votes to Frémont's 1,342,345 with Fillmore receiving 873,053. The Convention that nominated Frémont also entertained Lincoln's name as a nominee for Vice President, reflecting his growing prominence in Republican circles. However, the eventual Vice Presidential nominee to run with Frémont was William Dayton, a New Jersey Senator. Republican strategists recognized that the Republicans could win the White House in 1860 if the party could head off another third party effort and win two more States, such as Pennsylvania and Illinois.

Douglas Opposes the Admission of Kansas under the Lecompton Constitution

THE FIGHT OVER whether Kansas would come into the Union as a Free or Slave State produced another battle, the battle of competing constitutions. The 1857 constitutional convention that was controlled by the "Border Ruffians" had produced the pro-slavery Lecompton Constitution. This was submitted to Congress and President James Buchanan announced his support for the admission of Kansas under it (*i.e.*, the admission of Kansas as a Slave State).

Earlier, there had been a Congressional investigation which found that the Border Ruffians had distorted the voting in Kansas and corrupted the process so as to make the result of the referendum approving the Lecompton Constitution, in the eyes of the Congressional investigators, invalid. Because of the way the constitution was put to the voters of Kansas, it was not a fair referendum on whether the State should be Slave or Free. The constitution the citizens voted on only presented two forms of slavery and made it clear Kansas would be a Slave State. This was too much for Douglas. This was not what Popular Sovereignty required. In an act of extraordinary political courage, Douglas broke with President Buchanan, the leader of his party, and opposed the admission of Kansas under the Lecompton Constitution. Douglas led the opposition in the Senate which ultimately defeated the Lecompton Constitution.

Later, a subsequent convention in Kansas, in 1859, produced the Wyandotte Constitution, which was approved by the electorate and allowed Kansas to be admitted as a Free State, but not until 1861.

The Dred Scott Decision – the Not-So-Final Word

THE ANTI-SLAVERY SOCIETIES, like the one in Illinois, had long advocated that if a slave were voluntarily brought into a Free State, such as Illinois, then the slave should be deemed free. State courts in the northern States had accepted this argument. This was exactly what happened when Owen Lovejoy was prosecuted for harboring runaway slaves in 1843. Based on the trial judge's instruction on the law, embracing that proposition, the Illinois jury acquitted Lovejoy. But up until 1857, the United States Supreme Court had not spoken on the constitutional validity of this route to emancipation. With the decision he crafted in the Dred Scott case, Chief Justice Taney intended to slam the door shut on this avenue. He thought he was penning the final word on the proper realm of slavery. He was wrong.

When Dred Scott first sued for his freedom in Missouri, he had reason to believe that Missouri would recognize that his stay in Illinois operated to make him free. In earlier cases, Missouri's courts had acceded to the decisions of other States as a matter of comity. Scott had been a slave belonging to Dr. John Emerson, a surgeon in the United States Army. In 1834, Dr. Emerson took Scott from Missouri to Rock Island, Illinois and later to Fort Snelling in the Upper Louisiana Territory (near present day Minneapolis, Minnesota). Scott married another slave. They had children. They returned to Missouri with Dr. Emerson. Dr. Emerson died in 1846. Scott tried to purchase his freedom but was unsuccessful. With the help of Peter Blow, who had owned Scott at an earlier point in time, Scott sued Irone Emerson, Dr. Emerson's widow, for his freedom. His position was that he had lived for several years in Illinois and the Northwest Territory and had been emancipated by virtue of the fact that slavery was prohibited in both.

The legal battle began in 1846 with the lawsuit in State court. Scott won at the trial court level. But when his case reached the Missouri Supreme Court in 1852, that Court did an about face and held that because Scott had voluntarily returned to Missouri he was still a slave. The Court's opinion held that Missouri courts should follow Missouri's law on slavery, not accommodate the law of a Free State like Illinois or accept the argument that Scott was free, as a matter of federal law, under the Missouri Compromise because he had resided in a part of the Louisiana Territory that prohibited slavery.[399]

Scott (again with the help of Blow) then brought a second lawsuit in federal court invoking diversity jurisdiction which grants federal courts the ability to hear actions between citizens of different States. Scott contended he was a citizen of Missouri and that the defendant, John Sanford, Irone Emerson's brother and the administrator of Dr. Emerson's estate, was a citizen of New York. He brought an action for trespass, accusing Sanford of holding a former slave against his will.

The Dred Scott case was argued twice because the Justices of the Supreme Court could not decide on what grounds to decide the case when they conferred

Dred Scott, a citizen of Missouri (a "Slave State"), sued his owner's widow arguing that he had lived for years in "Free States" and therefore should be given his freedom. The case went all the way to the U. S. Supreme Court which ruled that Scott was to remain a slave. (Library of Congress)

after the first argument. When it was argued the second time, the Court set aside four days for the argument, signaling the importance of the case. The questions that the Court had asked the attorneys to argue made it clear that the Court was about to rule on the fundamental legal issues defining the proper place of slavery in the fabric of the Union.

The case was fraught with political implications. Both outgoing President Franklin Pierce and incoming President James Buchanan wanted the Supreme Court to still the "agitation" that was roiling the nation in the wake of the Nebraska Act. Both were Democrats whose hold on power rested on appeasing the demands of the Southerners in their party. They both supported the Nebraska Act with its repeal of the Missouri Compromise. But the Nebraska Act spurred the anti-Nebraska factions that were demanding that

Roger Brooke Taney (1777–1864), fifth Chief Justice of the United States Supreme Court, ruled that the Constitution did not recognize Dred Scott as a citizen of the United States. (Chicago History Museum)

for the announcement he wanted to make. The decision was handed down on March 6, 1857.[401]

There were many who were skeptical that the Court could fairly decide any slavery issue. "I would rather trust a dog with my dinner," groused Horace Greeley, editor of the *New York Tribune*.[402] The reason was that the Court was dominated by Southerners. Chief Justice Taney was from Maryland, a Slave State. There were four Associate Justices from Slave States: Peter Daniel (Virginia), James Wayne (Georgia), John Campbell (Alabama), and John Catron (Tennessee). The Northerners were: Benjamin Curtis (Massachusetts), Robert Grier (Pennsylvania), John McLean (Ohio) and Samuel Nelson (New York). Even though the population in the Free States was greater than that in the Slave States, the Justices from Slave States outnumbered those from Free States five to four. This was due to the "peculiar arrangement of the circuits to which each of the Justices of the Supreme Court was assigned" at that time.[403] The configuration at that time resulted in the imbalance. Thus, it was no surprise that the resulting decision in the Dred Scott case reflected the sectional differences. However, the opinion Chief Justice Taney labored over, that is 54 pages long in the United States Reports, did more than simply echo the Missouri Supreme Court's holding that Scott's status was that he was still a slave.

In sweeping terms, the Chief Justice's opinion concluded (1) that slaves and their descendants were not citizens of the United States under the Constitution and therefore could not sue in the federal courts; (2) that Congress could not prohibit slavery in newly acquired Territories (which meant the Missouri Compromise was unconstitutional) and (3) that Scott remained a slave.

The starting point for the Chief Justice's analysis was whether there was jurisdiction to hear the case based on diverse citizenship. If Scott was not a citizen of Missouri, the courts below should never have let the case proceed. The Chief Justice posed the question: "Can a Negro, whose ancestors were imported into this country, and sold as slaves, become a member of the political community formed and brought into existence by the Constitution of the United States, and as

Congress restore the Missouri Compromise. Buchanan reasoned that if the Court were to declare the Missouri Compromise unconstitutional – by holding that Congress did not have the power to prohibit slavery in the Territories – then it would stop the clamor for the restoration of the Missouri Compromise. Buchanan, in an egregious breach of judicial independence, went so far as to communicate with the Court by writing Justice John Catron, one of the Justices of the Supreme Court, to promote his agenda. Buchanan hoped the Court would issue a decision before March 4 so that in his inaugural address he could proclaim that all three branches of government – the judicial, the legislative and the executive – were in agreement on the unconstitutionality of the Missouri Compromise.[400] Buchanan got the decision he wanted but not in time such become entitled to all the rights, and privileges, and immunities, guarantied [sic] by that instrument to the citizen?"[404] His answer was no, based on his view that the drafters of the Constitution viewed slaves to be distinct from citizens. He contended that "people of the United States" did not embrace slaves. Rather, slaves were a "subordinate and inferior class of beings." The Chief Justice said citizenship in the United States was different from citizenship of a particular State. It could not be conferred on Africans even if manumitted. He declared that slaves and their descendants, whether free or not, "had no rights which the white man was bound to respect."[405] Chief Justice Taney supported his conclusion by pointing to two clauses in the Constitution that he said treated slaves as persons distinct from citizens. The first, in Article IV § 2, was the provision that required that fugitive slaves be returned, and the second, in Article I §9, was the provision that prohibited Congress from outlawing the importation of slaves until 1808.

No Person held to Service or Labour in one State, under the Laws thereof, escaping into another, shall, in Consequence of any Law or Regulation therein, be discharged from such Service or Labour, but shall be delivered up on Claim of the Party to whom such Service or Labour may be due.
– U.S. Constitution Art. IV §2.

The Migration or Importation of such Persons as any of the States now existing shall think proper to admit, shall not be prohibited by the Congress prior to the Year one thousand eight hundred and eight, but a Tax or duty may be imposed on such Importation, not exceeding ten dollars each Person.
– U.S. Constitution Art. I §9.

He also pointed to colonial laws, one from Massachusetts and one from Maryland, that prohibited the intermarriage of free Negroes or mulattos with white women, to show that the drafters of the Declaration of Independence and Constitution were of a view that there was a "perpetual and impassable barrier" erected between the white race and the one

they had reduced to slavery. He added to this a statute passed by Congress directing that all "free able-bodied white male citizens" be enrolled in the militia.

He also confronted the Declaration of Independence and its exhortation that "all men are created equal." The framers could not have considered this to include slaves. Otherwise the statement would have been hypocritical.

The supporting authority for the proposition that slaves and their descendants could not be citizens of the United States that the Chief Justice pointed to was far from convincing. The only decided case that came close was an 1833 lower court decision in Connecticut where Prudence Crandall was prosecuted and convicted for violating the Connecticut law that made it illegal to establish a school for the instruction of "coloured persons not inhabitants of Connecticut." The trial court held that persons of the African race were not citizens of a State that were entitled to the privileges and immunities protected by the U.S. Constitution.[406] But when the case was reviewed on appeal, it was reversed on other grounds (because the indictment did not accuse her of operating a school in violation of the law, it merely recited the fact that she operated a boarding house which the law did not prohibit). So the lower court decision in the *Crandall* case was of dubious precedential value.

The two clauses in the Constitution that the Chief Justice relied on said nothing about slaves that had been freed. He ignored the three fifths clause which arguably considered slaves to be something different than mere property if they were to be counted in determining how many representatives a State should be allocated. The laws aimed at preventing miscegenation did not speak to whether a freed black person could vote, own property or exercise other rights of citizenship. And the Chief Justice's cabined view of the Declaration failed to grasp the broader purpose of that document, the meaning that Abraham Lincoln would illuminate in the 1858 Lincoln-Douglas debates.

The Three-Fifths Clause
Representatives and direct Taxes shall be apportioned among the several States which may be included within this Union, according to their respective Numbers,

which shall be determined by adding to the whole Number of free Persons, including those bound to Service for a Term of Years, and excluding Indians not taxed, three-fifths of all other Persons.
  – U.S. Constitution Art. I §2.

The first part of the Chief Justice's opinion, concluding that slaves and their descendants could not be citizens of the United States, was joined in only by two other Justices (Wayne and Daniel). This meant that it was not the majority opinion of the Court and was not a holding that bound inferior courts. However, the other two parts of the Chief Justice's opinion did command a majority. His view that Congress did not have the power to prohibit slavery in newly acquired Territories (which made the Missouri Compromise unconstitutional) and that Scott remained a slave, was joined by not only Wayne and Daniel, but also Catron, Campbell and Grier.

To hold that Congress did not have the power to prohibit slavery in newly acquired Territories, the Chief Justice had to go through some fancy footwork to construe certain provisions of the Constitution inapplicable and to nullify the precedential effect of the Northwest Ordinance. The provision that had to be overcome was the grant of power to "make all needful rules and regulations" in the Territories.

The Congress shall have Power to dispose of and make all needful rules and Regulations respecting the Territory or other property belonging to the United States....
  – U.S. Constitution Art. IV §3.

The Chief Justice did not dispute the validity of the Northwest Ordinance and its prohibition of slavery in the Northwest Territory. The Continental Congress adopted that measure with the explicit assent of all of the original 13 States. But, according to the Chief Justice's reading, the clause in the Constitution only applied to Territory that the United States already owned at the time the Constitution was adopted. He reasoned that the clause did not speak of *any* Territory nor did it use the term *Territories*. By using the singular,

the reference could only mean to the Territory then in existence. This distinguished the Territory ceded by Virginia that became the Northwest Territory and was in existence prior to the adoption of the Constitution from the Territory purchased from France in the Louisiana Purchase. The clause could not apply to the Louisiana Purchase. That was acquired after the Constitution was adopted.

The Territory ceded by Virginia had been accepted by a Congress acting under the Articles of Confederation. The Chief Justice did not regard the Continental Congress as having any legislative power as an independent sovereign. Rather it was more of a "congress of ambassadors." Thus, the Northwest Ordinance represented an agreement among the States. In contrast, the Missouri Compromise was enacted by Congress acting under the Constitution, a charter that gave the federal government only limited powers. Absent an express grant of power to exclude slavery from a Territory, the Chief Justice held that Congress could not do so.

It was one thing for the States acting together in the Continental Congress to establish a government for the Northwest Territory and agree to outlaw slavery. It was quite another for Congress to assume the power to outlaw slavery where there was no specific grant of a power to do so in the Constitution.

To bolster his conclusion, the Chief Justice then pointed to the Fifth Amendment and its limitation on what laws Congress could pass. Here was a provision as he construed it, that prohibited interfering with the rights of slave-holders. He reasoned that under the Fifth Amendment, Congress could not prevent any citizen from taking his "property" (*i.e.,* a slave) into any (new) Territory. He argued that the Constitution clearly gave citizens the right to own slaves as property pointing to the two provisions he cited in the first part of his decision. Thus, the Missouri Compromise was unconstitutional because it declared slavery and involuntary servitude shall be forever prohibited in that part of the Louisiana Territory above 36°30'.

The argument that the Missouri Compromise was unconstitutional had been bandied about for some time before Chief Justice Taney gave it his imprimatur. Here was the validation of the position that the late South Carolina Senator John C. Calhoun had advocated when he opposed the Wilmot Proviso and argued that there could be no action by Congress on the right to bring slaves into the Territories won in the Mexican War. Calhoun's view had been that the Territories were owned in common by the States and that Congress did not have the power to exclude slavery from them. This was a core tenet of the South's States' Rights platform. The Supreme Court embraced it, convincing the North that the Supreme Court was now a puppet of the slave-holders.

No Person shall be ... deprived of life, liberty, or property, without due process of law....
  – *U.S. Constitution, Amendment V.*

The States' Rights doctrine actually had its origin in the *Kentucky and Virginia Resolutions* written (anonymously) by Thomas Jefferson and James Madison in 1798 in response to the Alien and Sedition Acts passed by the Federalists. In their view, the Union was a voluntary association of States. When Congress exceeded its powers, any State could nullify that law. This was the same principle that the South would later employ to justify secession.

Resolved, that the several States composing the United States of America, are not united on the principle of unlimited submission to their general government; but that by compact under the style and title of a Constitution for the United States and of amendments thereto, they constituted a general government for special purposes, delegated to that government certain definite powers, reserving each State to itself, the residuary mass of right to their own self-government; and that whensoever the general government assumes undelegated powers, its acts are unauthoritative, void, and of no force: That to this compact each State acceded as a State, and is an integral party, its co-States forming, as to itself, the other party.... Each party has an equal right to judge for itself, as well of infractions as of the mode and measure of redress.
  –Kentucky and Virginia Resolutions[407]

The final part of the Chief Justice's opinion addressed the question of whether Scott was still a slave. This presented the question of whether Scott's stay in Illinois operated to emancipate him. The Chief Justice was able to point to a decision he had authored that the Court had handed down in 1851 in another case involving the status of slaves who had traveled to a Free State. In *Strader v. Graham*,[408] Graham was the owner of three slaves who boarded a boat owned by Strader, traveled to Cincinnati and then escaped to Canada. Graham sued the owners of the boat and its captain under a Kentucky statute that made ship owners and operators liable for the value of slaves that they transported if they were transported without the authorization of their owner and were lost. The defendants argued that Graham had previously let the slaves, who were musicians, travel to Ohio and that their stay there operated to free them. The Court rejected this holding that the status of Negroes depended on the law of the State of their domicile. In other words, Ohio's law did not need to be followed by Kentucky:

Every State has an undoubted right to determine the status, or domestic and social condition, of the persons domiciled within its territory; except in so far as the powers of the States in this respect are restrained, or duties and obligations imposed upon them, by the Constitution of the United States. There is nothing in the Constitution of the United States that can in any degree control the law of Kentucky upon this subject. And the condition of the Negroes, therefore, as to freedom or slavery, after their return, depended altogether upon the laws of that State, and could not be influenced by the laws of Ohio.[409]

Applying the rule from this case to Dred Scott's status meant that whether Scott was a slave or free had to be determined by Missouri and Missouri did not need to pay any attention to the law of Illinois.

That the Dred Scott decision meant Scott was still a slave was clear.[410] The other consequences of the decision were not immediately clear. If the Chief Justice's ruling applied more broadly, if a slave or former slave was not a "citizen" of the United States, then no black could ever rely on the Constitution's privileges and immunities clause, a consequence that Lincoln would spotlight. And if Congress did not have the power to prohibit slavery in the Territories, what did that do to Douglas's Popular Sovereignty Doctrine?

The citizens of each state shall be entitled to all Privileges and Immunities of Citizens of the Several States.
   –U.S. Constitution Art. IV §2.

The Chief Justice "thought he was performing a great public service" by resolving the issue of citizenship and the constitutionality of the Missouri Compromise.[411]

The Dissenters

T HE CHIEF JUSTICE had spent two hours reading his decision aloud to those assembled in the Supreme Court's courtroom on March 6. The next day Justices Curtis and McLean read their dissenting opinions which took five hours.[412] They, too, had written lengthy opinions on each of the questions. Justice Curtis pointed out that the Chief Justice's ruling on the Missouri Compromise was unnecessary if indeed Scott was not a citizen of Missouri. In that case, the court below never had jurisdiction and should not have heard the case. To give any opinion beyond that was *obiter dicta*, a discussion unnecessary to the decision, not to be considered part of the ruling. Justice Curtis hoped to blunt the impact of the Court's ruling by providing an analysis that limited its reach.

Justice Curtis had concluded that Scott was a citizen and that the court below had correctly treated him as a citizen of Missouri. Pointing to the provision in the Constitution that set forth the eligibility requirements for President, he said the question as to who is a citizen could be answered by looking at who were citizens at the time the Constitution was adopted.

No person except a natural born Citizen, or a Citizen of the United States, at the time of the adoption of the Constitution shall be eligible to the Office of President....
   –U.S. Constitution Art. II §1.

He pointed out that five of the original 13 States – New Hampshire, Massachusetts, New York, New Jersey, and North Carolina – gave all free inhabitants, though descended from slaves, the vote on equal terms with other citizens. He considered this the hallmark of citizenship. Scott had married, something slaves were not allowed to do, and there were precedents in the Missouri Supreme Court that supported Scott's claim of being free by virtue of his stay in Illinois. Justice Curtis pointed out the fallacious reasoning in the Chief Justice's reliance on the legislation organizing the militia. The enrollment of "free, able-bodied, white male citizens" did not imply that freed blacks could not be citizens any more than it implied that people who were not "able-bodied" or "male" could not be citizens.[413]

Because he concluded that diversity jurisdiction did exist, based on Scott's citizenship, Justice Curtis considered it appropriate for him to discuss the merits of the dispute, the constitutionality of the Missouri Compromise. The Chief Justice's interpretation of the grant of power over Territory was flawed because at the time the Constitution was written the drafters knew that there were other Territories that Congress would have to govern. While Virginia had already ceded its claim to the Northwest Territory, Georgia and North Carolina both had Territories they were expected to cede as well. It made no sense for the framers of the Constitution to give Congress the power to govern the Northwest Territory and not the other Territories that Congress would have to deal with in the foreseeable future. Moreover, Congress had previously exercised its authority to legislate with regard to slavery in a series of prior acts. Congress had erected governments over Territories prohibiting slavery when it established the Indiana Territory (1800), the Michigan Territory (1805), the Illinois Territory (1809), the Wisconsin Territory (1836), the Iowa Territory (1838), and the Oregon Territory (1848). It refused to interfere with slavery already existing when it established the governments for Louisiana (1804), the Territory of Orleans (1805), the Missouri Territory (1812), and the Territory of Florida (1822).[414]

Justice McLean pointed out that the Constitution, in Article III §2, gave the federal judiciary jurisdiction over "all Cases in Law and Equity, arising … between citizens of different States…." The practical way to determine citizenship was to look at to whom the State granted the right to vote. The Chief Justice's view, that a free black could be a citizen of a State and not a citizen of the federal Union disregarded what the States had done.[415]

Justice McLean reviewed the precedents of the Missouri Supreme Court which, as a matter of comity, had acceded to the law of Illinois and deemed slaves taken there voluntarily to be free. Absent special legislation by the Missouri legislature rejecting the doctrine of comity, Justice McLean reasoned that the Missouri Supreme Court could not reject that common law doctrine. Commenting on the result reached by the majority of the Court, he stated: "I am unable to reconcile this result with respect due to the State of Illinois." If Missouri could disregard the law of Illinois then the people of any Slave State could introduce slavery into any Free State for any period of time.[416]

Repercussions from the Dred Scott Decision

THE DRED SCOTT decision immediately became a sensation. *The Chicago Tribune* editorialized with the question, "Is Illinois Still a Free State?"[417] The paper concluded that it is not because the Dred Scott decision would allow Douglas to "bring his plantation Negroes … into Illinois, and set them to farming … and no law of the State of Illinois can interfere to prevent him." Similarly, Illinois could not prevent the "opening of a Slave pen and an auction block for the sale of black men, women, and children right here in Chicago."

While Chief Justice Taney thought his decision would quiet the "agitation" over slavery, it had the opposite effect.[418] It actually propelled Lincoln to national prominence. Lincoln pointed to the Dred Scott decision as one of the threats to the spread of slavery along with Douglas's doctrine of Popular Sovereignty. Lincoln would make these two milestones the centerpiece of his attacks on Douglas and the policies of the Democrats as he took on Douglas in their famous debates. The Dred Scott decision presented a dilemma for Lincoln. Lincoln had always been an advocate for the rule of law. While he thought the Dred Scott decision was wrong, how was he going to confront it without advocating disobeying its mandate?

Lincoln Deconstructs Dred Scott

O N JUNE 12, 1857, having recently returned to Illinois after Congress adjourned, Douglas spoke in Springfield on three topics, one of which was the Dred Scott decision.[419] He wrote out his remarks after giving the speech and they were widely reprinted. Douglas was the leading spokesman of the Democratic Party, so his remarks were recognized as announcing the policy that the Democratic Party would run on in 1860. Lincoln, in a continuation of the challenge to Douglas begun with his Peoria speech in 1854, spoke two weeks later on June 26, 1857. Lincoln's remarks would be the Republican answer to the Little Giant's platform.

Douglas had said that anyone who denounced the correctness of the Dred Scott decision was offering violent resistance to it. Lincoln scoffed at this: "But who resists it? Who has, in spite of the decision, declared Dred Scott free, and resisted the authority of his master over him?"[420] Lincoln pointed out that judicial decisions have two uses: first they decide the controversy before the court and secondly, they establish a policy to indicate how similar cases should be decided in the future. The latter aspect of judicial decisions is their precedential effect. In the Dred Scott case, the Court had decided that a Negro could not sue in the U.S. Courts resolving the controversy before the Court, the first aspect of a decision. The Court also said Congress could not prohibit slavery in the Territories, an expression of a principle intended to govern future cases, the precedential or second aspect.

Lincoln pointed out that respect for judicial decisions, "when fully settled," was the proper course. But, a judicial opinion's weight as a precedent depended on the circumstances:

> If this important decision had been made by a unanimous concurrence of the judges, and without any apparent partisan bias, and in accordance with public expectation ... and had been in no part, based on assumed historical facts which are not really true ... it then might be ... revolutionary, to not acquiesce in it as a precedent.[421]

Lincoln then turned the tables on Douglas. He quoted Douglas as saying: "[W]hoever resists the final decision of the highest judicial tribunal, aims a deadly blow to our whole Republican system of government...." Lincoln reminded his listeners of the national bank controversy and President Jackson's veto of the bill for the re-charter of the national bank despite a Supreme Court decision upholding the constitutionality of the national bank. He quoted President Jackson's veto message:

> It is maintained ... that its constitutionality ... ought to be considered as settled ... by the decision of the Supreme Court. To this conclusion I cannot assent. Mere precedent is a dangerous source of authority, and should not be regarded as deciding questions of constitutional power, except where the acquiescence of the people and the States can be considered well settled.[422]

President Jackson went on to describe the basis for the opposite conclusion. Of course, everyone in Lincoln's audience knew that Douglas had forged his political career as a staunch defender of President Jackson and his war on the national bank. With Lincoln's argument in hand, the Republicans could continue to denounce the Dred Scott decision as erroneous and now had a principled basis for advocating that it was inapplicable to future cases.

Douglas and Lincoln Spar over Negro Equality

DOUGLAS DID NOT just defend the Dred Scott case in his speech. He went further, accusing the Republicans of favoring "Negro equality." If the Republican interpretation of the Declaration of Independence's exhortation "all men are created equal" meant Negro equality then we must "repeal all laws making any distinction whatever on account of race or color, and authorize Negroes to marry white women on an equality with white men!"[423] That meant emancipating all the slaves, repealing the provision in the Illinois Constitution that prohibited Negroes from coming into Illinois, giving them the right to hold office and a host of other horribles. Douglas was loudly applauded and cheered for this tirade. Douglas claimed that the phrase "all men are created equal" had to be construed as the signers of the Declaration meant it. They referred to the white race alone echoing Chief Justice Taney's claim that Negroes were universally regarded as an inferior race.

Douglas had appealed to the prevailing white supremacy attitude and had struck a chord. Lincoln addressed this head on recognizing the antipathy most of his listeners had to intermarriage of the races – what they referred to as "amalgamation:"

> There is a natural disgust in the minds of nearly all white people, to the idea of indiscriminate amalgamation of the white and black races; and Judge Douglas evidently is basing his chief hope, upon the chances of being able to appropriate the benefit of this disgust to himself.[424]

Lincoln then challenged the argument that Douglas made that if the Republicans contend that the term "all men" in the Declaration includes the Negro, then that means the Republicans "want to vote, and eat, and sleep, and marry with Negroes!"

Lincoln refuted this "counterfeit logic." Because "I do not want black woman for a *slave*" does not mean I "want her for a *wife*."[425] Lincoln elaborated to explain the distinction between his view of what the Declaration meant and the view espoused by Chief Justice Taney and Judge Douglas. Lincoln admitted that declaring all men equal did not place blacks immediately on an equality with whites. It did not place all whites on an equality with one another. The signers of the Declaration did not mean to declare all men equal *in all respects*. They did not mean all were equal "in color, size, intellect, moral development, or social capacity."[426] In what respects did they consider all men to be created equal? In "certain inalienable rights, among which are life, liberty, and the pursuit of happiness." They did not assert that all were enjoying this equality. They meant simply "to declare the *right*." This was stated as a standard maxim for our free society.

Once again Lincoln had chosen an image that helped bolster his argument. He did not talk about a male slave like Dred Scott. He spoke of a female slave when he said "In some respects she is certainly not my equal; but in her natural right to eat the bread she earns with her own hands without leave of asking anyone else, she is my equal and the equal of all others."[427]

Lincoln made another argument that placed the amalgamation threat in a different light. He pointed out that in 1850 there were 405,751 mulattoes in the United States. The overwhelming majority of this population was not to be found in the Free States. It was the product of black slaves and white masters. In other words, the population of free blacks in the Free States was not the source of the amalgamation that was already occurring.

Finally, Lincoln pointed out the illogic of Douglas's construction of the Declaration. Douglas had said the signers "were speaking of British subjects on this continent being equal to British subjects born and residing in Great Britain." He pointed out that this definition excluded white people outside of Great Britain and America and was frozen in time. So Douglas included the English, Irish and Scotch but left out the French, Germans and other white people of the world who came to America. Mocking Douglas he said when the Fourth of July is celebrated next week in Springfield, after reading the Declaration as written, they should read it as Judge Douglas construes it: "We hold these truths to be self-evident that all British subjects who were on this continent 81 years ago, were created equal to all British subjects born and then residing in Great Britain."[428] This was contrary to Lincoln's view that the Declaration contemplated progressive improvement.

The arguments that Lincoln and Douglas made from their differing constructions of the Declaration would be repeated and refined in the debates that would soon capture the attention of the nation. By following Douglas around and offering the Republican counterpoint, Lincoln was becoming recognized as a spokesman for his party and an able opponent to Douglas.

The Illinois Republicans Slate Lincoln to Unseat Douglas

WHEN DR. DYER and the other delegates headed to Springfield for the June 16, 1858 Republican State Convention the issue of party unity was their greatest concern.[429] Lincoln had been attacking Douglas and was recognized by most Illinois party members as the logical candidate to challenge Douglas for the Senate seat that would be contested that year. Having stepped aside for Trumbull in the last race for a Senate seat, most party members thought they owed it to Lincoln. However, there were two threats. First was some unwelcome meddling by Horace Greeley, the editor of *The New York Tribune*. There was a movement afoot, spurred by Greeley, to throw Republican support to Douglas as a reward for Douglas's rejection of the Lecompton Constitution and his repudiation of President Buchanan. Greeley and other Republicans in the east were suggesting that Douglas deserved to be re-elected to the Senate and should have the support of the Illinois Republicans believing that would strengthen the fledgling Republican Party. This so concerned Lincoln that his law partner Herndon took it upon himself to travel to New York to try to dissuade Greeley from further promoting the scheme. Greeley rebuffed Herndon, saying: "Forget the past and sustain the righteous."[430]

The other threat was from "Long John" Wentworth. Wentworth earned his nickname because he was six feet, six inches tall and weighed more than 300 pounds. Born in New Hampshire and a graduate of Dartmouth College, Wentworth came to Chicago in 1836 to be the managing editor of the *Chicago Democrat*. He later became its owner and publisher. Wentworth studied law, practiced in Chicago and ran for public office. He ran for Congress as a Democrat and served in the House of Representatives for several terms between 1843 and 1855. In 1857, he was elected Mayor of the City of Chicago. Wentworth was an anti-Nebraska Democrat, but he surprised everyone when he went to the May 29, 1856 Bloomington Convention that gave birth to the Republican Party in Illinois. Wentworth was one of the disaffected Democrats whose stance on the Nebraska Act meant he could no longer accept Douglas or the platform of the regular Democratic Party. In his Mayoral race in 1857, he gave a speech in which he said, "I'll tell you why they hated me. It is because they know that I shall leave no stone unturned to put that man (pointing to Lincoln) in the seat now disgraced by Stephen A. Douglas."[431] While Wentworth had publicly supported Lincoln, the *Tribune* thought he "smelled no better as a Republican than he did as a Democrat" and reported that Wentworth actually wanted the Senate nomination for himself.[432]

Greeley's machinations and Wentworth's ambition worried Lincoln's supporters and spurred them into action. Norman Judd, now a Lincoln partisan, was the chairman of the Republican Party of Illinois. Judd

met secretly in Springfield with Lincoln, Charles H. Ray and William Bross right before the Illinois State Republican Convention that would take place June 16, 1858.[433] They devised a plan to squeeze out any room for interlopers or mischief-makers. When the Convention was called to order, Judd orchestrated the proceedings. First he nominated Richard Yates to be chairman. They appointed the usual committees. Next the chair entertained a motion from a member of the Cook County delegation that the Convention *endorse* Abraham Lincoln as the "first and only" candidate of the Illinois Republicans to run against Douglas.[434] This was a signal for the Cook County delegation to rise and march around the hall behind a banner they unfurled: "Cook County for Abraham Lincoln." Over the clamor, there was a second motion, from a delegate from Peoria. He asked that the banner be amended to read; "Illinois for Abraham Lincoln." The "first and only" motion was seconded and immediately voted on and the chair declared it carried unanimously.

All of this was highly irregular since, at that time, it was not the province of the political parties to nominate candidates for the U.S. Senate. That right belonged to the General Assembly which nominated and elected the Senators. Whether Wentworth was actually plotting a coup is not certain.[435] Nevertheless, Judd's maneuver sewed up the nomination for Lincoln. Judd's craftiness and skillful orchestration of convention protocol to advance Lincoln's candidacy in 1858 was harbinger of the stratagems he would employ in Chicago in 1860 as one of the leaders of the promoters of Lincoln's candidacy for the Presidential nomination.

The "House Divided Speech"

LINCOLN KNEW HE would be the candidate of his party and he carefully prepared the speech he would deliver at the convention after he had secured the endorsement of his party. This, perhaps his most famous speech, is known as the "House Divided Speech" from the biblical imagery he employed. He had written the speech out, tried it first on Herndon and then read it to a small group of supporters. Many of his close friends thought it was too radical with its house divided metaphor. Herndon urged Lincoln to deliver it as written. He did.

Thus, at 8:00 P.M. on the evening of June 16, 1859, the delegates reassembled at the Statehouse in Springfield after having adjourned their Convention at 5:00 P.M. The Convention had named its candidates and the delegates were ready to celebrate. Lincoln proceeded to read his speech attacking Douglas and was interrupted by cheers and applause throughout. (This was the only time Lincoln delivered a speech from a prepared manuscript.[436])

As he often did, Lincoln set the stage at the very beginning of his speech, identifying the issue he would expound on. In this instance, he would take on slavery and the threat of its extension:

> *If we could first know* where *we are, and* whither *we are tending, we could then better judge* what *to do, and* how *to do it.*
>
> *We are now in the* fifth *year, since a policy was initiated, with the* avowed *object, and* confident *promise, of putting an end to slavery agitation.*
>
> *Under the operation of that policy, that agitation has not only*, not ceased, *but has been* constantly augmented.
>
> *In* my *opinion, it* will *not cease, until a crisis* shall *have been reached, and passed.*
>
> *"A house divided against itself cannot stand."*
>
> *I believe the government cannot endure, permanently* half slave *and half* free.
>
> *I do not expect the Union to be* dissolved – *I do not expect the house to* fall – *but I* do *expect that it will cease to be divided.*
>
> *It will become* all *one thing, or* all *the other.*
>
> *Either the* opponents *of slavery, will arrest the further spread of it, and place it where the public mind shall rest in the belief that it is on the course of ultimate extinction; or its* advocates *will push it forward, till it shall become alike lawful in* all *the States, old as well as* new – North *as well as* South.[437]

The Old State Capitol in Springfield, Illinois where Lincoln gave his "House Divided" speech in 1859. (Chicago History Museum)

Here was the platform that Lincoln would run on in trying to unseat Douglas for the Senate seat and here was the platform that the Republicans could hammer away on to capture the White House in 1860. Lincoln described the events that presented the threat of the expansion of slavery, focusing particularly on the Nebraska Act and the Dred Scott decision, though he also raised questions about the statements of former President Franklin Pierce and incumbent President James Buchanan. He derided Douglas's "sacred right of self government" calling it "squatter sovereignty." His definition of squatter sovereignty? "If any *one* man, chooses to enslave *another*, no *third* man shall be allowed to object."[438]

Lincoln went on to discredit Douglas's call for another vote in Kansas pointing out that Douglas had said he "did not care" whether slavery was voted up or down, as long as the doctrine of popular sovereignty was followed. This gave Lincoln an opportunity, indirectly, to rebuke the Republicans, like Greeley, who were enamored with Douglas and flirting with the idea of supporting him. If Douglas did not care whether Kansas voted in slavery, how "can he oppose the advances of slavery?"[439] Clearly Douglas was not aligned with the Republicans on the issue of whether the domain of slavery should expand.

Lincoln also offered up another one of his well designed metaphors. After describing the steps taken to advance slavery – Douglas's authorship of the Nebraska Act and the Act's qualification "subject to the Constitution," the statements of Presidents Franklin Pierce and James Buchanan that the nation should let the Supreme Court decide whether Congress has the power to prohibit slavery in the Territories, and Chief Justice Roger Taney's decision that Congress has no such power – he suggested that these four were working together to promote the spread of slavery:

> *[W]hen we see a lot of framed timbers, different portions of which we know have been gotten out at different times and places and by different workmen – Stephen, Franklin, Roger and James – for instance – and when we see these timbers joined together, and see they exactly make the frame of a house or a mill, all the tenons and mortises exactly fitting … we find it impossible to not* believe *that Stephen and Franklin and Roger and James all understood one another from the beginning, and all worked up a common* plan *or* draft *before the first lick was struck.*[440]

He then pointed out that the Supreme Court had left open the question of whether States had the power to prohibit slavery, suggesting that it was just a matter of time before the Supreme Court took the next step to make slavery universally lawful throughout the Union by holding that no State had the power to exclude slavery. Such a decision "*is* probably coming … unless the power of the present political dynasty shall be met and overthrown."[441] Here was the call to arms to the Illinois Republicans. The Convention went wild with cheering and applause. Here was a candidate and a cause that united the old Whigs, the Free-Soilers and

the anti-Nebraska Democrats. Dr. Dyer, Eastman and Lovejoy were now coreligionists with Trumbull, Judd, Wentworth and Davis.

The Lincoln-Douglas Debates

L INCOLN HAD FOLLOWED Douglas and given speeches in reply to Douglas on a number of occasions. The two had frequently crossed swords and the crowds looked forward to being entertained by these two able debaters. And there were frequent lighter moments. Douglas told a crowd that Lincoln had previously run a grocery store and "sold whiskey." Lincoln's response: "But the difference between Judge Douglas and myself is just this, that while I was behind the bar, he was in front of it."[442]

On July 9, 1858, Douglas gave a speech in Chicago from the balcony of the Tremont Hotel and invited Lincoln to be present. Lincoln spoke from the same balcony the next night.[443] They both spoke in Springfield on July 17th. Recognizing that Lincoln would be his opponent, Douglas's speeches directly attacked Lincoln. The *Press and Tribune* (the *Chicago Tribune's* name for several years) suggested that Lincoln and Douglas canvass the State together.[444] Lincoln wrote Douglas on July 24th proposing joint debates and dispatched Norman Judd to meet with Douglas to work out the arrangements.[445] Seven were agreed to. These would take place in the following Illinois towns:

Ottawa – August 21, 1858
Freeport – August 27, 1858
Jonesboro – September 15, 1858
Charleston – September 18, 1858
Galesburg – October 7, 1858
Quincy – October 13, 1858
Alton – October 15, 1858

The format called for the first person to speak for an hour, his opponent to speak for an hour-and-a-half, then the first person would reply for a half-hour. Douglas would open and close four times, Lincoln three. While this appears today to be a prodigious number of long speeches, both candidates spoke many more times for two hours or more each time as they canvassed the State. Lincoln gave 63 speeches during the campaign and Douglas gave 130.[446] Needless to say, both candidates repeated the same points many times over.

The debates themselves were true spectacles. Each candidate was surrounded by his supporters. There were torch light parades, canons blasting and bands playing. The newspaper reports confirmed that "[i]n every community favored with a visit from one or both senatorial candidates, there were weeks of preparation, spurred by a fierce resolve to outdo the enemy in numbers, noise, and display."[447] Ten thousand people turned out for the Ottawa debate. In Freeport there were 15,000. The *Press and Tribune* arranged a special 17 car train to Freeport and similar arrangements were made for the other cities.[448]

Douglas made Lincoln's House Divided Speech one of his chief targets in the debates: Lincoln was advocating dissolution of the Union. Quoting Lincoln's phrase that the Union "cannot endure permanently half Slave and half Free," Douglas said the Union had already endured 70 years. Of course the Union could continue indefinitely half Slave and half Free.[449] That was the genius of Popular Sovereignty. That doctrine let each State decide for itself whether to be Slave or Free. The Nebraska Act did not legislate slavery into any Territory or exclude it from any. It left the people free to regulate their affairs their own way. People in the North should not be overly concerned about slavery spreading. The climate is not suitable for cotton farming and thus slavery in the North would not be profitable.

From the very beginning, with the debate at Ottawa, Douglas sought to brand Lincoln as an abolitionist with his own version of the birth of the Illinois Republican Party: In 1854, "Lincoln went to work to abolitionize the old Whig Party all over the State."[450] Lincoln was in league with Lyman Trumbull, who, according to Douglas, had attempted to abolitionize the Democratic Party. Together they were going

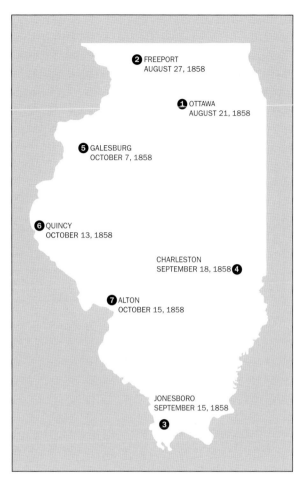

Sites and dates of the Lincoln-Douglas Debates. (Private Collection)

to deliver their members to the "Abolition Party."[451] Though Lincoln was not at the 1854 meeting that issued a platform on October 5th, Douglas sought to tie him to this supposed Republican platform with the most extreme of abolitionist positions. He used the first debate to read the platform of that meeting and pose seven questions based on it to Lincoln, hoping to pin Lincoln to the reviled abolitionists.

Douglas also tarred Lincoln with his opposition to the Mexican war which he described as "taking the side of the common enemy against his own country."[452] But he saved his most savage attack for Lincoln's condemnation of the Dred Scott decision. Lincoln opposed the Dred Scott decision because it deprived the Negro of the rights and privileges of citizenship. As Douglas saw it, that meant that Lincoln favored "Negro equality."

In Ottawa, Douglas stirred up the crowd with a series of questions: "Are you in favor of conferring upon the Negro the rights and privileges of citizenship? Do you desire to strike out of our State Constitution that clause which keeps slaves and free Negroes out of the State, and allow free Negroes to flow in, and cover your prairies with black settlements? Do you desire to turn this beautiful State into a free Negro colony in order that when Missouri abolishes slavery she can send 100,000 emancipated slaves into Illinois to become citizens and voters, on an equality with yourselves?"[453] The crowd responded to each question with roars of "No, no!" When he got to Freeport, Douglas tried a different approach to demonizing Lincoln's embrace of the Declaration's "all men are created equal." Douglas told his listeners that he had seen Frederick Douglass sitting in a carriage with a white woman: "[I]f you, Black Republicans, think that the Negro ought to be on a social equality with your wives and daughters, and ride in a carriage with your wife, whilst you drive the team, you have a perfect right to do so."[454]

In Ottawa, Lincoln was mostly on the defensive. He denied that he had a hand in the 1854 platform that Douglas tried to pin him to. He read an excerpt of his Peoria speech to show that he was opposed to the extension of slavery and did not call for the repeal of the Fugitive Slave Act. He defended his earlier conspiracy theory about Frank and Doug and Roger and James conceding he had no direct evidence to support it; only the circumstantial evidence he had recited. He made it clear that the threat the nation faced was the extension of slavery and that he and Douglas were on opposite sides of the issue. Douglas was indifferent to its spread and opened the door to slavery with Popular Sovereignty.

In Freeport, at the second debate, Lincoln answered the seven questions Douglas had put to him and seized the initiative by challenging Douglas to answer as many from him. The questions Lincoln answered made it clear he did not embrace the extreme position of the abolitionists. Rather he stood on the ground of seeking to prevent the spread of slavery. He repeated each of Douglas's questions and answered as follows:

Question 1. *"I desire to know whether Lincoln to-day stands, as he did in 1854, in favor of unconditional repeal of the fugitive slave law?"*
Answer. *I do not now, nor never did, stand in favor of the unconditional repeal of the fugitive slave law.*

Question 2. *"I desire him to answer whether he stands pledged to-day, as he did in 1854, against the admission of any more Slave States into the Union, even if the people want them?"*
Answer. *I do not now, nor ever did, stand pledged against the admission of any more Slave States into the Union.*

Question 3. *"I want to know whether he stands pledged against the admission of a new State into the Union with such Constitution as the people of that State may see fit to make?"*
Answer. *I do not stand pledged against the admission of a new State into the Union with such Constitution as the people of that State may see fit to make.*

Question 4. *"I want to know whether he stands to-day pledged to the abolition of slavery in the District of Columbia?"*
Answer. *I do not stand to-day pledged to the abolition of slavery in the District of Columbia.*

Question 5. *"I desire him to answer whether he stands pledged to the prohibition of the slave trade between the different States?"*
Answer. *I do not stand pledged to the prohibition of the slave trade between the different States.*

Question 6. *"I desire to know whether he stands pledged to prohibit slavery in all the Territories of the United States, North as well as South of the Missouri Compromise line?'*
Answer. *I am impliedly, if not expressly, pledged to a belief in the right and duty of Congress to prohibit slavery in all the United States Territories.*

Question 7. *"I desire him to answer whether he is opposed to the acquisition of any new Territory unless slavery is first prohibited therein?"*

Answer. *I am not generally opposed to honest acqui-sition of Territory; and in any given case, I would or would not oppose such acquisition, according as I might think such acquisition would or would not do to aggravate the slavery question among ourselves.*[455]

Douglas had based his questions on what he thought was the platform of the Springfield meeting in 1854. But he had been mistaken and the mistake had been discovered.[456] Lincoln now could point out that the Judge was wrong and had read resolutions from a Kane County group that had met that year.[457] While the Kane County group advocated repeal of the Fugitive Slave Act and the other extreme measures alluded to in Douglas's questions, as the Republicans fused, those positions were suppressed. The Springfield meeting had included Lovejoy, the person Douglas continually fingered as the leading abolitionist. But when Lovejoy spoke to the convention in Springfield he moderated his positions knowing the light in which he was looked upon and recognizing it was his "opportunity to make friends" with the anti-Nebraska Democrats and the Whigs. Bringing the former antagonists together was an extraordinary feat. Lovejoy "never put in a better day's work" helping accomplish it.[458]

Lincoln poked fun at Douglas's representation that what he read was *in fact* the platform of the Republicans. Each debater challenged the other to prove that what he relied on was factual. Douglas's mistake provided Lincoln with the opportunity to con-trast Douglas's certainty over the supposed fact about the authenticity of the Republican platform adopted in Springfield with Lincoln's more cautious "I believe it to be so" accusation of a conspiracy between Frank, Doug, Roger, and James that Douglas had been attacking as lacking a factual basis. Each debater chal-lenged the other to prove his facts and, as the debates went along, Lincoln offered more to build his case that Douglas had been part of a conspiracy to spread slavery and Douglas continued to try to pin Lincoln to the more extreme abolitionist statements implying he favored Negro equality.

At Freeport, Lincoln recounted that Senator Salmon Chase of Ohio had offered an amendment to the Nebraska Act that would have explicitly stated that the people of the Territory would have the right to exclude slavery. Judge Douglas, and those who were with him, voted it down. Lincoln argued that this made no sense if the intention of the Nebraska Act was, as Douglas said, to let the people have or not have slav-ery as they might decide. But if Douglas and the other supporters of the Nebraska Act looked forward to a Supreme Court decision saying that slavery could not be excluded from the Territories, then voting down the Chase Amendment made perfect sense.[459] Of course, Douglas responded that the amendment was one-sided which is why he voted against it.

To magnify the danger that the conspirators posed, Lincoln again suggested that the wording of the Nebraska Act left the way open for the Supreme Court to take the next step in making slavery universal: hold-ing that the Constitution did not allow the States to exclude slavery.

As with most conspiracy theories, Lincoln asked his listeners to draw inferences from the facts he tied together that seemed plausible but were somewhat far-fetched. As Douglas would point out the sequence of events did not seem to fit and Buchanan was out of the country serving as ambassador to the Court of St. James during much of the saga making his par-ticipation in a series of coordinated acts unlikely. But Lincoln persisted, using the specter of a conspiracy to underscore the threat posed by the supposedly inde-pendent events that all promoted the spread of slavery.

The two debaters explained in easily understood terms their respective sophisticated legal arguments as to the proper construction of the Dred Scott decision and how far it reached. Lincoln reminded everyone that the Court had found that it had no jurisdiction. That was the basis for the Court's decision and meant that everything else that the Justices said – that the Constitution did not permit Congress to exclude slav-ery from the Territories – was *obiter dicta*. Lincoln explained this legal concept – that statements in judi-cial opinions that are not the reason for the way the case is decided are not binding in the future. They are just observations of the Court as to how they might rule on the question. Thus, Lincoln could continue to advocate that Congress had the power to exclude slavery in the Territories, as he did in answer to one of Douglas's questions.

Because Douglas and the Democrats thought that the Dred Scott case was correctly decided and that the Justices properly ruled on the constitutional issue, this gave Lincoln the opportunity to construct his questions to Douglas to pose a dilemma for Douglas. If the constitutional issue was correctly decided and Congress had no power to exclude slavery in the Territories, then the people of a Territory could not exclude slavery and Popular Sovereignty was of no avail.

Among the four questions Lincoln put to Douglas at Freeport was a zinger aimed at showing how the Dred Scott decision gutted Popular Sovereignty and paved the way for the spread of slavery. The first question that Lincoln asked had a different target. It pointed out that the English Bill (named after Democratic Congressman William Hayden English) would have raised the barrier for Statehood for Kansas by imposing a requirement for a larger population if the voters of Kansas sought to exclude slavery than would be required if they approved the pro-slavery constitution. Lincoln's questions were, as follows:

Question 1. *If the people of Kansas shall, by means entirely unobjectionable in all other respects, adopt a State Constitution, and ask admission into the Union under it,* before *they have the requisite number of inhabitants according to the English Bill – some ninety-three thousand – will you vote to admit them?*

Question 2. *Can the people of a United States Territory, in any way, against the wish of any citizen of the United States, exclude slavery from its limits prior to the formation of a State Constitution?*

Question 3. *If the Supreme Court of the United States shall decide that States can not exclude slavery from their limits, are you in favor of acquiescing in, adopting and following such decision as a rule of political action?*

Question 4. *Are you in favor of acquiring additional Territory, in disregard of how such acquisition may affect the nation on the slavery question?*

When it was his turn, Douglas countered Lincoln's explanation about the erroneous Republican platform by saying that Lincoln was objecting to the "spot" where the platform was made, reminding his audience of Lincoln's objection to the Mexican War. Whether Lincoln was on the committee that issued the platform Douglas had quoted was irrelevant. The Republican delegates who adopted the platform he quoted were pledged to its planks. Their endorsement of Lincoln showed that Lincoln was committed to the same platform. Throughout the debates Douglas sought to impute all abolitionist positions to Lincoln and the Illinois Republican Party. Douglas said Lincoln's refusal to accept the Supreme Court's decision was essentially an act of rebellion.

Douglas gamely answered Lincoln's questions. As to the first, he would let Kansas in without requiring the extraordinary pre-conditions of the English Bill. (This, of course, further alienated Douglas from the Buchanan wing of the Democratic Party whose members had promoted the English Bill.) In response to the second question Douglas articulated what became famously known as the "Freeport Doctrine," Douglas's explanation of how Popular Sovereignty could still operate without disregarding the mandate of the Dred Scott decision. In response to the third question, rather than give a direct answer, he scoffed at the suggestion that the Supreme Court would ever declare that the States could not exclude slavery. In response to the fourth, he said he was in favor of acquiring more Territories whenever the country's growth and progress required it and that he favored acquiring Territories without reference to slavery and would leave it to the people there to do as they please about it under the "great principle" of Popular Sovereignty.

The Freeport Doctrine

WITH REGARD TO whether the people of a Territory could act to exclude slavery in light of the Dred Scott decision, Douglas said:

It matters not what way the Supreme Court may hereafter decide as to the abstract question whether slavery may or may not go into a Territory under the Constitution, the people have the lawful means to introduce it or exclude it as they please for the reason that slavery cannot exist a day or an hour anywhere, unless it is supported by local police regulations.[460]

This is the answer that ultimately lost Douglas the support of the Southern States and led to the fracture in the Democratic Party in 1860. The slave-holders thought they had won a victory in the Supreme Court and Douglas's answer took away their victory. Lincoln had forced a concession from Douglas that created a schism among the Democrats. Lincoln would press this home in future debates asking Douglas whether he would vote for legislation if the people in a Territory wanted federal legislation to protect their right to hold slaves in the Territory. Lincoln tried to tighten the screws by pointing out that, as a Senator, Douglas took an oath to uphold the Constitution and that it would be a violation of his oath of office to refuse to pass legislation seeking to enforce the constitutional right recognized by the Supreme Court. Douglas wriggled out of the trap saying that another of the "great principles" that his party followed was that the federal government should not interfere with the rights of the States to regulate their own affairs.

Lincoln and White Supremacy

IN EVERY DEBATE Douglas hammered away at the theme that Lincoln's advocacy that the Negro was included in the Declaration's "all men are created equal" invocation meant that Lincoln and the "Black Republicans," as Douglas liked to call them, wanted the Negro to be given full civil rights, to hold office, vote, intermarry with whites and enjoy political and social equality. The crowds cheered Douglas when he expressed the view that Negroes should not be extended this equality.

When they debated in Charleston in their fourth debate, Lincoln sought to put this exaggeration of his position to rest. He did so by saying he was against extending these rights to the Negro and that he thought there never could be social and political equality:

I will say that I am not, nor ever have been in favor of bringing about in any way the social and political equality of the white and black races, that I have not nor ever have been in favor of making voters or jurors of Negroes, nor of qualifying them to hold office, not to intermarry with white people; and I will say in addition to this that there is a physical difference between the white and black races which I believe will for ever forbid the two races living together on terms of social and political equality. And inasmuch as ... there must be a position of superior and inferior ... I as much as any other man am in favor of having the superior position assigned to the white race.[461]

If Lincoln thought this concession would rein in Douglas's attacks, he was mistaken. In the fifth debate at Galesburg, Lincoln spoke second and started off by saying that Douglas had just delivered the same speech he had delivered before. When it was Douglas's turn to reply, he said the problem with Lincoln was that he did not give the same speech everywhere in the State. When he was in the North, he talked about the Negroes being equal and when he was in the South, he talked about their inferiority.

Harping on this, in the Sixth debate, in Quincy, Douglas quoted from two of Lincoln's speeches to drive the point home. He said that in Charleston Lincoln said the Negro "belongs to an inferior race" and contrasted that with a speech he gave in Chicago where he said:

> My friends, I have detained you about as long as I desire to do, and I have only to say let us discard all this quibbling about this man and the other man – this race and the other race being inferior, and therefore they must be placed in an inferior position, discarding our standard that we have left us. Let us discard all these things, and unite as one people throughout this land until we shall once more stand up declaring that all men are created equal.

Douglas delighted in arguing that Lincoln declared all distinctions of race should be blotted out when addressing the Chicago abolitionists but took the opposite tack when addressing the citizens of Illinois in the Southern part of the State.

Lincoln began his rejoinder in Quincy by refocusing the issue on the question of whether slavery should be set on the road to extinction. He pointed out that in his attack on Lincoln's "House Divided" speech, Douglas said "why cannot the nation, part slave and part free, continue as our fathers made it *forever*?"[462] Lincoln objected to the premise that the fathers of our government "made it" part slave and part free. His view was that they left slavery as they found it as a matter of *necessity* because it was already here. But their intention was to set that institution on the course to its ultimate extinction. Douglas's policy, which would let it continue *forever*, was contrary to what the fathers intended.

With regard to Douglas's accusation that he gave one speech up North and another down South, Lincoln said he gave the same speech in both places and that his speeches were published for everyone to see. He explained that his view of the Declaration was the same as Henry Clay's: it enunciated a principle. The signers announced to the world the independence of the 13 colonies declaring that "all men are created equal." Clay had said that "as an abstract principle, *there is no doubt of the truth of that declaration*, and it is desirable in the *original construction* of society, and in organized societies, to keep it in view as a great fundamental principle."[463] Lincoln said that Douglas refused to recognize that there was any middle ground and, returning to the imagery he had employed before, said: "I have lived until my fiftieth year, and have never had a Negro woman either for a slave or a wife…."[464]

In the final debate in Alton, Lincoln said Douglas garbled Lincoln's meaning by quoting extracts from two of Lincoln's speeches. Lincoln then read an excerpt Douglas had skipped over that explained Lincoln's concept of "necessity" and his view of equality as the ideal:

> It may be argued that there are certain conditions that make necessities and impose them upon us, and to the extent that a necessity is imposed upon a man he must submit to it. I think that was the condition in which we found ourselves when we established this government. We had slaves among us, we could not get our Constitution unless we permitted them to remain in slavery, we could not secure the good we did secure if we grasped for more; and having by necessity submitted to that much, it does not destroy the principle that is in the charter of our liberties. Let that charter remain as our standard.[465]

Lincoln followed this quotation with another where he explained that the signers of the Declaration did not declare all men equal *in all respects*.

Lincoln concluded by reiterating that he thought slavery a great wrong and that this was a defining difference between the Republicans and the Democrats. He claimed that the Republicans were being faithful to the purpose of the founders and the Democrats were not. The founding fathers showed that slavery was disfavored by including a provision to banish the slave trade and by excluding slavery from the Territories. In the three instances to which slavery was alluded in the Constitution, the words "slavery" and "Negro" do not appear. Why did they use this "covert language?" They wanted a document that would endure forever so that "when it should be read by intelligent and patriotic men, after the institution of slavery has passed from among us – there should be nothing on the face of the great charter of liberty suggesting that such a thing as Negro slavery had ever existed among us."[466]

Lincoln Is Defeated by Douglas

THE CITIZENS OF Illinois went to the polls on November 2, 1858. They elected Republican office holders for the first time. However, the Democrats held control of the legislature due to the prior apportionment. When it came time for the legislature to elect a Senator, on January 6, 1859, Douglas was re-elected with 54 votes to Lincoln's 41.[467]

The debates brought wide recognition to both men. Douglas was the leading spokesman of the Democratic Party and the Democrats had already been considering him as the standard bearer of the party in 1860. While Lincoln was defeated for the Senate seat, he was now seen as an able foil to Douglas and his arguments had been followed across the country.

Was Lincoln a Racist?

LINCOLN'S EMBRACE OF the white supremacy view of Negro inferiority, the view he expressed in Charleston in the fourth debate can only be described as "racist," given that the definition of "racist" is "the notion that one's own ethnic stock is superior."[468] White supremacy was the prevalent attitude. Lincoln's recitation about Negroes being inferior restated the conventional wisdom of the day. It would have been political suicide in 1859 to advocate a different view.

To understand the extent of Negrophobia and its persistence throughout Lincoln's political life, it is useful to consider the history of the Illinois Constitution of 1848 and the Black Laws and their progeny. When

Article XIV of the Illinois Constitution of 1848, which empowered the legislature to pass acts which shall "effectively prohibit free persons of color from immigrating to and settling in this State,"[469] was submitted to the electorate, it was passed by a majority of 28,182 votes.[470] In January of 1853, John A. Logan introduced a bill in the Illinois General Assembly making it a *crime* to introduce a free colored person into the State. The bill passed the Illinois House by a vote of 45 to 23. It passed the Senate by a majority of four. The Act was intended to meet constituents' demands to keep Negroes out of the State, to conciliate neighboring States that allowed slavery and to thwart the abolitionists.

The prevalence of these attitudes did not end when Lincoln was elected President. Illinois had a Constitutional Convention in 1862. While that Constitution was voted down by the electorate, the delegates to the Convention passed the following Article XVIII:

Sec.1. No Negro or Mulatto shall migrate or settle in this State, after the adoption of this Constitution.

Sec. 2. No Negro or Mulatto shall have the right of suffrage, or hold any office in this State.

Sec. 3. The General Assembly shall pass all laws necessary to carry into effect the provisions of this Article.[471]

These provisions were approved by the delegates by votes of 57 to seven for the first, 42 to 20 for the second and 45 to 18 for the third.[472] While the 1862 Constitution was voted down, the Negro article was submitted separately to the electorate. Section 1 was approved by a majority of 100,590. Section 2 was approved by a majority of 176,271 with only 35,649 voting against it. The third section was approved by a 154,524 majority.[473]

Lincoln's explanation of "necessity" and Herndon's explanation of Lincoln's method for arguing the cases he tried suggest that Lincoln's Charleston recitation embracing the white supremist view was probably a strategic concession in crafting his argument to win a greater point. Herndon said Lincoln would concede major points to his opponent but draw the line on the issue he had determined he could win on. Agreeing with his audience on white supremacy gave Lincoln the ability to focus his audience on his issue – the threat of the spread of slavery. Lincoln chose the issue on which to pitch the battle – he opposed the spread of slavery and Douglas and the Democrats were pursuing policies that accommodated the spread of slavery. Slavery was wrong and this was the line. If Lincoln "had grasped for more," he would not have been able to win support for stopping the spread of slavery. Persuading his listeners, and ultimately the nation, to endow the Declaration's "all men are created equal" as the standard to guide the nation, not only set the course for extinguishing slavery, it opened the door for the development of greater civil rights.

John Brown Ignites the Powder Keg

JOHN BROWN'S LAST foray before starting his insurrection at Harpers Ferry took place in December of 1858, when Brown rode into Vernon County, Missouri with 20 men to free 11 Missouri slaves. This episode began when one of the slaves snuck across the State line in a disguise to tell one of Brown's comrades that he and his family were about to be sold to a slave-owner in Texas. On the night of December 20, Brown's band went to three different farms, liberated the slaves, and took supplies and property to use on the trek to Canada and pay for expenses. One of the slave-owners resisted and was killed. This was the start of a journey that lasted two and a half months.[474]

Brown led his pursuers on a merry chase. First he went back to Kansas. There was now a price on Brown's head. Brown did not take the precaution of posting scouts. This made his party appear less militant and allowed them to pass through a road block because his pursuers did not know they were looking at John Brown or suspect that the members of his entourage were the marauders they were supposed to be looking for. In another encounter when federal troops came to a cabin where they were resting, Brown's men aimed a rifle at the troop's leader and ordered him to surrender. He did and his troops ran off. This was followed by the "Battle of the Spurs." The troops, reinforced, reappeared, outnumbering Brown's band four to one. Yet Brown ordered his men to attack across a muddy stream, which they did, and the troops spurred their horses and ran off. Brown's men captured the stragglers. They now had five prisoners.[475] Brown soon let them go, leaving them to find their way home on shanks' mare as he headed into Nebraska with his band.

On February 5, 1859, he reached Tabor, Iowa where he expected a warm welcome. However, the Quakers in that community denounced him for slave-stealing that consisted of murder and robbery. Brown's band went on across Iowa to Grove City and Des Moines and, on February 20, stopped in Grinnell where they were enthusiastically received. They were housed and fed and spoke to admiring audiences.[476] Next they went to Springdale and remained there until March 9. From there they went to West Liberty where they were put on a box car that was to be added to a train en route to Chicago.[477]

Back in Chicago, John Jones went downstairs to answer his doorbell and found himself staring at Brown and his men. Mary Jones described them as "the roughest looking men I ever saw." She said they had "boots up to their knees, and their pants down in their boots, and they looked like they were ready to fight."[478] Brown explained that they had not eaten in a while and the Joneses offered to feed them breakfast. After that, John Jones and Brown's men went off to arrange the next leg of the journey. Then Alan Pinkerton knocked on Jones' door and asked to meet with Brown. Pinkerton told Brown that he had been to see the fugitives and that they were "going to be looked after."

Then Dr. Dyer arrived. He was concerned that Brown could be apprehended in Chicago. He suggested that Brown needed a suit of clothes which would be a good disguise for him. One man, who was about the same size as Brown, went downtown with Dr. Dyer and Freer. Using the stand-in as a surrogate, they bought a new suit of clothes for Brown which they brought back and Brown put on. Later, when Mary Jones told of this episode, she said, "I guess John Brown was hung in these same clothes," referring to Brown's fate a few months later after his unsuccessful effort trying to start a slave revolt with his October 16, 1859 raid on Harper's Ferry.[479]

Brown had seized the armory with 21 men and held it for two days, but a company of U.S. Marines led by Lt. Col. Robert E. Lee retook the armory, killing several of Brown's men and capturing Brown and those of his men who survived. Brown was charged with murdering four whites and a black, with treason against the State of Virginia, and with conspiring with slaves to rebel. Brown was tried in a week-long trial that commenced October 27th, found guilty by the jury, and hanged on December 2, 1859. Though it did not slow matters down, Brown's lawyer argued that Brown could not be guilty of treason against the State of Virginia because he was not a *citizen of Virginia* and therefore owed no duty to Virginia.

Dr. Dyer – An Ambassador for Chicago

IN 1859 CHICAGO was reaching out to its neighbors to promote the City and the opportunities for commerce as new railroads were built. In the space of 10 short years, Chicago had gone from having only 90 miles of track leading to or from the city to 4,569 miles.[480] On Tuesday, February 22, 1859, a new railroad line opened that connected Chicago and St. Joseph, Missouri. The Hannibal and St. Joseph Railroad connected the eastern Missouri city of Hannibal, on the Mississippi River, to the western city of St. Joseph, bordering Kansas. By connecting with

the Chicago, Burlington and Quincy Railroad travelers from the east could now reach St. Joe, the jumping off point for Kansas, Nebraska and the gold fields of California, without going through St. Louis "in the short space of 26 hours."[481] Moreover, Chicago was now well positioned to compete with St. Louis for the grain that would be harvested on the plains west of the Missouri River.

A delegation led by the president of the Chicago Board of Trade, James H. Ramsey, rode the first train to St. Joseph. Besides the directors of the Board of Trade, other members of the delegation included John Van Nortwick, the President of the Chicago, Burlington and Quincy Railroad; William Bross from the *Chicago Press and Tribune*, who was also a Chicago Alderman; and Dr. Dyer. Bross, also known as "Deacon Bross," because he was a fervent Presbyterian and the mainstay of the Second Presbyterian Church, had merged his newspaper, *The Democratic Press*, into the *Tribune*, which is why the *Tribune* was known for several years as the *Press and Tribune*. This newspaper's representative reported: "A new and splendid night car on the Burlington and Quincy made us as comfortable as we could have been had our heads rested on our own pillows."[482] The trip included "wit, fun and frolic, song and satire." In Hannibal, the party met with Mr. Osborne and Major Bucklin. The former was one of the men who built the Hannibal and St. Joseph line, and who also had been a contractor on the Illinois and Michigan Canal. The latter had "laid out the town of Chicago in 1830." The reporter relished the occasion: "An evening with them and Dr. Dyer, talking over incidents in the early history of our city, is a rare treat, not soon to be forgotten." (Unfortunately, the reporter forgot to share this treat with the *Press and Tribune's* readers.)

While the railroad crossed miles of prairie, the *Press and Tribune* observed that the country along the Burlington's route "needs but cultivation to make it one continuous garden." The country along the Hannibal-St. Joseph line was similarly blessed with rich soil. What was the potential? The President of the Burlington told the delegation that in the past year the railroad had brought more grain to Chicago from

Galesburg (from farms in Knox County, Illinois), than was produced in the entire State of Connecticut.[483]

In St. Joseph on Wednesday morning, the delegation from Chicago was joined by delegations from St. Louis and other cities for a grand celebration. There was a procession of delegations and a ceremony mixing waters brought from the Atlantic Ocean and the Mississippi River with the Missouri. Then there were speeches commemorating the event. Dr. Dyer was called to the platform and "convulsed" the audience with his "hits."[484]

Later in June of 1859, 700 citizens of Chicago took a train to Lake Forest for an outing.[485] Deacon Bross and Dr. Dyer were also on this trip and both were called on to make remarks.

Then, on August 4, 1859, Chicago hosted the St. Joseph delegation, reversing the trip the Chicagoans had made when the line opened. Mayor Haines was absent from the city and Dr. Dyer was called upon to act as host. The delegation was greeted at the Tremont. There were the usual speeches and expressions of welcome. The spokesmen on both sides could not avoid referring to the slavery issue. Both sides acknowledged that the delegations came from States that differed on that issue but were united in their desire to do business with each other. The Missourians cheerfully responded saying that while they came from a State that upheld that "peculiar institution," they valued free labor and that "if ever the flag of our country loses a star, or if even a stripe is obliterated, it will not be the fault of the "Border Ruffians."[486] (And, indeed, when the break came, Missouri did not secede.)

The weather did not cooperate. A steamboat trip on the *Planet* had been planned and, at 8:00 P.M., a number of the stalwarts ventured out on the lake despite rough waves and heavy rain. The steamer was absent from her dock a little over an hour. Not a few "paid tribute" when wind and waves demanded it.

Regaining their appetites, the excursionists were feted at the second annual supper of the Audubon Club of the city. The *Press and Tribune's* reporter enjoyed the feast, describing it in great detail:

It was in itself one of the finest and most brilliant affairs of the season. Mine hosts of the Tremont outdid themselves in the surprising excellence of cuisine and good taste in ball and table decorations. Appropriately in the latter the superb cabinet of the Audubon club yielded up its feathered treasures. Thus from these posts along the groaning tables loaded with delicacies, birds and fowl of great variety and brilliant plumage, many of them of rare value, looked with their glass eyes upon the funeral honors paid to their kindred dispatched to their last resting places in such good company and cookery.

The Bill of fare included:

Roast Canvas Back Ducks, Champagne sauce. Roast Brandt, Roast Mallard Ducks, Roast Wood Ducks, Roast Wild Goose, Roast Red Heads, Roast Teal Ducks, Roast Bittern, Roast Blue Wing Teal, Roast Pigeon, Roast Grey Ducks, Roast Broad Bills, Roast Dippers, Roast Lake Duck, Roast Sand Hill Crane, Roast Prairie Chicken Stuffed and Larded, Roast Partridge, Broiled Plover, Broiled Red Bird, Broiled Blue Birds, Broiled Marsh Birds, Broiled Woodcock on toast, Broiled Blue Wing Teal, Broiled Prairie Chicken, Broiled Wild Pigeon, Broiled Rail.

Two hundred and fifty guests attended this feast. The Light Guard Band played at intervals. The passengers who had been on the *Planet* "made good their losses." Overcoming the "din of popping corks," the president of the club recounted the club's purpose and invited the traditional toasts. The purpose of the club he noted was to secure better observance of the game laws of the State and to collect specimens to add to the club's "cabinet." The cabinet already boasted 800 specimens. There were toasts to Audubon, Daniel Webster, the press and more. The party lasted "until a late or rather early hour."[487]

Lincoln's Cooper Union Speech

THE LINCOLN-DOUGLAS DEBATES had brought prominence to Lincoln. The speeches of Lincoln and Douglas had been printed in newspapers across the country. Though not as well known as William Seward and Salmon Chase, Lincoln was becoming recognized as an effective spokesman of the Republican opposition to Douglas. There was talk of him being a possible Presidential candidate and Lincoln took a number of steps to build the case for his candidacy. In 1859 he gave speeches in Illinois, Iowa, Indiana, Wisconsin and Kansas.[488] He asserted leadership in the Republican cause beyond Illinois seeking to keep the party focused on the uniting principle of opposition to the expansion of slavery. When the Ohio Republican Party adopted a plank calling for the repeal of the Fugitive Slave Act, Lincoln wrote Salmon Chase, Governor of Ohio, to warn him against introducing any such plank at the national convention telling Chase that to do so would "explode" the convention.[489]

He collaborated with *Press and Tribune* editor John Locke Scripps who prepared a biography of Lincoln that his promoters could publish. Norman Judd, who had managed his campaign against Douglas, may have used his influence with the editors of the *Press and Tribune* to precipitate the editorial that was published on February 16, 1860, that endorsed Lincoln for the Presidency.[490] In describing his qualities, the editorial said: "he has that radicalism which a keen insight into the meaning of the anti-slavery conflict is sure to give; but, coupled with it, that constitutional conservatism which could never fail in proper respect for existing institutions and laws…."[491]

Judd was instrumental in advancing Lincoln's candidacy in another way. Judd was a member of the committee of the national Republican Party that would decide what city would host the next convention. Judd proposed Chicago as a (supposedly) neutral venue. Chicago won by one vote over St. Louis.

Lincoln's backers knew that he needed exposure to Republicans in the East. He had been invited to speak at Henry Ward Beecher's Plymouth Church in Brooklyn, New York. The Young Men's Republican Union assumed sponsorship of his appearance, the event was moved to the Cooper Institute and scheduled for February 27, 1860. When the day came, a crowd of 1,500 attended the speech.

Lincoln had accepted the invitation the prior October and had spent many hours researching historical records to support the argument he intended to make. Herndon described Lincoln's Cooper Union speech as a legal brief. And indeed, it was a memorable speech that was built exactly the way a lawyer's closing argument was, mustering each piece of evidence that proved the conclusion he asked his listeners to embrace.

Lincoln chose as his text a statement by Senator Douglas from one of his recent speeches:

Our fathers, when they framed the Government under which we live, understood this question just as well, and even better, than we do now.

With this as a starting point, Lincoln went on to identify who could properly be called the "fathers of our Government." This description could best belong to the 39 signers of the Constitution. "This question" was whether the federal government could, under the Constitution, regulate slavery in the Territories. Lincoln then went on to identify actions taken by a majority of the 39, showing that they thought there was no constitutional impediment preventing the federal government from regulating slavery in the Territories.

The Northwest Ordinance prohibited slavery in the Northwest Territory. This measure was passed by the Confederation three years before the Constitution. Four of the 39 were in that Congress and voted for it. While the Convention was framing the Constitution, two more of the 39 were there and voted for it. The first Congress passed an Act to enforce the Northwest Ordinance's prohibition on slavery. Sixteen of the 39 were there when it unanimously passed. George Washington signed the bill, another of the 39.

Lincoln then showed that other legislation reflected the belief that the federal government could regulate slavery in the Territories. Even the acceptance of the Territory ceded by North Carolina to create Tennessee and the Territory Georgia ceded to create Alabama and Mississippi, which included a condition that the federal government should not prohibit slavery there, included other measures that "interfered" with slavery – the prohibition of bringing slaves in from outside the United States.

When he was finished, Lincoln had identified 23 out of the 39 who had supported measures that showed that they believed that the federal government could regulate slavery in the Territories. Recognizing that the Supreme Court in Dred Scott had relied on the Fifth Amendment and that Senator Douglas occasionally cited the Tenth Amendment as the source for saying that Congress did not have the power to regulate slavery in the Territories, Lincoln also showed those two provisions were before Congress at the same time and no one then expressed the view that either Amendment limited the federal government's power over slavery in the Territories.

Lincoln pointed out that he did not advocate that the people were bound to follow implicitly whatever the fathers were shown to have done. That would ignore the wisdom of experience gained since. But if we are to deviate from the understanding they had of the Constitutional scheme, it should be based on "evidence so conclusive, and argument so clear, that even their great authority, fairly considered and weighed, cannot stand…." This would be highly improbably where "they understood the question better than we."

Lincoln did not object to anyone arguing that the Constitution forbade regulating slavery in the Territories. But to argue that "our fathers who framed the government under which we live" were of the same opinion was misleading and a deception.

Lincoln went on to address the Southern people as if he were speaking directly to them, a powerful rhetorical device: "You say we are sectional. We deny it."[492] Yes, Washington warned against sectional parties in his farewell address. But he approved and signed the prohibition on slavery in the Territories

and wrote LaFayette to say the prohibition was a wise measure and that he looked forward to the day when the United States would be a confederation of free States. The Republicans were the conservatives, seeking to enforce the policy of the fathers, and those who sought to open the Territories up to slavery were the radicals, repudiating the vision of the founders. The Republicans were not responsible for the acts of John Brown. The Republicans have no policy to make war on slave holding. They merely insist that the policy of our fathers be observed.

Recognizing that Southerners could point to the Dred Scott decision as having decided in their favor the question of whether the Constitution prohibited Congress from regulating slavery in the Territories, Lincoln explained why they could not rely on that decision to settle the question:

> Perhaps you will say the Supreme Court has decided the disputed Constitutional question in your favor. Not quite so. But waiving the lawyer's distinction between dictum and decision, the Court has decided the question for you in a sort of way. The Court have substantially said, it is your right to take slaves into the federal Territories, and to hold them there as property. When I say the decision was made in a sort of way, I mean that it was made by a divided Court … they not quite agreeing with one another in the reasons for making it … mainly based upon a mistaken statement of fact- the statement in the opinion that "the right of property in a slave is distinctly and expressly affirmed in the Constitution."

Here Lincoln unveiled a new analysis of the Dred Scott decision that went beyond his prior criticism of the decision and masterfully demonstrated its false premise. Focusing on the words "distinctly and expressly," Lincoln showed that there was no distinct provision recognizing slavery nor was there any provision expressly affirming the right asserted. The Constitution does not include the words "slave" or "slavery" nor the word "property" in connection with language alluding to slavery. When a slave is alluded to, he is called a "person." The phrase "service or labor due" is spoken of as a debt. To argue that the right is implied was disproven by Lincoln's analysis of the actions of the 39 signers. Lincoln then asked: "When this obvious mistake of the Judges shall be brought to their notice, is it not reasonable to expect that they will withdraw the mistaken statement, and reconsider the conclusion based on it?"

Lincoln then addressed the Southerners' threat to break the Union if their "rights" are not recognized and to blame the Republicans for dismembering the Union. This was no different than a highway man putting a pistol to one's head and saying "Stand and deliver or I will kill you, and then you will be a murderer!" This was simply extortion. In the one case for money, in the other for one's vote.

Then Lincoln addressed his fellow Republicans and exhorted them to stand firm. What would satisfy the Southerners? Surrendering the Territories to them? No. They want us to "cease calling slavery *wrong*, and join them in calling it *right*." That would mean repealing our state constitutions that prohibit slavery and every other law limiting it. Thinking it right they want its full recognition. Thinking it wrong, the Republicans cannot waiver. He concluded with: "Let us have faith that right makes might, and in that faith, let us, to the end, dare to do our duty as we understand it."

Lincoln's Cooper Union Speech brought the crowd to its feet with a rousing ovation. Copies were published and widely distributed. Lincoln made a series of other speeches while in the east and elevated his stature among Republicans.

Lincoln Becomes the Favorite Son of Illinois

WHEN DR. DYER and the other delegates to the Illinois Republican Convention traveled to Decatur on May 9–10, 1860, there were several simmering disputes within the party to be ironed out.[493] Wentworth had been feuding

with Judd and the *Press and Tribune*. However, both relented, not wanting to see a Democrat elected Mayor of the city that would host the Republican National Convention. With the *Press and Tribune's* support, Wentworth was elected Mayor. Judd, Leonard Swett and Richard Yates all sought the party's nomination for Governor. Yates won the hotly contested battle after several ballots.

Before the Convention, Lincoln had written Norman Judd, who, besides having managed Lincoln's campaign against Douglas, was chair of the Republican Party of Illinois, expressing his interest in having the Illinois delegation nominate him as its favorite son.[494] When the delegates finally got to the nomination of their Presidential candidate, there was no dissension. Lincoln was nominated and the delegates were instructed to "vote as a unit" in his favor. The solidarity of the Illinois delegation for Lincoln contrasted with the split support Chase had from the Ohio delegation and Cameron had from the Pennsylvania delegation.[495] Lincoln also had support from the Indiana delegation. Though he had fewer pledged delegates than Seward, he would go the convention in a strong position.

There was a dramatic episode in the Decatur convention when Richard Oglesby informed the delegates that there were some old Democrats from Macon County who wanted to make a contribution to the proceedings. Two old men circled the convention floor with two split rails and a banner that read: "ABRAHAM LINCOLN. The Rail candidate for President in 1860. Two rails from a lot of 3,000 made in 1830 by Thos. Hanks and Abe Lincoln – whose father was the first pioneer in Macon County." The cheering and shouting literally brought the house down as part of the roof fell in.[496] Lincoln was not only pronounced Illinois's favorite son, he was now "The Rail Splitter."

The "Second Choice" Strategy

LINCOLN HAD THE unwavering support of the Illinois delegation. But he also had a strategy for reaching beyond Illinois. He had devised a "second choice" strategy that he described in a letter he sent on March 24, 1860 to Samuel Galloway, a political ally in Ohio:

Of course I am gratified to know I have friends in Ohio who are disposed to give me the highest evidence of their friendship and confidence.... If I have any chance it consists mainly in the fact that the whole opposition would vote for me if nominated. (I don't mean to include pro-slavery opposition of the South, of course.) My name is new in the field; and I suppose I am not the first choice of a very great many. Our policy then is to give no offence to others – leave them in a mood to come to us, if they shall be compelled to give up their first love.[497]

The "*whole* opposition" statement revealed the other part of the strategy of Lincoln's backers. While Seward was the front runner, there were pockets of Republicans who would not support him. While Lincoln did not go to Chicago for the Republican National Convention which began May 16, 1860, reflecting the custom of the times, this idea that Seward could not win if nominated was exploited by David Davis, Leonard Swett and Judd who led the Illinois delegation and sought out support from other delegations.

Like Lincoln, Seward did not go to the Chicago convention. He waited at his home in Auburn, New York and left it to Thurlow Weed to manage his campaign. Seward was the presumptive front runner. But Seward and "Boss" Weed had alienated their former ally, Horace Greeley, the editor of the *New York Tribune*. The New York Republican Convention, under the control of Weed and Seward, did not send Greeley to Chicago as a delegate. Greeley became a vociferous "anybody but Seward" voice, got to Chicago as a delegate for Oregon, and promoted the candidacy of Missouri's Edward Bates. Seward had also feuded with the Fillmore branch of the party and castigated the Know Nothings. While Seward had gone to visit Simon Cameron during the year before the convention to secure a pledge of support from the Pennsylvanian, Weed ignored a request from Cameron to meet with him prior to the convention.[498] Seward and Weed mistakenly took Cameron's support for Seward for granted.

The city saw its population surge as the delegations arrived. There were bands, parades by the Illinois and Indiana "Wide Awake" Clubs. The "Wide Awakes" were marching clubs. The special 13 car train carrying Seward's delegates and supporters spilled forth uniformed marching clubs for Seward called the "Irrepressibles."[499] Weed had come to Chicago a few days early and shrewdly rented the Wigwam for a Seward rally the night before the convention. However, a Pennsylvania delegate pretending to offer a routine motion took the floor and refused to yield, speaking until close to midnight, causing the Seward rally to fizzle.[500]

It would take 233 votes to win. The biggest blocks of votes belonged to New York which had 70; Pennsylvania 54; Ohio 46; Indiana 26; Illinois 22 and Missouri 18. Indiana committed 26 first ballot votes to Lincoln. On the first ballot, it quickly became clear that the two leading candidates were Lincoln and Seward. Seward had 173-½ votes and Lincoln 102. The remaining votes (not counting a few abstentions) were split among various favorite sons. There were 50-½ for Simon Cameron of Pennsylvania, 49 for Salmon P. Chase of Ohio, 48 for Edward Bates of Missouri, 12 for John McLean of Ohio, 10 for Jacob Collamer of Vermont, three for Benjamin Wade of Ohio, and one each for William Dayton of New Jersey, Charles Sumner of Massachusetts, and John C. Freemont of California. With the first ballot out of the way, the question became how will the delegates vote on the second ballot? Will they turn to their second choice and, if so, who will that be?

Weed was supposedly telling delegations that Lincoln could not win votes east of Indiana, could not raise money for a campaign and could not offer jobs, contracts and other inducements equivalent to what Seward could offer. Lincoln's managers supposedly made lavish promises of cabinet positions to secure delegations for Lincoln. Lincoln's team, led by Judge Davis, included Norman Judd, Jesse Fell, Stephen T. Logan, Isaac N. Arnold, Leonard Swett, John Palmer, Joseph Medill, Charles Ray and Billy Herndon. Their headquarters was the Tremont House. Ray had written a note to Lincoln asking for authority to cut deals. Lincoln responded with a telegram: "I AUTHORIZE NO BARGAINS AND WILL BE BOUND BY NONE." When this arrived it stopped the campaigners dead in their tracks. But then Davis said: "Lincoln ain't here, and don't know what we have to meet."[501] Davis supposedly went on to make commitments to swing delegations to Lincoln.

Lincoln's backers had outmaneuvered the New Yorkers in two other ways. Judd had devised a seating plan for the convention that isolated the New York delegation and placed it at a distance from the delegations that Illinois hoped to sway. Pennsylvania, a key delegation, was seated right next to the Illinois delegation. There is also a colorful story that Lincoln's supporters printed counterfeit tickets for admission to the Wigwam and handed them out to supporters with instructions to show up early on the third day of the convention. Seward's supporters planned a grand march around the city that would end at the Wigwam. When they got there, supposedly they could not get in because the seats had all been taken by Lincoln's supporters. This story has been disputed by David Davis's biographer, based on an in-depth review of Davis's papers.[502] Nevertheless, the Wigwam was full of Lincoln supporters brought from every corner of the State and their cheers, every time Lincoln's name was mentioned, were louder than the cheers for Seward, helping to propel Lincoln's advancement.

Senator Seward of New York, the expected favorite, was not expected to win the nomination on the first ballot. When delegates voted on the second ballot, if the "second choice" strategy were to work, delegates would switch to Lincoln which would give Lincoln's candidacy momentum. This was a strategy that the Lincoln strategists held close to their vests. If Lincoln's rivals knew what the Lincoln camp was up to, they might have found ways to thwart it.

The Cameron Club

THERE IS NO record proving that Dr. Dyer was in league with Lincoln to effect the "second choice" strategy. But then again what Dr. Dyer and his friends in Chicago did fit exactly with that game plan.

On September 29, 1859, eight months before the Republican National Convention, Dr. Dyer called a meeting to organize the "Cameron Club," a political organization dedicated to the support of Simon Cameron, the Senator from Pennsylvania, who would be Pennsylvania's favorite son. The first meeting was held at the offices of James Bell. In addition to Bell and Dr. Dyer, it was attended by Calvin DeWolf, Dr. Charles Leib, George F. Crocker, Simeon Whitely, C.P.I. Arion, and John Lyle King. Dr. Dyer was elected President, DeWolf, Vice-President and Bell, Secretary-Treasurer, for a term running through September 29, 1861. The club would meet every Thursday at 7:00. A resolution was passed and recorded in the Club's Minute Book that expressed the purpose of the organizers:

RESOLVED that the Cameron Club will use all fair measures and its utmost endeavors, to secure the nomination of the Honorable Simon Cameron of Pennsylvania by the National Republican Convention for the office of President of the United States and that all of our endeavors shall be exerted to secure his election when thus nominated.[503]

At its weekly meetings, new members were welcomed, the club would hear speakers, and discuss the effort to write letters to friends and letters to the editor and otherwise promote Cameron's candidacy. The club would go on to meet in Dr. Dyer's offices and then move to a permanent home at 205 Randolph.

The club's membership would ultimately grow to 300 and it would proselytize to promote clubs in other cities and states. They began to correspond with Cameron's campaign manager in Pennsylvania, Judge Joseph Casey.[504] And, of course, members of the club wrote a stream of letters to "General" Cameron between June of 1859 and May of 1860.[505] (Cameron had been Adjutant General of the Pennsylvania militia.)

While the club's formation sounded antagonistic to Lincoln's candidacy, the club almost immediately changed its name to the "Cameron-Lincoln Club" at its fourth meeting on October 20, 1859. This was done in recognition of Lincoln's growing popularity and anointed Lincoln as the club's Vice Presidential candidate. The resolution making Lincoln the club's choice for Vice President explained:

> *His name is identified with the history of the Republican Party, and his able defense of its principles. His honesty and the noble qualities of his heart and mind have given him a strong hold upon the affection of our people.*[506]

In keeping with the political methods of the day, one member composed a song dedicated to the Cameron-Lincoln Club.[507]

The club invited speakers to its weekly meetings and many prominent Illinois Republicans came. Zebina Eastman spoke to the club on November 17th; "Long John" Wentworth endorsed Cameron at the January 27, 1860 meeting; on February 10, 1860, Norman Judd, addressed the club, attacking Buchanan; he was followed by Isaac Newton (I.N.) Arnold who said he was a Seward man but told the club he supported Cameron as his second choice. The club invited editors of newspapers from Sterling, Waukegan and other cities in Illinois.

The Cameron-Lincoln Club members took steps to prepare for the convention. They contributed money to build the Wigwam, the building where the convention would be held. They made arrangements for the arrival of the Pennsylvania delegation: they appointed a 50 person committee, with Dr. Dyer as chair, to welcome the delegation when it came to town and to assist it with arrangements during its stay. The headquarters for the Cameron delegates during the Convention would be the Briggs House, at the Northeast corner of Randolph and Fifth Avenue (later Wells Street). On the eve of the convention, the club met and heard from Judge Casey and Robert M. Palmer, speaker of the Pennsylvania Senate.

One has to wonder whether the Pennsylvanians accepted this outpouring of Illinois support uncritically. If they had inquired, they would have discovered that Dr. Dyer was a close personal friend of Lincoln's and had been a delegate at the two most recent Republican State Conventions which endorsed Lincoln unanimously first for his run against Douglas for the Senate in 1858 and then as Illinois's favorite son for the Presidency in 1860.[508] DeWolf had also been a delegate for Cook County at the 1860 Illinois Republican Convention in Decatur that made Lincoln Illinois's favorite son. And if they had looked closely at the speakers who addressed the club, they would have discovered that it was a roster of Lincoln's principal supporters that included Wentworth, Judd and Arnold. The facts suggest that the Cameron-Lincoln Club was more of a Trojan Horse than a pure tribute to Cameron. This may not have been obvious immediately because the Illinois State Republican Convention that took place in Decatur was held May 9 and 10, just six days before the Republican National Convention in Chicago which started on May 16th.

Dr. Charles Leib, who had come from Pennsylvania, and like Cameron, was a former Democrat, was the Cameron-Lincoln Club member who took the lead in corresponding with General Cameron. Dr. Leib's path to becoming an Illinois Republican reflected an opportunistic streak: he started off as a Douglas Democrat. Then he split with Senator Douglas when Douglas opposed the Lecompton Constitution.[509] Leib sided with President Buchanan, scheming to control the patronage positions in Chicago as Buchanan purged appointees who had been sponsored by Douglas.[510] Douglas attacked Leib savagely and accused him of trying to destroy the Democratic Party in Illinois.[511] As the Democratic Party in Illinois fractured, Leib, on the outs with Douglas, became a Republican.

THE REPUBLICANS IN NOMINATING CONVENTION, IN THEIR WIGWAM AT CHICAGO, MAY, 1860.

Inside the Chicago Wigwam, where, on the third ballot,
Abraham Lincoln became the Republican Party's nominee for
President on May 18, 1860. (Chicago History Museum)

In 1859, Dr. Leib met with Cameron in Philadelphia and volunteered to be his unofficial campaign manager, "his chief bugler," in the west.[512] In June of 1859 he wrote Cameron to provide his assessment of the Republican Party's chances in 1860 and Dr. Leib's view of how Cameron stood among Republicans in Illinois and Wisconsin. Dr. Leib began enlisting supporters for Cameron's candidacy and boasted in his letter on September 2, 1859 that "Dr. C.V. Dyer, a wealthy and leading citizen and Republican, has declared for you...."[513] Another early supporter that he enlisted was E.M. Haines, a member of the legislature and brother of Chicago's Mayor.[514] This was on the eve of the birth of the club. Over the next several months, Dr. Leib went on to chronicle the activities of the Cameron-Lincoln Club and its growth, to explain

to Cameron the support the club would be giving Lincoln as its Vice Presidential candidate, and to ask for copies of Cameron's speech in the Senate on the tariff during the Polk administration to use in his proselytizing efforts.

As the date of the Convention came closer, Leib, DeWolf and others wrote Cameron to report on their discussions with delegates and friends of delegates speculating about whom the delegates might support.

One intriguing letter is Dr. Leib's of March 24, 1860, in which he reported that Lincoln was in Chicago and that Dr. Leib had two conversations with him. Dr. Leib optimistically reported to Cameron that Lincoln was "evidently anxious for the Vice Presidential nomination and I think sees the importance of your nomination."[515] At the same time, he reported that Lincoln had said, "There is an impression abroad, although I have no confidence in it, that Cameron is not a candidate and is for Seward." Dr. Leib assured Lincoln that Cameron was a candidate, that Pennsylvania would be nominating him and that Cameron did not support Seward. This was undoubtedly intelligence that Lincoln was glad to hear. Perhaps not recognizing the import it would have on Cameron's prospects, Dr. Leib also reported that Lincoln told him that "some of his friends are talking about him for President but that he has no such idea and that his name shall not be used to make trouble."[516] According to Dr. Leib, Lincoln told him he would be at the Convention and invited the Club members to greet him when he came to the City. However, Dr. Leib told Cameron that Lincoln "feels that if Seward should be the nominee he would be out of the running…" [for Vice President] because Seward would need a former Democrat to balance the ticket.

Was Lincoln being coy about his intentions when he talked to Dr. Leib? The correspondence and the Club's minute book do not provide the answer. The date of Dr. Leib's encounter with Lincoln is the same as the date of the letter Lincoln wrote to Samuel Galloway explaining the "second choice" strategy. It may be that Dr. Leib was playing his role as part of the second choice strategy when he wrote Cameron. Or it may be that Lincoln did not take him into his confidence.

Pennsylvania Switches to Lincoln

ON THE EVENING after the first day of the convention, there was a meeting of delegates opposed to Seward. Representatives from the delegations from Illinois, Indiana, Pennsylvania and New Jersey met to see if they could agree on a candidate instead of Seward. This "committee of 12" exchanged views as to who would be the strongest candidate. Horace Greeley, the editor of the *New York Tribune*, learned of the meeting, came by and asked if they had agreed on a candidate. He was told no and

wired his newspaper that Seward was unstoppable and could expect to be nominated the next day.[517]

After Greeley left, there was a suggestion that the delegates take a straw vote to see how many votes each candidate had. This was done and Lincoln, having Illinois and Indiana, had more votes than anyone else. The New Jersey and Pennsylvania delegates agreed to hold caucuses to see if their state delegations would support Lincoln on the second ballot.[518] The New Jersey delegates caucused that night and came on board the Lincoln bandwagon. Pennsylvania caucused the next morning.

Some historians have said that Pennsylvania's support was secured only after Swett and Judge Davis promised a cabinet position to Pennsylvania's Simon Cameron.[519] Davis's biographer disputes this version based on a review of the correspondence between Davis and Judge Joseph Casey, Cameron's representative at the convention. While Judge Casey surely asked for a cabinet position for Cameron and specifically asked for the Treasury, "Davis and Swett responded cautiously that Pennsylvania would have a place in Lincoln's cabinet and that they would personally recommend Simon Cameron for it."[520]

On the second ballot, Seward's support stalled and Lincoln's climbed dramatically. New Hampshire gave 10 votes to Lincoln, Vermont switched to Lincoln and Connecticut and Rhode Island gave Lincoln votes. When Pennsylvania announced its votes for Lincoln it was clear that the momentum favored Lincoln. The roll call resulted in Seward having 184-½, Lincoln 181, Bates 35, Cameron two, McLean 8, Chase 42-½, Dayton 10 and Cassius Clay, of Kentucky, two.

The third ballot was called for and Lincoln's tally rose to 231-½ while Seward slipped back to 180. Lincoln was 1-½ votes short of victory. A delegate from Ohio rose and asked to be recognized to switch four votes from Seward to Lincoln, thus putting Lincoln over the top. Pandemonium erupted. The crowd roared, the canon on the roof of the Wigwam was fired and the noise was deafening.

As soon as the convention was over, the Cameron-Lincoln Club changed its name again and became the "Lincoln-Hamlin Club."[521] Then its members went to work to campaign for that ticket. The Illinois Republicans rewarded Dr. Leib. After Lincoln won the nomination, Dr. Leib became the editor of *The Railsplitter*, the campaign's newspaper published in Chicago from June through October of 1860.[522] Dr. Leib and several other Lincoln-Hamlin Club members would have roles to play in the Lincoln Administration.

Twenty-eight years later, on March 8, 1888, the survivors of the Cameron-Lincoln Club celebrated Simon Cameron's ninetieth birthday with a banquet at the Sherman House in Chicago. Cameron was unable to attend. Among the speakers was Simeon Whiteley who had been employed in the War Department under Cameron. Whitely gave a toast and remarked that the Cameron-Lincoln Club had made the nomination of Lincoln "not only possible but certain."[523]

The "Baby Waker" canon was operated by Wide-Awake cadets who fired it while marching for "Honest Old Abe." (Private Collection)

Dr. Dyer and the "Wide-Awakes" Campaign for Lincoln

D R. DYER CAMPAIGNED vigorously for the Lincoln-Hamlin ticket. On the evening of July 23, 1860, he joined Norman Judd, to address the "German Picnic," a gathering at Wright's Grove ("near the northern limits of the city"). This was attended by the South Side Wide-Awakes, the Lincoln Rangers (mounted), and the West Side Wide-Awakes. The "Wide-Awakes" were marching clubs. The standard Wide-Awake uniform "consisted of a full robe or cape, a black glazed hat, and a torch six feet in length to which a large, flaming, pivoting whale-oil container was mounted. Its activities were conducted primarily in the evening and consisted of several night-time torch-lit marches through cities in the northeast and border States.

The Wide-Awakes adopted the image of a large eyeball as their standard banner."[524] At the German Picnic, Judd and Dr. Dyer gave "stirring speeches" and "[t]he Lumbards gave some capital singing. Altogether, the affair was a success, and a happy augury of the campaign soon to be fully opened."[525]

On Sept 6, 1860, *The Chicago Press and Tribune* reported an "imposing demonstration" when 1,500 to 2,000 persons attended a meeting at Blue Island that had been intended as a "local affair." Once again there was a parade of Wide-Awakes. This time, 300 Wide-Awakes, were accompanied by "a company of Wide-Awake cadets … boys from 12 to 18 years – 33 in number. They are fully officered and equipped, and thoroughly drilled, and their fine appearance and manly bearing elicited the utmost enthusiasm from the crowd present. The boys also had a 'baby waker' which occasionally belched forth in loud tones its good will for 'Honest Old Abe.'" Dr. Dyer and Mayor Wentworth were among those who gave speeches and were "enthusiastically received."[526]

The Wide-Awakes Marching Club, famed for their night time torch parades, openly supported the Lincoln-Hamlin ticket. (Chicago History Museum)

On Friday night, October 5, 1860, Dr. Dyer and J.Y. Scammon spoke to a Peoria meeting of Republicans. Scammon attacked (Democratic) Governor Matteson's "canal script robbery" and Dr. Dyer "convulsed the audience with his side-splitters."[527] Earlier that week, on October 3, 1860, 10,000 Wide-Awakes marched in a three-mile procession. The story of this rally occupied eight columns of the *Chicago Tribune*. On October 11, 1860 Dr. Dyer was one of several speakers addressing the Republicans of Northern Illinois in Elgin.[528]

Dr. Leib campaigned for the Lincoln-Hamlin ticket publishing 18 issues of *The Railsplitter* between June 23, 1860 and October 27th. This newspaper featured biographies of Lincoln and Hamlin, the Republican Party's platform, reprints of speeches by Lincoln, Cameron and other leading Republicans and, of course, political cartoons and commentary skewering Douglas and other Democratic politicians. Subservience to the demands of the Southern wing of the Democratic Party was a regular theme. One politician was described as "crawl[ing] on his belly whenever the South required him to do so."[529] *The Railsplitter* reported on the election of officers for the Wide-Awake Club which held meetings in a hall rented on Lake Street every Tuesday and Friday evening.

In contrast to its treatment of Douglas and the Democrats, *The Railsplitter* described Lincoln as a paragon of virtue:

In his personal habits Lincoln is as simple as a child. He never drinks intoxicating liquors of any sort, not even wine. He never uses tobacco in any of its shapes. He never uses profane language – never indulges in games of chance – never incurs debt when he has the means to pay. And at the present time he owes no man a dollar. There are few public men, we think, who can fill this bill of qualities.[530]

Each issue of *The Railsplitter* included a political cartoon portraying Douglas and focusing on an issue where the Republicans thought he was vulnerable. On October 6, the cartoon showed Douglas in a circus ring trying to ride two horses standing with one foot on the back of each. The horses were labeled "Popular Sovereignty" and "Dred Scott." Douglas moaned at his inability to keep the unruly horses together. The caption quoted the clown saying, "I may be a fool … but I ain't such a fool as to try to ride a pair of horses as that. You had better ride one at a time, and even then, either one of 'em would throw you, or any other man."

The Democrats Fracture

DOUGLAS HAD EXPECTED to be the candidate of the Democratic Party, having been its champion for years. However, when the Party met, he faced a revolt. The Southerners could not stomach Douglas's Freeport Doctrine which robbed them of their victory in the Dred Scott case. If local laws could defeat the ruling, then slavery could still be excluded from the Territories and the slave-owner's right to take his property wherever he pleased would be infringed. (Exactly the point made by *The Railsplitter* cartoon.) Douglas's answer to the question Lincoln had posed in the Lincoln-Douglas debates two years earlier doomed his nomination and his candidacy. Lincoln's question had unmasked the irreconcilable conflict in Douglas's straddle.

The Democrats originally convened in Charleston on April 23, 1860. When the platform plank embracing

slavery was defeated, the Southerners walked out. This prevented Douglas from getting the needed votes of two-thirds of all delegates. In June the Convention reconvened in Baltimore. After a credentials fight Douglas won the nomination. But the States that had walked out held their own convention and nominated John C. Breckenridge.

Lincoln Wins the Presidency

WHEN AMERICANS WENT to the polls in November of 1860, the Republicans emerged victorious because the Democrats were split. Lincoln had the greatest popular vote, 1,865,908. But it was only 39.8% of the popular vote. Stephen Douglas had 1,380,202 or 29.5%, John Breckenridge had 848,019 and John Bell had 590,901. In Illinois, Lincoln got 172,171 votes (50.7%) to Douglas's 160,215 (47.2%), while Breckenridge got 2,331 (0.7%) and Bell 4,914 (1.4%).

The vote was very much along sectional lines. Lincoln won most of the Northern States: California, Connecticut, Illinois, Indiana, Iowa, Maine, Massachusetts, Michigan, Minnesota, New Hampshire, New York, Ohio, Pennsylvania, Rhode Island, Vermont and Wisconsin.

Douglas won Missouri and New Jersey. Breckenridge won Delaware, Florida, Georgia, Louisiana, Maryland, Mississippi, and North Carolina. Bell won Kentucky, Tennessee and Virginia.

With the election of Lincoln the Slave States recognized that the nation now had a leader who was antagonistic to their interests. Without waiting for Lincoln to be sworn in, on December 24, 1860, South Carolina adopted its Secession Declaration enumerating among its reasons for seceding: "an increasing hostility on the part of the non-slaveholding States to the institution of slavery, [which] has led to a disregard of their obligations [to apprehend and return fugitive slaves]…."[531] South Carolina's Declaration identified Illinois as one of the States that had either "nullified" laws such as the Fugitive Slave Act or "rendered use-less any attempt to execute them."[532] On January 29, 1861 Georgia followed suit, issuing its Declaration stating that, "The party of Lincoln, called the Republican party, under its present name and organization, is of recent origin. It is admitted to be an anti-slavery party [A]nti-slavery is its mission and its purpose."[533] The Secession Declarations show that the citizens of the slave-owning States knew what Lincoln's election meant for the institution of slavery.

PART III

1860–1865:

Emancipation – Triumph of the Abolitionists

The Road
to the Extinction of Slavery

LINCOLN WAS SWORN in as President March 4, 1861. His election did not end slavery. It would take a Civil War and "rivers of human blood"[534] before the nation eradicated the scourge of slavery. Lincoln has been immortalized as "The Great Emancipator." The foundation for this epitaph is his issuance of the Emancipation Proclamation and his role in persuading Congress to adopt the Thirteenth Amendment.

In 1862 and 1863, using his powers as Commander-in-Chief, President Lincoln issued the two executive orders, known as the "Preliminary Emancipation Proclamation" and the "Final Emancipation Proclamation," which freed slaves in the States in rebellion against the Union. This officially revised the federal government's policy and made an explicit purpose of the Civil War the abolition of slavery. With the War's conclusion, President Lincoln pushed to get Congress to pass the Thirteenth Amendment and succeeded in his efforts when Congress, on January 31, 1865, proposed that Amendment to the legislatures of the States. Prior to his death on April 15, 1865, the Thirteenth Amendment had been ratified by 21 States. It was declared passed on December 18, 1865 when 27 of the then 36 States had ratified it.

As if these were the only steps Lincoln took, Lincoln's role in ending slavery has been criticized by some who have called him an "accidental emancipator."[535] The argument for this position is that Lincoln was a racist and issued the Emancipation Proclamations only as a last resort to win the war by making use of black troops (who, according to this view, tipped the balance making the Union's ultimate victory possible).

The Final Emancipation Proclamation took effect January 1, 1863, 22 months after he was sworn in as President. So, this "delay" has also caused some commentators to doubt Lincoln's commitment to abolishing slavery. During this period of "delay," President Lincoln rescinded emancipation orders of two military commanders who had issued emancipation orders prior to his embrace of that policy and he rebuked Simon Cameron, his Secretary of War, for advocating a policy of arming the freed slaves, before Lincoln was prepared to adopt that policy. And he wrote the famous letter to Horace Greeley on August 22, 1862, expressing the view that if he could save the Union without freeing a single slave, he would do so. These are all actions that can be legitimately pointed to in support of the argument that Lincoln was not committed to abolition.

Portraying Lincoln as a reluctant agent in the fight against slavery, however, grossly distorts the record. When the complete picture is examined it is clear that Lincoln took measured steps that led in only one direction. Between 1861 and 1865 Lincoln used his powers, as the Chief Executive and as Commander-in-Chief, to hasten slavery down the road to its ultimate extinction in a number of ways. Lincoln even called upon Chicago's leading abolitionist, Dr. Charles Volney Dyer, to effect one of these initiatives.

While emancipation was not an initial policy of his Administration, the slowness in adopting that policy must be weighed in context. Lincoln recognized the limits of his authority under the Constitution, he had legitimate concerns about whether the border States might join the Confederacy if he acted too soon, and he needed to mollify political opponents who stood ready to fan the flames of racism if Lincoln made freeing slaves the primary war aim.

Lincoln's Record Opposing Slavery before his Inauguration

LINCOLN'S OPPOSITION TO slavery was a consistent policy of long standing. Before being sworn in as President, Lincoln's record as an opponent of slavery between 1837 and 1861 can be briefly recapped, as follows:

- In 1837, as a member of the Illinois General Assembly, he issued a protest to the resolutions accepting the Southern States' position on slavery in which he said, "slavery is founded on both injustice and bad policy."

- In 1841, in his argument to the Illinois Supreme Court, in *Bailey v. Cromwell*,[536] Lincoln argued that "Nance," a putative slave, was presumed to be free under the Northwest Ordinance.

- In 1847, when he reached Congress, Lincoln prepared a bill to abolish slavery in the District of Columbia.

- In 1847–49, when he was in Congress, he consistently voted for the Wilmot Proviso which would have required all territory won in the Mexican War to be free.[537]

- Between 1854 and 1860, he gave speeches on the repeal of the Missouri Compromise that asserted his unwavering opposition to the institution of slavery. For example, in his speech on the Kansas-Nebraska Act (the "Peoria Speech"), on October 16, 1854, he said:

> *This* declared *indifference, but as I must think, covert real zeal for the spread of slavery, I can not but hate. I hate it because of the monstrous injustice of slavery itself. I hate it because it deprives our republican example of its just influence in the world....*[538]

- In his August 24, 1855 letter to Joshua Speed, he reiterated his opposition to slavery, the restoration of the Missouri Compromise and defended the rejection of the Lecompton constitution.

- In his House Divided Speech, his seven debates with Stephen Douglas, and his Cooper Union speech, he forcefully opposed the expansion of slavery making it clear that neither the Nebraska Act nor the Dred Scott decision should stand in the way of a national policy aimed at containing slavery.

- After his election but before his inauguration, he opposed any compromise with the seceding States. In his letter to William Kellogg on December 11, 1860, Lincoln said: "Entertain no proposition for a compromise in regard to the extension of slavery.... The tug has to come, and better now than later."[539]

- In his letter of December 15, 1860 to John A. Gilmer, Lincoln said: "On the territorial question I am inflexible. On that there is a difference between you and us, and it is a substantial difference. You think slavery is right and ought to be extended; we think it is wrong and ought to be restricted."

The assessment of the secessionists that Lincoln was an enemy of slavery was correct.

The "Hands Off" Policy of Lincoln's First Inaugural Address

WITH LINCOLN'S ELECTION, the fight against slavery now was in the hands of a President and a Republican Congress committed to stopping the expansion of slavery. The seceding States obviously thought the Republicans' agenda went further. In his first inaugural address, on March 4, 1861, Lincoln began by defining his duty as preserving the Union. He quoted from one of his earlier speeches to address the apprehension of the Southern States: "I have no purpose, directly or indirectly, to interfere with the institution of slavery in the States where it exists. I believe I have no lawful right to do so, and I have no inclination to do so."[540] He quoted the Constitution's "shall be delivered up" clause regarding the return of "persons held to service" and said that he and every member of Congress was duty bound to enforce the Fugitive Slave Act. In other words, his election and the election of a Republican Congress did not change the rights of the Southern people to maintain slavery.

He then addressed the Acts of Secession. While his predecessor, James Buchanan, thought the federal government was powerless to prevent secession, Lincoln erected a legal argument from which he could mold federal policy to restore the Union and hold the secessionists responsible for any repercussions from their Acts of Secession: He proclaimed that the Acts of Secession were legally void. His reasoning was simple and compelling: Proclaiming that the Union was perpetual, he said that the Constitution was a contract and that one party to a contract cannot rescind it without the other's consent. Any acts within any State against the authority of the United States would be insurrectionary. He appealed to the Southern States to reconsider their actions and not to precipitate a civil war.

While he wished no bloodshed or violence, he made clear that he would preserve the property of the government:

[T]here needs to be no bloodshed or violence; and there shall be none, unless it is forced upon the national authority. The power confided in me, will be used to hold, occupy, and possess the property, and places belonging to the government, and to collect the duties and imposts; but beyond what may be necessary for these objects, there will be no invasion – no using of force against, or among the people anywhere.[541]

This conciliatory approach fell on deaf ears. The South's leaders were defiant. On April 10, 1861, Fort Sumter was fired upon and Brigadier General Pierre Beauregard demanded its surrender. The Civil War had begun, 37 days after Lincoln's inaugural address. Lincoln recognized this as the watershed. He observed, "the last ray of hope for preserving the Union peaceably, expired at the assault upon Fort Sumter."[542] The olive branch had been rejected and the South would now test the Union's resolve to "hold, occupy and possess" government property and its ability to curb the rebellion.

First Steps

LINCOLN HAD ALWAYS expressed the view that slavery should be set on the road to its ultimate extinction. This was the line in the sand proclaimed in his House Divided speech. After being sworn in on March 4, 1861, he lost no time in showing how this policy could be pursued even while a perilous rebellion loomed on the horizon. As President, Lincoln had to uphold the Constitution. He acknowledged that the Constitution permitted those States that wanted it to permit slavery. This was part of the "original bargain." The border States of Delaware, Kentucky, Maryland, and Missouri had not seceded and all had slave populations. Nevertheless, without interfering with the rights of those States, there were steps he could take as President to restrict slavery.

President Lincoln took one of the first of those steps when, on May 2, 1861, he directed the Secretary of the Interior to take over the responsibility for administering the laws that prohibited the slave trade. This centralized the uncoordinated efforts of the U.S. marshals, district attorneys, the State, Navy and War Departments.[543]

Addressing the slave trade was a serious blow to the institution of slavery. The *New York Times* reported, in a crusading article on November 17, 1862, that "no commerce was ever more profitable than the traffic in Africans, provided those engaged could go unmolested." The *Times* reported that the trade was "flourishing" at the time of the inauguration of the Lincoln Administration because of "officials in power who winked at the fitting out of slavers." The *Times* reported that 30,000 slaves had been landed in Cuba in the past year. It claimed to have the names of over 150 vessels engaged in that trade from 1858 to 1861, the names of the captains and crews and those who fitted them out. And it published a number of those. The list included:

[T]he schooners Weather Gage, Cogswell *and* Josephine, *barks* J.J. Cobb, C.E. Fay, Cora, *and* Kate, *the brigs* Achorn *and* Falmouth, *and ship*

Erie, *the* Storm King *and* Triton ... *the* Cignet *and* Williams. *The schooners* Wanderer *and* Lyra *and steamer* City of Norfolk....

The *Times* concluded that the evidence showed that there had been an extensive trade but "little effort to suppress it." This led to an appraisal of what the Lincoln Administration had done since taking office:

> *The inauguration of the present Administration, with principles avowedly opposed to the increase of the African population in this country and the extension of slavery, although coming into power with a gigantic rebellion on its hands, had time nevertheless, to displace officials derelict of their duty, and appoint others competent and disposed to energetically enforce laws for which they were appointed.*
>
> *The result of this change has been amply apparent, and furnishes abundant evidence that the trade can be completely suppressed.*[544]

This stepped up enforcement had immediate effects: At the end of the year President Lincoln was able to report the results to Congress with great satisfaction:

> *The execution of the laws for the suppression of the African slave trade, has been confided to the Department of the Interior. It is a subject of gratulation that the efforts which have been made for the suppression of this inhuman traffic, have been recently attended with unusual success. Five vessels being fitted out for the slave trade have been seized and condemned. Two mates of vessels engaged in the trade, and one person in equipping a vessel as a slaver, have been convicted and subjected to the penalty of fine and imprisonment, and one captain, taken with a cargo of Africans on board his vessel, has been convicted of the highest grade of offence under our laws, the punishment of which is death.*[545]

In the very first year of his Presidency, Lincoln could point to the success of his policy to enforce more rigorously the laws against the slave trade.

The Confiscation Acts of 1861 and 1862

IN AUGUST OF 1861, Lincoln signed the First Confiscation Act which authorized the seizure of "property" being used in aid of the rebellion. Under this Act, the legal claims of "certain persons to the labor and service of certain other persons," as Lincoln put it, were forfeited as property being used for insurrectionary purposes.[546] The Act was intended to establish a uniform policy for the army with regard to slaves. Should slaves be considered contraband and, if so, should they be free? Or should they be returned to their owners as seemingly required by the Fugitive Slave Act? Using the circuitous language of persons "held to service," the Act made it clear that property, including persons "held to service," if used to assist the rebellion, was forfeited.

The First Confiscation Act did not explicitly emancipate slaves that reached Union lines. Nor did it make any provision for feeding or caring for the "forfeited property." Taking the next step, in his Annual Message to Congress on December 3, 1861, President Lincoln addressed these issues, calling for an appropriation and a declaration that such "persons" be deemed free.

This led to the Second Confiscation Act, which Congress passed on July 16, 1862. This Act provided that those supporting the insurrection who did not surrender within 60 days would be punished by having their slaves freed. The scope of this emancipation measure, however, was limited. The Act explicitly provided that fugitives from border States were to be returned to their owners if the owners could prove their loyalty to the Union.

Frémont's Blunder

THE FIRST MAJOR battle of the Civil War was the Battle of Bull Run which took place on July 21, 1861. However, the nation was quickly embroiled in a war being conducted in several theaters. Major General John C. Frémont, the former Presidential candidate, was the commander of the Army's Department of the West. Frémont ousted the pro-slavery governor of Missouri, installed a pro-Union regime and imposed martial law. He issued a proclamation that liberated *all slaves* in Missouri. President Lincoln wrote Frémont on September 2, 1861, asking him to rescind the order explaining that it might cause the border States such as Kentucky to side with the seceding States. (Lincoln supposedly said he *hoped* to have God on his side but he *had* to have Kentucky.[547]) In its place, he asked that Frémont issue an order that conformed to the (First) Confiscation Act of 1861 which confiscated property, including slaves, used to support the rebellion. Frémont refused and sent his wife to plead with the President. This was a blunder. President Lincoln then commanded Frémont to rescind the order as directed and relieved him of command.

Lincoln continued to be concerned about whether the border States would join the Confederacy throughout 1861. However, by December of 1861, he thought that the loyalty of the border States was more secure. He reported to Congress that after Fort Sumter "[t]he insurgents confidently claimed a strong support from north of Mason and Dixon's line; and the friends of the Union were not free from apprehension on that point. This, however, was soon settled definitely and on the right side."[548] He explained that the hostility to Union forces in Maryland had abated, an election there cemented the government to the pro-Union side and Maryland, Kentucky and Missouri, which had all originally refused to furnish soldiers, by December had provided 40,000 troops for the Union cause.

Another General who had to be reminded of the Chain-of-Command was David Hunter, who was the Major General commanding the military department of the south with jurisdiction over Georgia, Florida and South Carolina. General Hunter issued an order declaring all persons previously held as slaves in the three States free. The President countermanded that with a Proclamation on May 19, 1862 stating that General Hunter was not authorized to issue it and making it clear that as Commander-in-Chief it was his prerogative to determine whether and when to issue such an order. This was a policy decision as to whether such a measure was necessary to the maintenance of the government and not a matter for commanders in the field.

Recognizing Haiti and Liberia

IN A SEPARATE request in his first Annual Message to Congress, on December 3, 1861, President Lincoln asked that Congress recognize the independence of Hayti (sic) and Liberia. The South had opposed the recognition of Haiti for over 35 years. In 1826, John C. Calhoun, then Vice President under John Quincy Adams, objected to the recognition of Haiti and the idea that the United States would send and receive ministers from a Republic governed by freed slaves. Calhoun had asked; "What would be our social relations to a Black minister in Washington? ... Must his daughters and sons participate in the society of our daughters and sons?"[549]

President Lincoln not only asked that the two Republics be recognized, he asked for "an appropriation for maintaining a chargé d'affairs near each of these new states."[550]

In 1861, President Lincoln also directed that the indictment pending against Calvin DeWolf in Chicago for interfering with the recapture of a slave, as discussed above, be dismissed.

Suspending the Enforcement
of the Fugitive Slave Act

Consistent with the purpose of the Confiscation Acts, Congress passed "An Act to Make an Additional Article of War" which President Lincoln approved on March 13, 1862. This Act instructed the officers of the military services, the Army and the Navy, that they were "prohibited from employing any of the forces under their respective commands for the purpose of returning fugitives from service or labor, who may have escaped from any persons to whom such service or labor is claimed to be due…." Any violation was grounds for court martial. While this Act only established a military policy, it gutted enforcement of the Fugitive Slave Act.

Abolishing Slavery
in the District of Columbia

Lincoln had always believed that Congress had the authority to abolish slavery in the District of Columbia.[551] When he served in Congress he had resided near a warehouse he referred to as a Negro livery stable from which slaves were sold. The Compromise of 1850 had eliminated the slave trade in the District of Columbia so there were no more auction blocks or Negro livery stables when he lived in the White House. However, there were slaves living in the District as domestic servants or working as laborers. The "Act for the Release of Certain Persons Held to Service or Labor in the District of Columbia" that President Lincoln signed on April 16, 1862, emancipated these slaves and also included provisions for compensation and colonization.

Compensation was intended to reduce the friction with slave-owners who might be reluctant to allow their slaves to be emancipated. Colonization was aimed at reducing the objections of Northerners who were fearful of being overrun by that "unwanted population," freed slaves. (Lincoln's continued promotion of colonization has also been cited to support the view that he was a racist and not fully committed to abolishing slavery.)

The District of Columbia had become a city of refuge with a large free black population. The compensation system (which included a process by which dissatisfied slave owners could petition for relief) worked and became a model for future emancipation initiatives.

Abolishing Slavery
in the Territories

Defying the Dred Scott decision, the Republican platform in 1860 had asserted that Congress had the power to prohibit slavery in the Territories. In 1862, the Republicans in Congress passed a bill that did just that. President Lincoln signed it with great satisfaction. It provided:

That from and after the passage of this act, there shall be neither slavery nor involuntary servitude in any of the Territories of the United States now existing, or which may hereafter be formed or acquired by the United States, otherwise than in punishment of crime, whereof the party shall have been duly convicted.

The Republicans had finally enacted the principle of the Wilmot Proviso. However, in 1862, it did not apply just to Texas, Utah and New Mexico (including present day Arizona). The Union now included the territories of Colorado, Dakota and Nevada. The provision was passed in defiance of the Dred Scott decision which had not been reversed, overruled or supplanted by a Constitutional Amendment. The Republicans viewed that part of the Supreme Court's decision that said Congress did not have the power to prohibit slavery in the Territories as *obiter dicta*, an argument that Lincoln had made in the Lincoln-Douglas debates. In other words, the question had not been directly presented and ruled on in the Dred Scott case because the Court had no jurisdiction once it decided that Scott was not a citizen of a State diverse from Sanford, the man he sued. The Republicans were prepared to defend the new measure and the principle it embraced in the Supreme Court if there were a test. That never happened. The Dred Scott decision was rendered a nullity by the Thirteenth Amendment.

Exhausting the Peaceful Extinction of Slavery Option

IN 1855, SIX years before he became President and faced the task of setting the government's policy in response to secession and insurrection, Lincoln had expressed the view that there was no hope to eradicate slavery peacefully when he wrote George Robertson, the Kentucky lawyer who had represented the heirs of Robert Todd, Lincoln's father-in-law. Robertson had given Lincoln copies of his speeches and writings discussing slavery to which Lincoln responded as follows:

> *You are not a friend of slavery in the abstract. In that speech you spoke of the "peaceful extinction of slavery," and used other expressions indicating your belief that the thing was, at some time, to have an end. Since then we have had thirty-six years of experience, and this experience has demonstrated, I think, that there is no peaceful extinction of slavery in prospect for any of us.*[552]

Despite viewing "peaceful extinction" as a dismal prospect, as President, Lincoln pursued two policies – compensation and colonization – that sought to end slavery peacefully.

With regard to compensation, Lincoln had urged Congress by a special message dated March 6, 1861, to prod the States to adopt policies of gradual emancipation with compensation as an incentive. Congress did so and passed the following Resolution:

> Resolved, *That the United States ought to co-operate with any State which may adopt a gradual abolishment of slavery, giving to such State pecuniary aid, to be used by such State in its discretion to compensate for inconveniences, public and private produced by such change of system.*[553]

Aimed particularly at the border States, Lincoln was frustrated that this offer produced no takers. He pointed out that the cost of compensating slave owners paled in comparison to the cost of the war. He wrote James A. McDougall on March 14, 1862 pointing out that if $400 a head were paid for all the slaves in Delaware according to the last census, it would cost $719,200 which was less than the cost of a the war for half a day, which was $2,000,000.[554] He did the math for all the border States and concluded that freeing the slaves in all the border States and the District of Columbia would equal the cost of 87 days of the war ($174,000,000).

With regard to colonization, Lincoln's critics point to his efforts to promote colonization as evidence of his lack of commitment to emancipation and as evidence of his racism. Further, they argue that he was never committed to assuring equal rights for freed blacks. One critic has construed Lincoln's position to say that he was dreaming of an "all-white nation."[555] However, promoting colonization served another purpose. By advocating that freed slaves should be sent to Liberia or later Chiriqui (now a province of Panama), Lincoln made emancipation more palatable. He used colonization "to sweeten the pill of emancipation" for political opponents in the North and slave-holders in the border States.[556] Lincoln had to contend with the fact that there were members of his own party who were against emancipation and there were others in the North who strongly opposed the war. These were the Copperheads and Peace Democrats who would have settled the war on terms that preserved slavery. The most prominent Copperhead was former Congressman Clement L. Vallandigham who professed that the war was not being fought to save the Union but to free the blacks.

Lincoln had embraced colonization for many years. In his eulogy on Henry Clay in 1852 he lauded Clay who had been a slave-owner but also the President of the American Colonization Society. He quoted one of Clay's speeches to point out that colonization was not merely aimed at relieving slave-holders of the "troublesome presence" of freed slaves, but also was a meritorious policy because it offered to repatriate Africans with their ancestors where "they will carry back to their native soil the rich fruits of religion, civilization, law and liberty."[557] By 1854, he realized this was Pollyannaish when he gave his speech on the Kansas-Nebraska Act where he acknowledged the impracticality of sending freed slaves to Liberia:

My first impulse would be to free all the slaves and send them to Liberia, – to their own native land. But a moment's reflection would convince me that … its sudden execution is impossible. If they were all landed there in a day, they would all perish in the next ten days…

Nevertheless, Lincoln continued to hold out colonization as the avenue for dealing with freed slaves and quoted the Kansas-Nebraska speech passage in his reply to Douglas in their first debate on August 21, 1858. This was part of his answer to Douglas who charged Lincoln with favoring Negro equality.

It is important to recognize that the American Colonization Society supported *voluntary* colonization. When Lincoln promoted colonization, he was promoting voluntary emigration. In other words, blacks that chose to go to Liberia would be furnished the means to get there. He did not advocate forcible removal of freed blacks.

In the first year of his Presidency, in October of 1861, Lincoln directed the Secretary of the Department of the Interior, Caleb B. Smith, to investigate the feasibility of settling free blacks in Central America on the isthmus of Chiriqui.[558] In his first Annual Message, he asked Congress for funds to support colonization. He explained that this would ameliorate the burden of caring for slaves freed under the First Confiscation Act, it would be an incentive to States considering voluntary gradual emancipation, and it could be promoted to free colored people already in the United States, "so far as individuals may desire, [to] be included in such colonization."[559] He suggested acquiring new territory for this purpose. Congress responded by appropriating funds. Recognizing that Liberia had failed to attract many freed slaves, Congress authorized acquiring territory in the Western Hemisphere (*i.e.*, Chiriqui). This led to appropriations that totaled $600,000. Lincoln signed contracts with a promoter who supposedly would organize a colony on Chiriqui. The effort to colonize Chiriqui fizzled when Central American countries objected to any colonization without a treaty.

Colonization met with opposition in Congress, from abolitionists, and from free blacks. However, the Preliminary Emancipation Proclamation continued to couple emancipation with colonization. President Lincoln stated that he would "continue the effort to colonize persons of African descent, with their consent, upon this continent, or elsewhere, with the previously obtained consent of the Governments existing there…."[560] Colonization had become a will o' the wisp. It was never an effectual policy. Lincoln's appraisal in his December 1, 1862 Annual Message to Congress was that freed slaves had no interest in going to Liberia or Haiti.[561] The explanation that it was promoted for political reasons to appease opponents of emancipation would appear to be more likely to be true than a supposed motivation to deport freed slaves to create an all-white nation. Lincoln needed to exhaust the peaceful extinction options and he did so.

Arming the Slaves – Cameron Rebuked

SIMON CAMERON WAS President Lincoln's first Secretary of War. He served in that capacity for only ten months. When Lincoln issued the call for 75,000 voluntary troops, it became Cameron's responsibility to equip them and provide transportation. Undistracted by hopes of a peaceful resolution to the conflict, he pursued an aggressive policy to prepare the country for war. He did not enjoy the unalloyed support of his fellow Cabinet members.

One problem that faced military commanders was what to do with the slaves that came under their control by virtue of the First Confiscation Act. As they were employed to build defensive works, they often worked at exposed points. Military commanders were given instructions to "employ such persons in such service as they may be fitted for – either as ordinary employees, or if special circumstances seem to require it, in any other capacity, with such organization (in squads, companies, or otherwise) as you may deem most beneficial to the service." President Lincoln, when he saw this order, added: "This, however, is not to mean a general arming of them for military service."[562]

When President Lincoln submitted his first annual report to Congress, it was accompanied by the usual reports from the Cabinet officers. Cameron's report had been printed and mailed to postmasters to be released as soon as the telegraph should announce the reading of the President's report. In the closing paragraphs, the report advocated arming the slaves and using them in the military:

> Those who make war against the Government justly forfeit all rights of property, privilege, or security derived from the Constitution and laws against which they are in armed rebellion; and as the labor and service of their slaves constitute the chief property of the rebels, such property should share the common fate of war…. It is as clearly a right of the Government to arm slaves, when it may become necessary, as it is to use gunpowder taken from the enemy…. If it shall be found that the men who have been held as slaves are capable of bearing arms and performing efficient military service, it is the right, and may become the duty, of the Government to arm and equip them, and employ their services against the rebels….[563]

Arming the slaves and organizing them into military units was beyond where President Lincoln was and he was certainly not prepared to issue a public announcement embracing such a policy in December of 1861. The reports were recalled and a new final paragraph substituted.[564] Recognizing the difficult position he had put the President in and to avoid further embarrassment, Cameron offered to resign.

In January the President wrote him to accept his resignation as Secretary of War and to appoint him to be Minister to Russia:

> MY DEAR SIR:
>
> As you have more than once expressed a desire for a change of position, I can now gratify you, consistently with my view of the public interest. I therefore propose nominating you to the Senate, next Monday, as Minister to Russia.
>
> Very sincerely, your friend,
> A. Lincoln[565]

In late 1861 and early 1862 Lincoln was still worried about whether the border States might bolt to the South and about fueling the rhetoric of political opponents in the North. He could not afford to antagonize them. Lincoln appointed Cameron's chief aide, Edwin M. Stanton, in his stead not realizing that it was Stanton who had actually drafted the offending passage. Later in the war, Lincoln adopted the policy Cameron (and Stanton) had advocated.

Of course, citing the employment of slaves in the army as the precipitating cause for Cameron's resignation takes the view of Cameron's admirers. Cameron had his share of detractors. Other cabinet members opposed him and his chief detractor was Thaddeus Stevens, a powerful Congressman and rival from Pennsylvania who chaired the House Ways and Means Committee, the committee that funded the Civil War. Stevens attacked Cameron as corrupt, pointing to deals Cameron made that favored railroads he owned. Stevens told Lincoln that "the only thing Cameron wouldn't steal was a *red hot stove.*" This comment got back to Cameron's friends and Stevens was called on to apologize. Stevens went to Lincoln and said, "I have been asked to apologize for what I said about General Cameron. I believe I said that the only thing he wouldn't steal was a red hot stove.... *I take it back.*"[566]

After being appointed to be Minister to Russia, Cameron went to St. Petersburg, met Czar Alexander II, and congratulated him for his March 3, 1861 decree freeing the serfs, an extraordinarily progressive measure in Czarist Russia. He told the Czar that Lincoln would soon free the slaves. Cameron succeeded in establishing warm relations with Russia. Russia's friendship with the United States was a significant factor influencing England and France not to recognize the Confederacy. (Czar Alexander was assassinated by a bomb in 1881.)

When Cameron became Minister to Russia, the person he replaced was Cassius M. Clay, who had been appointed to that post in April of 1861. Clay was an abolitionist of long standing, a leader of the Republican Party in Kentucky, and a veteran of the Mexican War. Clay came back from Russia to accept a commission as a general. However, he soon resigned to protest the failure to proclaim the slaves in the Southern States free. Lincoln had promised him he could have the Ministry to Russia position back if Cameron resigned. When Cameron resigned, Clay returned to Russia in 1862 and served in that capacity until 1869.

An Insurrection or a War?

PRESIDENT LINCOLN TOOK care to term the acts of the seceding States as an "insurrection" and not a "war." There were two reasons for being precise about this terminology. First there was the question of what authority did the President have to call out the Army or the Militia? Second there was the question of what status should the seceding States have as a matter of international law?

When President Lincoln issued the call for 75,000 voluntary troops on April 15, 1861, he did so without any express Congressional authorization. Congress was not in session. Here is the Constitutional problem the President faced. One of the hallmarks of the form of government established by our Constitution is the separation of powers. The Constitution, in Article I, allocated to Congress the following powers:

> *To declare War ....;*
> > *To raise and support Armies....;*
> > *To provide and maintain a Navy;*
> > *To make Rules for the Government and Regulation of the land and naval Forces;*
> > *To provide for calling forth the Militia to execute the Laws of the Union, suppress Insurrections and repel Invasions;*
> > *To provide for organizing, arming, and disciplining, the Militia....*[567]

The Constitution, in Article II, allocated to the President the following powers:

> *The President shall be Commander-in-Chief of the Army and Navy of the United States, and of the Militia of the several States, when called into the actual service of the United States....*[568]
> > *[H]e shall take Care that the Laws be faithfully executed....*[569]

The Constitution, in Article IV, also guaranteed the States a republican form of government:

The United States shall guarantee to every State in this Union a Republican Form of Government, and shall protect each of them against Invasion; and on Application of the Legislature, or of the Executive (when the Legislature cannot be convened) against domestic violence.[570]

Thus, under the Constitution's scheme of the separation of powers, there was no express grant of power to the President to call out the militia under the circumstances he faced. (While he could act without authorization from Congress, to protect States against domestic violence, those conditions did not appear to exist.) President Lincoln chose to describe the rebellion as an insurrection and to *assume* the implied power to act when Congress was not in session. Fortunately, a Constitutional crisis was averted when Congress ratified all of his actions on August 6, 1861 which made valid all acts, proclamations and orders issued by the President after March 4, 1861.

President Lincoln also implemented a blockade on April 27 and 30, 1861. Under the blockade several ships were captured and brought as prizes to ports under control of Union forces. The Supreme Court was asked to decide the legality of the blockade as to four of the ships (*The Brig Amy Warwick; The Schooner Crenshaw; The Barque Hiawatha;* and *The Schooner Brilliante*) testing the legality of the President's actions. Because Congress had never declared war and a blockade was a measure that could only be recognized when there was a state of war, the ship owners claimed the capture of their ships was illegal. Though the cases were not decided until March 10, 1863, the Court upheld the exercise of power and explained its reasoning as follows:

If a war be made by invasion of a foreign nation, the President is not only authorized but bound to resist force by force. He does not initiate the war, but is bound to accept the challenge without waiting for any special legislative authority. And whether the hostile party be a foreign invader, or States organized in rebellion, it is none the less a war, although the declaration of it be "unilateral."[571]

This validated the power that President Lincoln had exercised. However, had the White House not been occupied by Lincoln, a Commander-in-Chief who saw his duty to meet force with force, the seceding States might have succeeded in their attempt to establish a separate and independent republic. So, the abolition of slavery is due in no small part to Lincoln's view of the Constitution and the war powers he assumed believing they were implied in the Constitution.

With regard to the blockade, the Supreme Court recognized that a belligerent, engaged in war, has a right to blockade the ports of its adversary. Neutral countries are bound to respect the blockade. Where a vessel of an adversary or a neutral violates the blockade, it can be captured and taken as prize. Looking at the factual record in each instance, the Supreme Court upheld the determinations of the courts below that all of the vessels in question were validly taken pursuant to the blockade. The ships owned by citizens of the Southern States were owned by persons residing in territory occupied by the hostile party and properly treated as enemies. The one ship owned by a Mexican citizen (*The Brilliante*) was a ship owned by a neutral on notice of the blockade and also properly taken when it sought to run the blockade. The war between the United States and the "so-called Confederate States," was a civil war, giving the President the right to proclaim a blockade to the same extent as if the country were engaged in a foreign war.

The Trent *Affair –*
Keeping the Lion at Bay

THE BRITISH WERE watching the Civil War unfold with great interest. Cassius Clay's view of the British position was that, "They hope for our ruin."[572] Great Britain's mills depended on cotton and a blockade of the Southern ports was an irritation. Jefferson Davis thought that Great Britain would recognize the Confederacy because of its need to get cotton. Great Britain had abolished slavery in 1833. The fact that the war was not being fought to end slavery (prior to January 1, 1863) deprived the United States of the high moral ground.

President Lincoln had taken care to refer to the actions of the seceding States as an "insurrection." If the Confederate States were recognized as a foreign nation by other nations, then the Confederacy might enlist support from governments, be able to purchase arms, commission the building of ships, seek alliances, and enlist foreign allies to help break the blockade.

On May 13, 1861, Britain issued a declaration of neutrality. This had the effect of recognizing the Confederate States as belligerents and meant that ships of the Confederacy could use British ports around the world to refuel and re-equip, though British citizens were prohibited from equipping ships for military use. Secretary of State William Seward sent instructions to Charles Francis Adams, the United States Minister to Great Britain, to protest this action which the United States saw as a first step to full recognition. France, the Netherlands, Spain and Brazil followed Great Britain's lead. President Lincoln and his Cabinet all believed that if the European nations intervened in the Civil War it would doom the effort to preserve the Union.

In August of 1861, Jefferson Davis appointed new ministers to represent the Confederacy in Europe. These were John Slidell of Louisiana and James Mason of Virginia. Their appointment was well known and the first problem Slidell and Mason had was getting to Europe in light of the blockade. On October 1, they were in Charleston looking for a ship to run the blockade. On October 12, they succeeded, eluding the blockade on *The Theodora*. They were trying to connect to a British ship to take them to England and proceeded to Havana, Cuba where a British ship, the *RMS Trent*, was expected.

Charles Wilkes, Captain of the *U.S.S. San Jacinto* learned of their whereabouts and determined to intercept the *Trent*. On November 8th, Wilkes intercepted the *Trent*, fired two shots across her bow, boarded and took Slidell and Mason prisoner. The *Trent* was allowed to proceed on its way absent the two passengers.

The initial reaction to the capture of Slidell and Mason in the United States was euphoric. Wilkes was proclaimed a hero. But the legal justification for intercepting a British ship at sea and removing two passengers was dubious. Upon reflection President Lincoln realized that the United States could not violate the neutrality of Great Britain by boarding her ships and taking prisoners, conduct very like that objected to in the Declaration of Independence where the colonists listed their grievances with the King.

The British were incensed and considered the *Trent* affair an insult to the country. Dispatches were prepared to be sent to Lord Lyons, the Minister of Great Britain to the United States. Britain demanded release of the envoys and an apology. There were some in Great Britain who thought that the United States was deliberately provoking Great Britain and urged the country to prepare for war. On June 14, Lord Lyons sent a letter to Sir Alexander Milne, the British commander for the North American station to be prepared for the possibility of a declaration of war by the United States against Great Britain. Milne wrote the Admiralty and asked for reinforcements.

Seward had sent a dispatch to Adams on November 30 that reached Adams on December 17th. Seward told Adams to tell the British that Captain Wilkes had acted without orders. This qualification set the stage for a diplomatic resolution. In the United States when Lord Lyons delivered the official British demand, the Cabinet met to determine what response to make. Seward wrote out a response that announced the release of Slidell and Mason, reiterated that Captain Wilkes acted without orders but included no apology. This resolved the crisis. Slidell and Mason were sent on their way. Though they reached England, they did not succeed in their mission to obtain recognition for the Confederacy.

The Lyons-Seward Treaty

SEWARD HAD SEVERAL strategies for persuading Great Britain not to grant full diplomatic recognition to the Confederate States. Adams was told to tell the British that recognition would be considered an unfriendly act and that Great Britain should recognize the danger of recognition in light of her own far flung possessions and a homeland that included Scotland and Ireland.

There was also an opportunity to engender sympathy for the North by joining with Great Britain to strengthen the enforcement of both nations' ban on the international slave trade. Great Britain had banned the slave trade in 1807 and entered into treaties with a number of countries prohibiting the international slave trade. The United States had entered into an earlier treaty with Great Britain, the Webster-Ashburton Treaty of 1842, calling for an end to the slave trade and committing both parties to enforcement of the treaty. Starting in 1843, the United States had stationed ships, the Africa Squadron, on the west coast of Africa to protect U.S. shipping and suppress the slave trade. When slavers were interdicted and captives freed, the United States sent them to Liberia which had been established by the American Colonialization Society in 1817.

When President Lincoln imposed the blockade of Southern ports, the Navy moved ships from the Africa Squadron making it difficult for the United States to continue to meet its obligations under the Webster-Ashburton Treaty. Other countries had treaties with Great Britain that allowed the British warships to stop and inspect their ships. The United States had refused to give the British that authority. Now Secretary Seward had two reasons to do so.

The treaty he negotiated, known as the Lyons-Seward Treaty, gave mutual rights of search and established procedures for adjudicating the legitimacy of seizures.

Lincoln Appoints Dr. Dyer to Be a Judge

ON APRIL 10, 1862, President Lincoln sent to the Senate for its consideration and ratification the Treaty between the United States and her Britannic Majesty for the Suppression of the Slave Trade (the Lyons-Seward Treaty).[573] On April 24, 1862, Secretary of State Seward wrote President Lincoln to congratulate him on the Senate's unanimous ratification of the Treaty to End the African Slave Trade. This treaty gave special instructions to the navies of the two countries to "visit" merchant vessels of the two countries suspected of engaging in the African Slave trade or being fitted out for that purpose. Such vessels were to be detained and "brought to trial" before a special tribunal, the Mixed Court for the Suppression of the African Slave Trade. The court was to judge whether a vessel was properly detained and there was no appeal from its decision. President Lincoln told Congress that this would bring the "odious traffic" in African slaves to an end.[574]

On February 19, 1863, Lincoln wrote Seward to nominate Dr. Charles V. Dyer of Chicago to serve as the representative of the United States on the court to be convened in Sierra Leone. In his letter to Seward, Lincoln said that he had been asked by I.N. Arnold to nominate Dr. Dyer but went on to say: "I also know Dr. Dyer and believe him to be a proper man. Please send me a paper ... nominating Dr. Dyer."[575] Dr. Dyer wrote to accept on March 5, 1863 "for judge on the part of the United States at Sierra Leone under the Treaty with Her Brittanic Majesty of the 7th of April, last, for the Suppression of the African Slave Trade...." Later when Dr. Dyer saw the President, Lincoln said to him that "it was a great pleasure to appoint an old abolitionist to office."[576]

Toward the end of his long career as an abolitionist, Dr. Charles Volney Dyer was appointed by Lincoln to serve as U. S. representative to the Court at Sierra Leone under a Treaty with Her Britannic Majesty for the Suppression of the African Slave Trade. (Chicago History Museum)

in Washington as the events of the Civil War unfolded. When he was not sent back to Congress after his term, Lincoln appointed him to a position in the Treasury Department where he served until 1866. Other Illinois Republicans who served in the Lincoln Administration or received appointments from President Lincoln included: David Davis who was nominated to the Supreme Court, and Chicagoans Gustave Koerner who served as Minister of Spain, Norman Judd who served as Minister to Berlin, Zebina Eastman who was U.S. Consul to Bristol, England, Alan Pinkerton who ran the Union Intelligence Service, and Dr. Leib who became an assistant quartermaster for the Army.[577]

There were other close personal friends who sought positions and were disappointed: Leonard Swett did not get a major appointment but served as a mediator to handle a dispute overseen by the Department of the Interior. Orville Browning hoped to be appointed to the Supreme Court but lost out to Davis. However, Browning was appointed to fill the Senate seat vacated by Stephen Douglas's death, by Illinois Republican Governor Yates.

Dr. Dyer Goes to Africa

I N 1863, D R. Dyer traveled with his family to Sierra Leone to serve on the Mixed Court for the Suppression of the African Slave Trade, the tribunal to which he had been appointed by President Lincoln. During that trip, he attended a Fourth of July dinner at Tenerife, one of the larger Canary Islands off the coast of Africa. Several British officers had been invited. There was some tension in the air because, as everyone knew, Great Britain had been exhibiting some sympathy for the Confederate cause. The doctor had been asked to make the toast, "The President of the United States" followed by some appropriate remarks. One of the British officers sitting nearby interrupted with several snide remarks, such as, "Vicksburg isn't taken yet," etc. When the same officer was asked to respond to the Americans, he stood and made the

Republicans from Illinois Serving the Lincoln Administration

W HO WAS THIS I.N. Arnold that Lincoln was obliging? He was, of course, Isaac Newton Arnold, the Illinois Republican who had addressed the Cameron-Lincoln Club, supported Lincoln at the Convention in the Wigwam, and who had been elected to Congress to represent Chicago in 1860, in the same election in which Lincoln won the Presidency. Arnold was an intimate friend of Lincoln's, one of the people who spent time with him formal toast: "The Queen of England," which he followed with: "the sun never sets on her dominions!" Dr. Dyer was heard to say in a low voice, "Because the Lord can't trust an Englishman in the dark."[578]

Dr. Dyer was known for his quick wit. It was said that he had an uncommon fondness for "fictitious literature," that his conversation was "enriched by the choicest gems of poetry" and that "his anecdotes were always to the point," enlivened by wit and humor.[579]

On another occasion, after he was appointed to the Mixed Court, a neighbor known for his Kentucky leanings accosted him and said: "Why do you go to Africa at your time of life? Can't you get enough nigger in America?" To which the doctor replied without hesitating: "I have been looking all my life for a Negro without any Kentucky blood in him, and I am obliged to go to Africa to find one."[580]

Lincoln's Reply to Greeley

IN 1862, LINCOLN was under pressure to issue an emancipation proclamation. On August 19, 1862, Horace Greeley, publisher of the *New York Tribune*, wrote an editorial urging a proclamation:

> *I do not intrude to tell you – for you must know already – that a great proportion of those who triumphed in your election, and of all who desire the unqualified suppression of the rebellion now desolating our country, are sorely disappointed and deeply pained by the policy you seem to be pursuing with regard to the slaves of the Rebels.*[581]

President Lincoln responded saying that there should be no doubt as to his policy:

> *I would save the Union. I would save it the shortest way under the Constitution. The sooner the national authority can be restored; the nearer the Union will be "the Union as it was." If there be those that would not save the Union, unless they could at the same time*

save slavery, *I do not agree with them. If there be those that would not save the Union, unless they could at the same time* destroy *slavery, I do not agree with them. My paramount objective in this struggle* is *to save the Union, and is* not *either to save or destroy slavery. If I could save the Union without freeing any* slave *I would do it, and if I could save it by freeing* all the slaves *I would do it; and if I could save it by freeing some and leaving others alone, I would also do that. What I do about slavery, and the colored race, I do because I believe it helps to save the Union; and what I forbear, I forbear because I do not believe it would help to save the Union. I shall do* less *whenever I shall believe what I am doing hurts the cause, and I shall do* more *whenever I shall believe doing more will help the cause. I shall try to correct errors when shown to be errors; and I shall adopt new views so fast as they shall appear to be true views.*

> *I have here stated my purpose according to my view of* official *duty; and I intend no modification of my oft-expressed* personal *wish that all men every where could be free.*[582]

This letter provides the strongest evidence that the critics of Lincoln's emancipation policy have. It harkens back to Lincoln's initial policy as stated in his first inaugural address which offered to continue the Union with slavery if the seceding States recanted. Remarkably, the letter to Greeley does not even acknowledge the Confiscation Acts which had already changed the landscape and proclaimed slaves of the rebels to be free. Was Lincoln still wrestling with whether to issue a broader proclamation of emancipation? Or was he merely reminding Greeley and his readers of the fact that the only basis for acting on emancipation in light of the Constitution's acceptance of slavery would be as a military expediency? That would require him to determine that issuing such a proclamation would "help the cause."

Lincoln had already discussed issuing an emancipation proclamation with his Cabinet a month before. He would issue the Preliminary Emancipation on September 22, 1862, just one month after the Greeley letter. The letter to Greeley may have been intended to buy Lincoln time.

Timing – The Reply to the Chicago Emancipation Memorial

ANOTHER INSIGHT INTO what President Lincoln was thinking is in his "Reply to the Chicago Emancipation Memorial" remarks, made to a group of Chicago ministers on September 13th, in the interval between the letter to Greeley and the issuance of the Preliminary Emancipation Proclamation. The ministers had met earlier, on September 7, 1862, in Chicago and appointed a delegation to meet with the President and present a memorial from Christians of all denominations in Chicago in favor of national emancipation. The delegation met with the President on the 13th and returned to Chicago and reported the substance of their interview at a meeting held in Bryan Hall on Sunday, September 21, 1862.[583]

The President told the delegation that the "subject presented in the memorial is one upon which I have thought much for weeks past…." The President could not resist teasing the righteousness of the ministers:

> *I am approached by the most opposite opinions and advice, and that by religious men, who are equally certain they represent the Divine will. I am sure that either one or the other class is mistaken in that belief, and perhaps in some respect both. I hope it will not be irreverent for me to say that if it is probable that God would reveal his will to others, on a point so connected with my duty, it might be supposed he would reveal it directly to me; for unless I am more deceived in myself than I often am, it is my earnest desire to know the will of Providence in this matter.* And if I can learn what it is I will do it! *These are not, however, the days of miracles, and I suppose it will be granted that that I am not to expect a direct revelation.*[584]

In explaining why he had not yet issued an emancipation proclamation, Lincoln got to the crux of the matter: "What *good* would a proclamation of emancipation from me do?" He said he did not want to issue a document that the world would see as "inoperative." He made it clear that he was confident that as Commander-in-Chief, in time of war, he had the authority to "take any measure which may best subdue the enemy." He explained that he viewed whether to issue such a proclamation as a war measure "to be decided upon according to the advantages or disadvantages it may offer to the suppression of the rebellion."[585] "What good would it do?" also pointed out that the Union was then perceived as unsuccessful in its military campaigns. President Lincoln and his Cabinet did not want to issue a proclamation and adopt a policy that would appear to be issued out of desperation.

In the course of their discussion, the President observed that "slavery is the root of the rebellion, or at least its *sine qua non*. The ambition of politicians may have instigated them to act, but they would have been impotent without slavery as their instrument."[586] This revealed that, whether and when to issue an emancipation proclamation involved not just a question of military expediency, but also of justice and morality. The Chicago delegation explored these dimensions with him.

The delegation met with the President for over an hour and engaged in an exchange reviewing the reasons for and the possible objections to such a proclamation. The ministers put forth the case for issuing the proclamation: they defended the religious basis for the memorial saying that the Bible denounced oppression as the "highest of crimes," they argued that it would secure the sympathy of Europe and remove the threat of foreign intervention, they argued that it would draw the slaves to the Union, and they assured the President that it would galvanize opinion in the North in favor of the Union's cause. The President agreed with some of these arguments but recited some of the objections he was wrestling with. What would the Union do with more slaves coming into our lines? There were "fifty thousand bayonets" from the boarder States in the Army, would they defect to the other side?

In answer to what should be done with the slaves, the delegation criticized the "half measures" of the current policy under the Confiscation Acts. They advocated arming the slaves:

> *It is folly merely to feed and receive the slaves. They should be welcomed and fed, and then, according to Paul's doctrine, that they who eat must work, be made to labor and to fight for their liberty and ours. With such a policy the blacks would be no encumbrance and their rations no waste. In this respect we should follow the ancient maxim, and learn from the enemy. What the rebels most fear is what we should be most prompt to do; and what they most fear is evident from the hot haste with which, on the first day of the present session of the Rebel Congress, bills were introduced threatening terrible vengeance if we used the blacks in the war.[587]*

The delegation also had an answer to the concern that boarder State troops might defect. If they do, they will be easily replaced by troops from other Northern States reinvigorated in the cause: "[A] proclamation of general emancipation, 'giving Liberty and Union' as the national watch-word, would rouse the people and rally them to his support beyond any thing yet witnessed – appealing alike to conscience, sentiment, and hope."[588]

In closing the interview, the President cautioned the delegation not to construe his recitation of objections to suggest he had decided against a proclamation. He assured them he held the matter under advisement. He simply wanted them to recognize some of the difficulties he faced.

What role did the Chicago delegation play in the emancipation process? There were probably many advisers urging Lincoln to do one thing or the other with regard to freeing the slaves. The Chicagoans may have helped the President think through the "difficulties" and reach a resolution. The Emancipation Proclamation that the President issued certainly met all of their wishes.

The Emancipation Proclamation

ON SEPTEMBER 17 and 18, 1862, Union forces stopped the advance of Robert E. Lee's army in the Battle of Antietam. This provided Lincoln with a sufficient claim of a Union victory and allowed him to issue the Preliminary Emancipation. This document announced a policy that would go into effect in the future, January 1, 1863. It provided that if any Slave State ceased hostilities and adopted a program of gradual emancipation, that the federal government would provide funding to accomplish that emancipation. If, after January 1, the States were still in rebellion, then all persons held as slaves within any such State would thenceforth be free. The Proclamation reiterated an intention to offer voluntary colonization to freed slaves "with their consent."

Needless to say, no State accepted the offer to cease hostilities and adopt a policy of gradual emancipation. Thus, on January 1, 1863, the Final Emancipation Proclamation was issued which recited the conditions of the Preliminary Proclamation and identified the States still in rebellion. It then declared all persons held as slaves in those States forever free.

The President also addressed the issue of arming the slaves and explicitly approved employing freed slaves in the Army:

> *And I further declare and make known, that such persons of suitable condition, will be received into the armed service of the United States to garrison forts, positions, stations, and other places, and to man vessels of all sorts in said service.[589]*

Thus, as of January 1, 1863, the United States was committed to freeing the slaves in the States in rebellion. Though the boarder States were excluded, slavery was now much further down the road to its ultimate extinction (though it would require the North to win the war).

ICHI - 59557

On January 1, 1863, as the nation approached the third year
of Civil War, Lincoln issued the Emancipation Proclamation,
declaring that all slaves held within designated states
"henceforth shall be free." (Chicago History Museum)

The road to the ultimate extinction of slavery was not without twists and turns. In between the Preliminary and Final Emancipation Proclamations, the President on December 1, 1862, delivered his Annual Message to Congress in which he proposed an alternative emancipation program. If the seceding States were to recant, cease hostilities and adopt a voluntary program of gradual emancipation, Congress should provide compensation. How long a period did the gradual emancipation have to be? The legislation he proposed asked that the gradual emancipation adopted occur between 1863 and 1900. In other words, Lincoln would have accepted 37 more years of slavery in return for ending the war and bringing slavery to an end. He reasoned that the cost of the war more than justified this offer.

Arming the Slaves

THE (SECOND) CONFISCATION Act of July 17, 1862 authorized commanders to enlist fugitive slaves for any purpose. However, it was the Emancipation Proclamation that authorized arming the slaves and using them in combat. In January of 1863, Governor John Andrew of Massachusetts obtained permission to raise a regiment of African-American soldiers. (This is the subject of the movie *Glory*.) On May 22, 1863, the War Department issued General Order 143 which organized the Bureau of Colored Troops. According to the U.S. National Archives & Records Administration, the United States Colored Troops numbered 185,000 (including officers, who were not African-American). This was approximately 10 percent of all troops.

The black regiments saw action almost immediately, notably at Port Hudson, Louisiana in May of 1863 and Fort Wagner, South Carolina in July of 1863. They then appeared in most battles throughout 1864 and 1865.

President Lincoln viewed the use of colored troops as delivering a heavy blow to the Confederates. In the letter he wrote, on August 26, 1863, to James C.

Conkling defending the issuance of the Emancipation Proclamation, he described the contribution of the colored troops as follows:

> [S]ome of the commanders of our armies in the field who have given us our most important successes, believe the emancipation policy, and the use of colored troops, constitute the heaviest blow yet dealt to the rebellion, and that at least one of those important successes, could not have been achieved when it was, but for the aid of black soldiers.[590]

Conkling had apparently written to Lincoln to say that he would not fight to free Negroes. Lincoln's rejoinder: "Some of them seem willing to fight for you." Lincoln made it clear there was no turning back. Lincoln asked "Why should they do anything for us?" Answering this question, he said: If they stake their lives for us, they must be prompted by the strongest motive – even the promise of freedom. And the promise being made, must be kept."[591]

President Lincoln reiterated this commitment in remarks to two Wisconsin politicians, Alexander Randall and Joseph Mills:

> There are men base enough to propose to me to return to slavery our black warriors of Port Hudson and Olustee, and thus win the respect of the masters they fought. Should I do so, I would deserve to be damned in time and eternity. Come what may, I will keep faith with the black man.... No human power can subdue the rebellion without the emancipation policy.... I will abide the issue.[592]

Thirteenth Amendment

RECOGNIZING THAT "THE original proclamation has no constitutional or legal justification, except as a military measure," with
the end of the war in sight, President Lincoln wanted
to make certain that slavery would not be resusci-
tated in the South and that it would be extinguished
in the boarder States.[593] When the time for the 1864
Presidential election approached, the Republicans
joined with War Democrats to form a "Union Party"
with Lincoln and Andrew Johnson as its candidates.
In addition to taking an uncompromising position on
winning the war, Lincoln insisted that this Party make
abolishing slavery universally part of its platform. It
did with the following platform plank:

*Resolved, That as slavery was the cause, and now con-
stitutes the strength of this Rebellion, and as it must
be, always and everywhere, hostile to the principles of
Republican Government, justice and the National safety
demand its utter and complete extirpation from the soil of
the Republic; and that, while we uphold and maintain
the acts and proclamations by which the Government, in
its own defense, has aimed a deathblow at this gigantic
evil, we are in favor, furthermore, of such an amendment
to the Constitution, to be made by the people in confor-
mity with its provisions, as shall terminate and forever
prohibit the existence of Slavery within the limits of the
jurisdiction of the United States.*

The Democrat's platform declared the attempt to
restore the Union "by the experiment of war" a failure
and promised to convene a convention of the States to
bring hostilities to a stop and achieve peace. The nation
had a stark choice.

Lincoln was re-elected and then pressed Congress
to adopt the Thirteenth Amendment and send it
to the States for ratification. He succeeded after a
battle in Congress to get enough votes. According to
Charles A. Dana, Lincoln engineered the admission
of Nevada as a State to tip the balance. Dana quoted

Lincoln as saying: "It is easier to admit Nevada than
to raise another million soldiers."[594] The language of
the Amendment was patterned after the Northwest
Ordinance:

*Neither slavery nor involuntary servitude, except as
punishment for crime whereof the party shall have been
duly convicted, shall exist within the United States, or
any place subject to their jurisdiction.*

Illinois was the first State to ratify the Thirteenth
Amendment on February 1, 1865.

The Persistence of Racism – Nelson v. Illinois

LINCOLN WON RE-ELECTION with a vote
of 2,218,388 to McClellan's 1,812,807. The
electoral vote was 212 to 21. Illinois was solidly
in Lincoln's column. But while Illinois approved of
Lincoln and the Republican Platform which called for
an Amendment to the Constitution to abolish slavery
for good, it did not mean that the citizens of Illinois
had changed their views about welcoming blacks into
the State.

In 1864, the Illinois Supreme Court decided the
case of *Nelson v. Illinois*.[595] Nelson, a mulatto, was prosecuted under the Act of 1853 that prohibited Negroes
and Mulattoes from emigrating into Illinois. The Act
provided that if any Negro or Mulatto came into the
State and remained for 10 days or longer, he shall be
deemed guilty of a high misdemeanor and fined. If he
were unable to pay the fine the sheriff was commanded
to sell him to the highest bidder who would pay his fine
and costs.

When the case came before the Illinois Supreme
Court, the Thirteenth Amendment had not yet been
adopted. However, Nelson's attorneys argued that the
provision in the Illinois Constitution outlawing slavery
prohibited the penalty imposed. Like the Thirteenth
Amendment, the Illinois provision stated that "there

Created by Augustus Saint-Gaudens in 1887, this Chicago Landmark is one of the city's oldest public sculptures and is widely considered the most significant 19th Century sculpture of Abraham Lincoln. (Private Collection)

in, this State as an offense, and has declared the punishment. The courts are not authorized to say that such an act is not a crime.[596]

Nelson's attorneys also argued that the punishment violated Article IV of the United States Constitution which guarantees the citizens of each State the privileges and immunities of citizens of the several States. Echoing the Dred Scott decision, the Illinois Supreme Court dismissed this claim saying: "[T]his record contains no evidence that the plaintiff in error [Nelson] is a citizen of any State."

The Court explained that its reasoning for affirming was the precedent of *Eells v. The People*, the conviction of Dr. Eells for harboring a runaway slave. If the State can prevent the introduction of Negro slaves and punish those who introduce them (Eells), it can punish the slaves (Nelson) coming into the State.[597] Nelson's attorneys also made the creative argument that the Illinois provision conflicted with the Fugitive Slave Act because it prevented slave-owners from recovering their property. The Illinois Supreme Court decided it did not need to reach this issue since no master had stepped forward to reclaim his slave.

Thus, in 1864, when slavery was being hastened down the road to its ultimate extinction, Illinois, by judicial decree, sold Nelson, a fugitive slave who entered Illinois to seek refuge, into servitude.

shall be neither slavery nor involuntary servitude in this State, except as punishment for crime whereof the party shall have been duly convicted." The Court decided that Nelson had been convicted of a crime and the prohibition on slavery in the Illinois Constitution did not apply:

> *[A] State has the power to define offenses and prescribe the punishment, and the exercise of such powers cannot be inquired into by a court of justice. In the rightful exercise of this power, the legislature has declared the emigration of persons of color to, and their settlement*

Why Was Lincoln Assassinated?

THE ACTIONS THAT Lincoln took after being elected President as recounted above show that he was an enemy of slavery. The States that seceded reached this conclusion before the war. The case for labeling him an "accidental emancipator" does not withstand examination. The evidence that Lincoln was an enemy of slavery and led the nation to abolish slavery outweighs the case for the accidental emancipator thesis. One final piece of evidence should be added to this proof. Why was Lincoln assassinated?

John Wilkes Booth wrote a "To Whom It May Concern" letter in 1864 which he left in a sealed envelope for his brother-in-law, J.S. Clarke. Clarke opened the letter after Booth's death, read its contents and immediately gave it to federal authorities. Booth's letter was subsequently published in the *Philadelphia Press* on April 19th. Booth's letter, intended to explain and justify his actions, reveals that he viewed Lincoln's election as President to be a "war on Southern rights and institutions." The institution under attack was, of course, slavery, which Booth considered a "blessing:"

> *This country was formed for the* white, *not for the black man. And looking upon* African Slavery *from the same stand-point held by the noble framers of our Constitution, I, for one, have ever considered* it *one of the greatest blessings (both for themselves and us) that God ever bestowed on a favored nation. Witness heretofore our wealth and power; witness their elevation and enlightenment above their race elsewhere.*

Booth claimed that he had "aided" in the capture and execution of John Brown whom he labeled a traitor. He then equated "all abolitionists" with Brown and condemned them as traitors who "deserved the same fate as poor old Brown." Booth's intention at the time he wrote the letter was to make President Lincoln "a prisoner." Though not explained, he apparently intended to extort some bargain from the government to resurrect the Southern society as he envisioned it. Why was Lincoln assassinated? Because John Wilkes Booth considered Lincoln to be a "traitor." A traitor to what? To Booth's ideal of the South, a society based on slavery, sanctioned and established by the Constitution. How fortunate that Booth's view of the Constitution has been repudiated and that Lincoln's endures.

Dr. Dyer Learns of Lincoln's Assassination in Rome

BETWEEN 1863 AND 1865, when he was not on duty at the Mixed Court, Dr. Dyer traveled through Europe with his wife staying for short periods in Switzerland, Rome, Florence and Munich.[598] He was in Rome when news reached the Continent that Lincoln had been assassinated. As Americans gathered to "mingle their tears and sympathies," Dr. Dyer, being the only one present who had known President Lincoln intimately, was asked to deliver a eulogy:

> *In a most simple and pathetic manner, he spoke of the great and good man. As he proceeded, half suppressed sobs were heard on every side, and as he closed, scarcely able to control his own trembling utterance, the dew of grief moistened every eye.*[599]

On May 14, 1865, on the six hundredth anniversary of Dante's birthday celebrated in Florence, Dr. Dyer was again asked to speak on behalf of the Americans present. When he pronounced the name of Abraham Lincoln, "every Italian in that vast assembly of distinguished men rose reverently to his feet, and stood in profound silence. Each heart seemed thrilled with a pang of sorrow, and each countenance betrayed intense emotion. No language can portray the effect of this spontaneous homage to the memory of the Liberator."[600]

Has Chicago Forgotten the Abolitionists?

D R. DYER DIED on April 24, 1878, at the residence of his daughter Mrs. Adolph Heile (Cornelia, for whom Cornelia Street in Chicago is named) at the corner of Belmont and Halsted Streets. His funeral was attended by many of the prominent Chicagoans who survived him and had joined with him in fighting slavery as operators of the Underground Railroad and as promoters of political parties, causes and candidates. These included his pallbearers: William Bross, Mahlon Ogden, Henry Blodget, Amos Hall, I.N. Arnold, and Z. Eastman. Mourners included: John Wentworth, Allan Pinkerton, L.C.P. Freer, J.Y. Scammon, Calvin DeWolf, Philo Carpenter, Gurdon Hubbard and John Jones. There was an "innumerable caravan" of others, old, young, rich and poor. In one of the obituaries ("The Old Settlers of Chicago Took Final Leave of Another of Their Number"), there was a report of the tribute by the blacks of Chicago:

> The colored element had for their chief figure-head at the funeral John Jones, ex-county commissioner, who remembered the famous abolition record of Dr. Dyer with enthusiastic gratefulness.[601]

Over 100 carriages followed the hearse from the church to the Twenty-second street depot from which the casket was then taken to Oakwoods cemetery.

When Rufus Blanchard collected information about Dr. Dyer for his collection of biographies of early Chicagoans, L.C.P. Freer responded to his request saying that he began the study of law in the office of Calvin DeWolf at 71 Lake Street in 1846, and that Dr. Dyer occupied the same suite of offices. Dr. Dyer "was at that time recognized as the leading spirit among the anti-slavery people of this part of the state and our office might reasonably have been designated as 'The Chicago depot of the underground railroad.'"[602] Freer

also paid tribute to James Collins "who stood at the head of the Chicago bar, had his office nearly opposite, and next to Dr. Dyer was recognized the most devoted and energetic friend of the colored man."[603]

At one time Chicago had honored Dr. Dyer by naming a street after him. In fact Dyer was the original name for what is now Halsted Street, the longest street in the City of Chicago. The name was changed to honor William and Caleb Halsted, land developers, who were actually in Chicago only once.[604] Halsted was also know as the "Egyptian Road" because it led to the area in southern Illinois known as "Little Egypt," the epitaph colorfully employed by Stephen Douglas in the Lincoln-Douglas debates.

The City of Chicago has approximately 96 war monuments and memorials. Fifty-six parks and 38 schools are named for veterans of conflicts. In addition to Abraham Lincoln, Ulysses S. Grant, Philip H. Sheridan and John Logan, there are hundreds of other monuments and memorials in Chicago commemorating the lives of other people not associated with any war. To name a few, these include statues of William Shakespeare, Hans Christian Anderson, Louis Pasteur, Christopher Columbus, Nathan Hale, George Washington, Thaddeus Kosciuszko, and René-Robert Cavelier, Sieur de La Salle. Some have a stronger connection to Chicago and our cultural patrimony than others. In 2004, a life-sized bronze statue was unveiled of Bob Newhart, the actor who portrayed Dr. Robert Hartley a fictitious Chicago psychologist, in a television show popular in the 1970s. Displayed on Michigan Avenue originally, the statue's permanent home is to be Gateway Park, to the west of Navy Pier.[605]

There are no statues or memorials commemorating the abolitionists or their activities. Nor are there markers where their homes were that were used to hide runaway slaves or where the first meeting of the Anti-Slavery Society occurred. Chicago has many public buildings and streets named after politicians and celebrities but the names of Dyer, Freer, DeWolf, Carpenter, Bascomb, Eastman, Pinkerton, Hamilton, Collins, Childs, Fulton, Rossiter and Bradwell are uncelebrated.

In their lifetimes, these men never sought recognition for their deeds. They lived very full lives without the celebrity we sometimes bestow on public figures. A.T. Andreas captured the appropriate legacy for these men when he wrote of Dr. Dyer:

> *Dr. Dyer [was] one of the prominent officers of the celebrated "Underground Railroad" of Chicago, and helped in rescuing from slavery and the fangs of the human blood hounds who sought to overtake them, thousands of fugitives. To a resident of the State that gave birth to Abraham Lincoln, it would seem sufficient eulogy to say that a man was prominently connected with the underground railroad; no more grateful reflection can be entertained by Dr. Dyer's descendants, than that many former slaves can point to his grave and say "there lies the man who helped me to life and liberty."*[606]

Why is it the case that the deeds of the abolitionists in Chicago are not better known? Did the secrecy of operating the Underground Railroad leave too few traces? Were their papers and whatever other records existed destroyed in the Chicago Fire of 1871? Were their views about equality unpopular even after the Civil War? Was their example of civil disobedience too dangerous to extol? For whatever reason, there has not been any interest in celebrating the lives and accomplishments of abolitionists. Perhaps their story has not been fully told – up until now.

{ APPENDIX }

TABLE OF CASES

Bailey v. Cromwell, 4 Ill. 71 (1841).

Boon v. Juliet, 2 Ill. 258 (1836).

Chambers v. People of the State of Illinois, 5 Ill. 351 (1843).

Choisser v. Hargrave, 2 Ill. 317 (1836).

Cornelius v. Cohen, 1 Ill. 131, 1 Breese 131 (1825).

Crandall v. State, 10 Conn. 339 (1834).

Eells v. Illinois, 5 Ill. 498 (1843).

Harry v. Jarrott, 6 Ill. 120 (1844).

Jarrott v. Jarrott, 7 Ill. 1 (1845).

Kinney v. Cook, 4 Ill. 232 (1841).

Littleton v. Moses, 1 Ill. 393 (1831).

McElroy v. Clements (unreported).

Moore v. Illinois, 55 U.S. 13 (1852).

Nance v. Howard, 1 Ill. 242 (1828).

Phoebe v. Jay, 1 Ill. 268 (1828).

Prigg v. Pennsylvania, 16 Peters 627-32, 41 U.S. 539, 626-33 (1842).

Sarah, a woman of color, v. Borders, 5 Ill. 341 (1843).

Scott, a man of color v. Emerson, 15 Mo. 576 (1852).

Scott v. Sandford, 60 U.S. 393 (1857).

Somerset v. Stewart, 98 Eng. Rep. 499 (King's Bench, 1772).

Strader v. Graham, 51 U.S. 82 (1851).

Thornton's Case, 11 Ill. at 335.

Willard v. Illinois, 5 Ill. 461 (1843).

CONSTITUTIONS AND STATUTES

Illinois Constitution Article VI (1818).

Illinois Constitution (1848).

Illinois Constitution (1870).

U.S. Constitution

Article I §2.

Article I §9.

Article II §1.

Article IV §2.

Article IV §3.

Article VI.

Amendment V.

Amendment XIII.

Amendment XIV.

Amendment XVII.

Illinois Criminal Code § 149 (1843).

Act of February 7, 1865, *Public Laws of Illinois*, 24 G.A. 105.

Northwest Ordinance of 1787.

Presidents of the United States 1789–1865

Name	Term
George Washington	April 30, 1789 to March 3, 1797
John Adams	March 4, 1797 to March 3, 1801
Thomas Jefferson	March 4, 1801 to March 3, 1809
James Madison	March 4, 1809 to March 3, 1817
James Monroe	March 4, 1817 to March 3, 1825
John Quincy Adams	March 4, 1825 to March 3, 1829
Andrew Jackson	March 4, 1829 to March 3, 1837
Martin Van Buren	March 4, 1837 to March 3, 1841
William Henry Harrison	March 4, 1841 to April 4, 1841
John Tyler	April 6, 1841 to March 3, 1845
James Polk	March 4, 1845 to March 3, 1849
Zachary Taylor	March 5, 1849 to July 9, 1850
Millard Fillmore	July 10, 1850 to March 3, 1853
Franklin Pierce	March 4, 1853 to March 3, 1857
James Buchanan	March 4, 1857 to March 3, 1861
Abraham Lincoln	March 4, 1861 to April 14, 1865

Chief Justices of the Supreme Court 1789–1865

Name	Term
John Jay	October 19, 1789 to June 29, 1795
John Rutledge	August 12, 1795 to December 15, 1795
Oliver Ellsworth	March 8, 1796 to December 15, 1800
John Marshall	February 4, 1801 to July 6, 1835
Roger B. Taney	March 28, 1836 to October 12, 1864
Samuel P. Chase	December 15, 1864 to May 7, 1873

Governors of Illinois 1818–1865

Name	Term	Party
Shadrack Bond	1818–22	Democratic-Republican
Edward Coles	1822–26	Democratic-Republican
Ninian Edwards	1826–30	Democratic-Republican
John Reynolds	1830–34	Democrat
William Lee D. Ewing	1834	Democrat
Joseph Duncan	1834–38	Democrat
Thomas Carlin	1838–42	Democrat
Thomas Ford	1842–46	Democrat
Augustus C. French	1846–53	Democrat
Joel Aldrich Matteson	1853–57	Democrat
William Harrison Bissell	1857–60	Republican
John Wood	1860–61	Republican
Richard Yates	1861–65	Republican

Mayors of Chicago 1837–1865

Name	Term	Party
William Butler Ogden	1837–38	Democrat
Buckner Stith Morris	1838–39	Whig
Benjamin Wright Raymond	1839–40	Whig
Alexander Lloyd	1840–41	Democrat
Frances Cornwell Sherman	1841–42	Democrat
Benjamin Wright Raymond	1842–43	Whig
Augustus Garrett	1843–44	Democrat
Alson Sherman	1844–45	Independent Democrat
Augustus Garrett	1845–56	Democrat
John Putnam Chapin	1846–47	Whig
James Curtiss	1847–48	Democrat
James H. Woodworth	1848–50	Independent Democrat
James Curtiss	1850–51	Democrat
Walter S. Gurnee	1851–53	Democrat
Charles McNeill Gray	1853–54	Democrat
Isaac Lawrence Milliken	1854–55	Democrat
Levi Day Boone	1855–56	Know-Nothing
Thomas Dyer	1856–67	Democrat
John Wentworth	1857–58	Democrat
John Charles Haines	1858–59	Democrat
John Wentworth	1860–61	Republican
John Sidney Rumsey	1861–62	Republican
Francis Cornweell Sherman	1862–65	Democrat

11 *Foreword*

1. *New York Times*, April 25, 1878, Obituary of Dr. Dyer.

2. L. Bennett, *Forced Into Glory: Abraham Lincoln's White Dream*, Johnson Publishing Co. (2000).

PART I
1835–1850:
The Era of the Acceptance of Slavery

14 *The Role of Chicago in the Fight against Slavery*

3. P. Gilbert, *Chicago and Its Makers*, F. Mendelsohn (1929), p. 1029.

4. The popular vote for Lincoln was 1,865,593. Stephen Douglas had 1,382,713; John Breckenridge had 848,356; and John Bell had 592,906.

16 *The Legitimacy of Slavery*

5. W. L. Miller, *Arguing About Slavery*, Vintage Books (1996), p. 13.

6. *Id.*

7. The Constitution was drafted in 1787, but slavery had flourished in America for over 100 years before then. One source has reported that the first slaves in America were a group of Scottish women and children sold as slaves at Jamestown, Virginia in 1611. *See*, http://ngeorgia.com/history/why.html (visited 1/7/04). De Tocqueville put the date at 1621. A. De Tocqueville, *Democracy in America*, 1835 (Folio Society Ed. 2002), p. 330. In 1650, at the end of the English Civil War, 150 Scots captured by the British in the Battle of Dunbar, Oliver Cromwell's victory over forces supporting the claims of Charles Stuart (Bonnie Prince Charlie), were shipped to New England and sold into servitude. In November of 1651, another 300 Scots, taken prisoner when Cromwell finally defeated the royalists at the Battle of Worcester, were shipped to Boston. *The Highlander*, Sept./Oct. 2004, pp. 10–18, 71. In 1660, a monopoly was awarded to the Company of Royal Adventurers giving it the right to license British slave traders operating on the West African coast. *The Highlander*, Mar./Ap. 2004, at 24 ("Scotland's Terrible Trade"). Throughout most of the colonial period, slavery was recognized as a legitimate enterprise in England.

8. With the exception that every State would have at least one representative, even if it had fewer than thirty thousand "persons."

9. Counting slaves gave the pro-slavery States the ability to control the House of Representatives in the early years of the Republic.

10. A. Lincoln, *Speeches and Writings 1832–1858*, Library of America (1989), p. 801.

11. There was actually a third reference to slavery in the Constitution, again addressing the subject in a round-about fashion. Art. I §9, enumerating limitations upon the powers of Congress, provided:

    > *The Migration or Importation of such Persons as any of the States now existing shall think proper to admit, shall not be prohibited by the Congress prior to the Year one thousand eight hundred and eight, but a Tax or duty may be imposed on such Importation, not exceeding ten dollars for each person.*

    This meant that Congress could not curb the importation of slaves (the "slave trade") until 1808. The provision allowed the "slave trade" to flourish until at least that date and said nothing about curtailing slavery otherwise. In other words, it was assumed that slave owners could continue to own slaves and continue to sell slaves already here or their descendants.

12. In England, in a decision in 1772 authored by Lord Mansfield, a slave brought to England who escaped could not be returned to slavery or maintained in slavery in England. *Somerset v. Stewart*, 98 Eng. Rep. 499 (King's Bench, 1772). An Anti-Slavery Society was formed in 1787 to abolish slavery throughout the British Empire and end the slave trade. William Wilberforce, a Member of Parliament, campaigned to abolish slavery. Petitions were sent to Westminster starting in 1788. Parliament abolished slavery in the West Indies in 1833.

17 *A Nettlesome Question*

13. J.G. Whittier, *Justice and Expedience*, quoted in W.L. Miller, *Arguing about Slavery*, Vintage Books (1996), pp. 74–75.

14. Four women were invited to attend as "listeners and spectators." At that time, women were not supposed to participate in public affairs. W.L. Miller, *Arguing about Slavery*, Vintage Books (1996), p. 69.

15. England compensated slave owners when it abolished slavery.

16. W.L. Miller, *Arguing About Slavery*, Vintage Books (1996), pp. 65–79.

17. *Id.*, p. 76.

18. *Id.*, p. 29.
19. *Id.*, p. 37.
20. *Id.*, p. 39.
21. *Id.*

18   Elijah Lovejoy – Illinois's Abolitionist Editor

22. P. Simon, *Lovejoy, Martyr to Freedom*, Concordia (1964) p. 18–19.
23. *Presbyterian Life*, May 30, 1953, pp. 15–18.
24. In 1812, Congress admitted Louisiana as a State and its citizens were guaranteed the rights of American citizens, which included the right to own slaves where not prohibited. To the north and west was the Missouri Territory. Since Congress took no action to limit slavery there, it was permitted. Illinois, on the other hand, had been part of the Northwest Territory where Congress had acted to exclude slavery.
25. *St. Louis Observer*, Ap. 1835, quoted in Joseph and Owen Lovejoy, *Memoir of the Rev. Elijah P. Lovejoy Who Was Murdered In Defence of the Press At Alton, Illinois, November 7, 1837* (1838), p. 125.
26. *St. Louis Observer*, October 1835, quoted in Lovejoy, p. 127.
27. *St. Louis Observer*, October 21, 1835, quoted in Lovejoy, p. 136.
28. Joseph and Owen Lovejoy, *Memoir of the Rev. Elijah P. Lovejoy Who Was Murdered In Defence of the Press At Alton, Illinois, November 7, 1837* (1838), p. 136–37; M. Dillon, *Elijah P. Lovejoy, Abolitionist Editor*, University of Illinois Press (1961), p. 65.
29. *St. Louis Observer*, May 5, 1835, quoted in Joseph and Owen Lovejoy, *Memoir of the Rev. Elijah P. Lovejoy Who Was Murdered In Defence of the Press At Alton, Illinois, November 7, 1837* (1838), p. 168.
30. P. Simon, *Lovejoy, Martyr to Freedom* (1964), pp. 47–50. The judge, whose name appropriately enough was Luke Edward Lawless, was condemned widely by newspapers and public figures, including Abraham Lincoln. His conduct was even too much for his fellow Missourians. Shortly after this episode, a committee of St. Louis lawyers found Lawless unfit to discharge his official duties. *Id.* at 61.
31. The pledge was never fulfilled. M. Dillon, *Lovejoy, Abolitionist Editor*, University of Illinois Press (1961), p. 99.
32. *Presbyterian Life*, May 30, 1953, p. 16.
33. *See*, W.L. Miller, *Arguing About Slavery*, Vintage Books (1996), p. 180 et seq.
34. *Presbyterian Life*, May 30, 1953, p. 16.
35. P. Simon, *Lovejoy, Martyr to Freedom*, Concordia (1964), p. 67.
36. Joseph and Owen Lovejoy, *Memoir of the Rev. Elijah P. Lovejoy Who Was Murdered In Defence of the Press At Alton, Illinois, November 7, 1837* (1838), pp. 227–28.
37. *Id.*, p. 284.
38. P. Simon, *Lovejoy, Martyr to Freedom*, Concordia (1964), p. 109.
39. *Id.*, p. 112.
40. After another lull, the defenders reported to the mob that Lovejoy was dead and they proposed to leave. The mob would not guarantee safe passage and fired on them as they fled. Then they captured the warehouse, dragged the hated press out and destroyed it, throwing pieces of it in the river.

There were later two trials arising from this incident. The *defenders* were indicted and prosecuted. Gilman, the owner of the warehouse, was actually accused of starting the riot. However, the testimony corroborated the fact that the defenders were fired upon by the attackers and acted in defense. Incredibly, the Attorney General of Illinois, Usher P. Linder, was one of the prosecutors. Rather than advocate freedom of the press, he pandered to the mobites. He urged conviction saying, the defendants had brought to Alton "a press to teach the slave rebellion." Despite Linder's arguments the jury found the defenders not guilty.

Many of the attackers were indicted and tried for inciting a riot and destruction of property. The jury found these men not guilty and set them free. There were four men who claimed to be responsible for Lovejoy's murder. Paul Simon reported that each of them later met with misfortune – one was burned alive by Indians, another slit his own throat in prison. P. Simon, *Lovejoy, Martyr to Freedom*, Concordia, pp. 122–23 (1964). With biblical overtones, Simon pointed out that Alton, Illinois, once a rival to St. Louis as a port city on the Mississippi, sank into decline because of the reputation for lawlessness it earned from the mob killing of Lovejoy.
41. http://www.altonweb.com/history/lovejoy/a01.html.
42. In remarks made in dedicating a plaque to the memory of Lovejoy, then Governor Adlai Stevenson said: "We are also dedicating a stone to mark the grave of heresy ... the heresy that says you can kill an idea by killing a man, defeat a principal by defeating a person, bury truth by burying its vehicle." *Presbyterian Life*, May 30, 1953, p. 18.

22 Chicago's Response

43. P. Gilbert, *Chicago and Its Makers*, F. Mendelsohn (1929), p. 1029.

44. E.O. Gale, *Reminiscences of Early Chicago*, Revell Co. (1902), p. 269. ("The Saloon, despite its name, was an important factor in the progress of our city for many years. Here the Unitarians first gathered, then came the Universalists, followed by the Swedenborgians and all classes of respectable assemblages. Here we went to hear Temperance lectures and concerts, and the varied class of entertainments that is offered in every young city.")

45. J. Kirkland, *The Story of Chicago*, Dibble Publishing Co. (1892), p. 224; Z. Eastman, *Anti-Slavery Agitation in Illinois*, Chicago History Museum (undated), p. 661.

22 Chicago in 1838

46. C. Winslow, *Historical Events of Chicago*, Soderlund Printing (1937), p. 15.

47. *Western Citizen*, July 26, 1842, p. 4.

48. R. Fergus, *Fergus's Directory of the City of Chicago 1839*, Fergus Printing Co. (1870); E. O. Gale, *Reminiscences of Early Chicago*, Revell Co. (1902), p. 11. (The Miamis conveyed "one piece of land six miles square at the mouth of the Chickajo river … where a [French] fort formerly stood.")

49. *Western Citizen*, July 26, 1842, p. 4.

50. C. Winslow, *Historical Events of Chicago*, Soderlund Printing (1937).

51. Its official title is: "An Ordinance for the Government of the Territory of the United States Northwest of the River Ohio," passed July 13, 1787.

26 Dr. Dyer's Vermont Heritage

52. *The Biographical Encyclopedia of Illinois of the Nineteenth Century* (1875), reported that Dyer graduated with distinguished honors in December 1830.

53. New York prohibited the sale of slaves in 1788; in 1799, it declared the children of slaves to be born free; when De Tocqueville visited New York in 1831, there were still slaves present. A. De Tocqueville, *Democracy in America*, 1835, Folio Society Ed. (2002), p. 335.

54. *The Chicago Times*, April 25, 1878.

28 The Illinois General Assembly Condemns Abolitionist Societies

55. Basler, R., *Collected Works of Abraham Lincoln*, vol. I, p. 75.

56. Schurz, C., *Abraham Lincoln*, Houghton, Mifflin and Co. (1891) p. 15.

57. *Id.* (citing *House Journal*, Tenth General Assembly, First Session, pp. 817–18).

29 The Underground Railroad – the Beginning

58. J. Kirkland, *The Story of Chicago*, Dibble Publishing Co. (1892), p. 225.

59. A. Andreas, *History of Chicago*, Arno Press (1975), p. 606.

60. *The Chicago Times*, April 25, 1878.

61. F.R. Cook, *Bygone Days in Chicago*, McClurg & Co. (1901), p. 64.

30 The Case of Phoebe

62. *Phoebe v. Jay*, 1 Ill. 268 (1828).

63. *Id.*

64. The law provided, as follows:

     It shall be lawful for any person, being the owner or possessor of any negroes or mulattoes of and above the age of fifteen years, and owing service or labor as slaves in any of the states or territories of the United States … to bring the said negroes and mulattoes into this territory….

     The owner or possessor … shall, within thirty days … go with the same before the clerk of the court of common pleas … and in the presence of said clerk, the said owner or possessor shall determine and agree, to and with his or her negro or mulatto, upon the term of years which said negro or mulatto will and shall serve his or her said owner….

     If any negro or mulatto … shall refuse to serve … it may be lawful for such person, within sixty days thereafter, to remove said negro or mulatto to [a state or territory permitting slavery].

65. This was an application of the "Supremacy Clause" found in Article VI of the Constitution (The Constitution and Laws of the United States … shall be the supreme law of the land…"). Lockwood applied this principle to the laws of territorial legislatures which he viewed to be "inferior" to any laws passed by Congress because the territorial legislatures were created by Congress.

66. Illinois Constitution, Article VI (1818) (emphasis supplied).

67. *Phoebe v. Jay*, 1 Ill. 269 (1828).

68. Under the Supremacy Clause, both acts of Congress were entitled to equal weight. The last he construed as implicitly repealing the earlier law.

69. Illinois Constitution, Article VI, Section 3 (1818).

70. The form of a valid indenture, in one case, was that the indentured servant agreed to serve for *eighty* years, and, at the expiration of that term, would be paid fifty dollars for his services. *Harry v. Jarrott*, 6 Ill. 120 (1844).

71. Dunne, E.F., *Illinois, The Heart of the Nation*, The Lewis Publishing Co. (1933), pp. 263–264, 274, 276. Coles was an extraordinary figure in Illinois history. He brought his slaves to Illinois, freed them, giving each 160 acres. He ran for governor and was elected three years after moving to Illinois from Virginia. He advocated emancipating all slaves in Illinois.

72. The strength of the political sentiment in Illinois that was pro-slavery in the early years of statehood is probably best reflected by the fact that in 1824 the legislature of Illinois mustered the required two-thirds vote needed to call a new constitutional convention expressly for the purpose of admitting slavery into Illinois. The call was submitted to the electorate and defeated by the narrow margin of 1800 votes.

32 Other Illinois Supreme Court Decisions on Slavery Prior to 1850

73. *Nance v. Howard*, 1 Ill. 242 (1828).

74. *Sarah, a woman of color, v. Borders*, 5 Ill. 341 (1843).

75. *Littleton v. Moses*, 1 Ill. 393 (1831).

76. Another case that was similar was *Kinney v. Cook*, 4 Ill. 232 (1841). Kinney sought to recover compensation for services rendered. Cook asserted that Kinney had been his slave. The jury awarded $285. The Supreme Court affirmed, holding that there was a presumption in favor of liberty. The fact that Kinney had resided with the Cook during the time services were rendered did not disprove that Kinney was a free man. Cook, the defendant, had to prove that the Kinney was a slave or indentured servant as recognized by Illinois law and failed to present any evidence to meet that burden. The *Kinney* court pointed out that while in Slave States the burden might be placed on the putative slave to show that he or she was a free person, in Illinois the burden was on the party seeking to deprive someone of his or her liberty.

77. *Choisser v. Hargrave*, 2 Ill. 317 (1836).

78. Justice Lockwood decided a similar case in 1825, holding that Betsy, the child of an alleged indentured servant, was free because a signed indenture was never presented to the clerk. *Cornelius v. Cohen*, 1 Ill. 131, 1 Breese 131 (1825).

79. *Boon v. Juliet*, 2 Ill. 258 (1836).

80. *Jarrott v. Jarrott*, 7 Ill. 1 (1845).

81. Justice Scates, who wrote the opinion in *Jarrott*, allowed himself to express the following personal sentiment: "All philanthropists unite in deprecating the evils of slavery, and it affords me sincere pleasure, when my duty under the constitution and law requires me to break the fetters of the slave, and declare the captive free."

33 Harboring Runaway Slaves

82. *Eells v. Illinois*, 5 Ill. 498 (1843).

83. The story is told in S. Black and R. Bennett, *A City of Refuge – Quincy, Illinois*, Millennial Press (2000), p. 264.

84. *Eells v. Illinois*, 5 Ill. 498 (quoting *Prigg v. Pennsylvania*, 16 Peters 627–32, 41 U.S. 539, 626–33 [1842]). Actually Chief Justice Taney concurred in part and dissented in part. The excerpt relied on was part of his dissent. *Prigg* threw out a Pennsylvania law on the grounds that the constitution relegated to Congress the exclusive right to pass laws regarding the recapture of slaves. The majority in *Prigg* stated the rule of their decision as throwing out state laws whether they impeded *or assisted* the recapture of slaves. Taney would not have ruled out state laws that assisted. This question was left open by virtue of the facts in *Prigg*. Indeed, the *Eels* case presented that very issue when it reached the Court and was decided in 1852.

85. Justice Lockwood disagreed. In his dissent he cited two provisions of the Illinois Constitution: (1) the provision in Article 6 that "neither slavery nor involuntary servitude shall hereafter be introduced into this state" and (2) the provision in Article 8 "that all men are born equally free and independent." From this he reasoned "that all men, whether black or white, are, in this state, presumed to be free." He thought that the indictment of Eells was deficient because it did not allege that Eells *knew* that the person he was harboring was a runaway slave. Lockwood reasoned that Eells was entitled to presume that the person he aided was a free man. Alternatively, Justice Lockwood would have held that the Illinois law was unconstitutional based on his view that "the power of legislation, on the subject of fugitive slaves, is vested exclusively in congress, and that no state can pass any law to super-add to, control, qualify, or impede the remedy given by congress." But Lockwood's attempt to raise the bar for prosecutions for harboring and secreting did not carry the day.

86. *Western Citizen*, November 3, 1846 (Obituary of Dr. Eells).

87. S. Black and R. Bennett, *A City of Refuge – Quincy, Illinois*, Millennial Press (2000), p. 265.

88. *Moore v. Illinois*, 55 U.S. 13 (1852). (Moore was Eells' executor.)

89. *Western Citizen*, November 3, 1846 (Obituary of Dr. Eells).

90. Work was the father of the composer of *Marching Through Georgia* and other Civil War songs. C.A. Landrum, *Quincy in the Civil War*, Carl Landrum, p. xix (1966).

91. *Western Citizen*, July 26, 1842 and August 5, 1842.

92. Missouri did not allow a slave to testify against a white man. So, the slave-owners testified to what the slaves told them the defendants had said to them. This was rank hearsay. But the defendants' counsel's objections to that form of testimony were overruled. (One of the jurors was Mark Twain's father.) S. Black and R. Bennett, *A City of Refuge – Quincy, Illinois*, Millennial Press (2000), p. 208.

93. D.C. Grunwaldt, *Quincy, Illinois and the Underground Railroad* (unpublished), Historical Society of Quincy and Adams County (1961).

94. Thompson wrote a pamphlet, *Prison Life and Reflections*, which called attention to the episode and focused attention on the plight of fugitive slaves and those who sought to help them.

95. *Western Citizen*, July 26, 1842 and August 5, 1842.

96. S. Black and R. Bennett, *A City of Refuge – Quincy, Illinois*, Millennial Press (2000), p. 265.

35 The Chicago Harboring Evasion

97. Illinois Criminal Code § 149, *see Willard v. Illinois*, 5 Ill. 461 (1843).

98. Dyer may also have thought he could avoid prosecution for harboring and secreting if he did not acknowledge that he *knew* that his guests were runaway slaves. The Illinois Supreme Court was divided on the issue of whether an indictment had to allege *scienter*, *i.e.*, the legal requirement that the defendant must *know* that the act he is engaging in is illegal. In *Chambers v. Illinois*, two members of the Court, Chief Justice Wilson and Justice Lockwood, agreed with the majority to grant a new trial to Chambers who allegedly harbored a negro woman named Sarah. But while the majority thought that the evidence of the voluntary indenture agreement was insufficient, requiring a new trial, Wilson and Lockwood would have gone further and dismissed the case entirely for failure to allege *scienter*.

36 Lincoln's Path to Becoming a Lawyer

99. D.K. Goodwin, *Team of Rivals*, Simon & Schuster (2005), p. 47.

100. http://alabamamaps.ua.edu/historicalmaps/us_states/indiana/index.html.

101. *Id.*, pp. 51–52.

102. E.S. Miers, *Lincoln Day By Day*, Lincoln Sesquicentennial Commission, Vol. 1 (1960), p. x.

103. http://www.papersofabrahamlincoln.org/narrative_overview.htm.

40 Lincoln's Role in Fugitive Slave Cases

104. The Lincoln Legal Papers, a project of the Illinois Historic Preservation Agency, the Abraham Lincoln Association and the University of Illinois at Springfield, has compiled a documentary history of Abraham Lincoln's law practice for the years 1836 to 1861. Researchers for the project have scoured court house records throughout Illinois, enlisting the assistance of historical societies, collectors of autographs and historical documents, university archives and every other repository imaginable to compile as complete a catalog as possible of Lincoln's legal career before becoming President.

105. This case is also mentioned in E. Miers, *Lincoln Day By Day*, Lincoln Sesquicentennial Commission (1960), Vol. 1, p. 259.

106. One biographer of Lincoln has suggested that he made a feeble argument on Matson's behalf saying that the whole case turns on what Matson's intent was in bringing the Negroes to his farm, were they only crossing the State or were they located there indefinitely. If the former, they were *in transitu* and remained slaves. If the latter, they were emancipated. A. J. Beveridge, *Abraham Lincoln, 1809–1858*, New York (1928), Vol. 1, p. 392–98.

107. 4 Ill. 71 (1841).

108. The Court relied on its earlier decision in *Kinney v. Cook*, 4 Ill. 232 (1841) holding that every person in Illinois is presumed free.

109. R.W. Johannsen, *Stephen A. Douglas*, Oxford University Press (1973), p. 104.

110. E. Miers, *Lincoln Day By Day*, Lincoln Sesquicentennial Commission, Vol. 1 (1960), p. 287. (The Lincoln legal papers project has not yet found corroborating documentation as to these two cases.) The Project also has documented that Herndon separately handled two cases that arose after the Fugitive Slave Act of 1850 was passed. In 1857, he represented the fugitive slave in *McElroy v. Clements*. Clements had escaped

from Kentucky. The U.S. Commissioner ruled for McElroy, the slave-owner.

In 1860, Herndon represented another fugitive slave, Canton, who escaped from Missouri in 1857. The U.S. Commissioner ruled for Dickinson, the slave-owner. However, Canton later escaped again and passed through Springfield on his way to Canada and freedom.

41   Slaves "In Transit" and the Doctrine of "Comity"

111.   *Willard v. Illinois*, 5 Ill. 461 (1843).

112.   S. Currey, *Chicago: Its History and Its Builders*, S.J. Clarke Publishing Co. (1912).

113.   As of 2004, this data base was being maintained at the following web site: http://www.ilsos.net/departments/archives/servant.html.

42   The "Free Negro" Population in Chicago in 1840

114.   *Chicago American*, January 8, 1841.

42   Dr. Dyer, his Medical Practice and his Vision for Chicago

115.   Upton, G.P. and Colbert, E., *Biographical Sketches of Leading Men of Chicago*, Wilson & St. Clair (1868), p. 75. The relationship between Castleton and Middlebury College is explained in *New England Journal of Medicine*, April 7, 1933, pp. 729–735.

116.   *The Chicago Times*, April 25, 1878 (Obituary of Dr. Dyer). The story is also told in JAMA, May 20, 1968 and Castleton Medical College 1818–1862, p. 698, which additionally reported that Castleton expelled two students to appease the public.

117.   *The Chicago Times*, April 25, 1878.

118.   P. Gilbert and C.L. Bryson, *Chicago and Its Makers*, Mendelsohn (1929), p. 75. The library died of neglect in 1844. See also, Andreas, A.T., *History of Chicago*, Arno Press (1975), p. 522.

119.   A.T. Andreas, *History of Chicago*, Arno Press (1975), p. 522.

120.   *Id.*

121.   J. Kirkland, *The Story of Chicago*, Dibble Publishing Co. (1892), p. 235.

122.   C. Winslow, *Historical Events of Chicago*, Soderlund Press (1937), p. 17.

123.   *Illinois State Register*, June 19, 1840.

124.   Cornelia Street in Chicago was named after Cornelia Dyer (later Mrs. Adolf Heile). Dyer was living with her and her family in their home at 1607 North Halsted Street at the time of his death.

125.   Upton, G.P. and Colbert, E., *Biographical Sketches of Leading Men of Chicago*, Wilson & St. Clair (1868), p. 75.

44   Owen Lovejoy

126.   Blanchard, R., *Discovery and Conquests of the Northwest*, Vol. I (1879) and Vol. II (1900), p. 295.

127.   E. Magdol, *Owen Lovejoy: Abolitionist in Congress*, Rutgers University Press (1967), p. 32.

128.   *Id.* at 33.

129.   *Id.* at 34–35.

130.   *Id.* at 36.

46   Lovejoy's Indictment

131.   *Id.* at 41.

132.   *Id.* at 44.

133.   See, *Eells v. Illinois*, 5 Ill. 498 (1843); *Willard v. Illinois*, 5 Ill. 461 (1843), discussed above.

134.   *Western Citizen*, June 1, 1843.

47   Forming a New Political Party – The Liberty Party

135.   B. P. Thomas, *Theodore Weld, Crusader for Freedom*, New Brunswick (1950), p. 179 (quoted in E. Magdol, *Owen Lovejoy: Abolitionist in Congress*, Rutgers University Press [1967], p. 55).

136.   E. Magdol, *Owen Lovejoy: Abolitionist in Congress*, Rutgers University Press (1967), p.57.

137.   Z. Eastman, *Anti-Slavery Agitation in Illinois*, Chicago History Museum (undated), p. 661.

138.   The Cook County delegates were: Charles V. Dyer, Calvin De Wolf, L.C.P. Freer, R.E. Heacock, James H. Collins, Philo Carpenter, Nathaniel S. Cushing, Adam Johnston, R.B. Heacock, Doliver Walker, Philip Bean, Robert Freeman, D.L. Roberts, J.W. Ransom, James Martin, Joseph Mecker, N. Gilbert, S.D. Childs, E.M. Jones, Henry Ayer, William L. Lawrence, W.C. Vanosdell, W.H. Taylor, Benjamin Briggs, Henry Smith, Joseph Johnston, Charles Sweet, and T.E. Hamilton.

139.   N.D. Harris, *History of Negro Slavery in Illinois and the Slavery Agitation in that State*, A.C. McClurg & Co. (1904), p. 152.

140.   Z. Eastman, *Anti-Slavery Agitation in Illinois*, Chicago History Museum (undated), p. 661.

141.   N.D. Harris, *History of Negro Slavery in Illinois and the Slavery Agitation in that State*, A.C. McClurg & Co. (1904), p. 148.

48   The Birth of Western Citizen

142.   *Id.*, p. 125.

143.   Records of the Illinois State Anti-Slavery Society, Minute Book, Chicago History Museum.

144.   *Western Citizen,* July 26, 1842.

145.   Records of the Illinois Anti-Slavery Society, Chicago History Museum.

146.   Newton, J.F., *Lincoln and Herndon*, The Torch Press (1910), p. 62 n.1.

51   The "Black Codes"

147.   Z. Eastman, *History of the Black Codes of Illinois*, Chicago History Museum (undated).

148.   *Id.*

149.   The statute provided: "Every black or mulatto person who shall be found in this State, and not having such a certificate as required by this chapter, shall be deemed a runaway slave or servant, and it shall be lawful for any inhabitant of this State to take such black or mulatto person before some justice of the peace and should such black or mulatto person not produce such certificate as aforesaid, it shall be the duty of such justice to cause the black or mulatto person to be committed to the custody of the Sheriff of the county who shall keep such black or mulatto person and in three days after receiving him shall advertise him at the Court House door and shall transmit a notice and cause the same to be advertised for six weeks in some public paper printed nearest the place of apprehension of such black or mulatto person stating a description of the most remarkable features of the supposed runaway and if such person as committed shall not produce a certificate or other evidence of his freedom within the term aforesaid it shall be the duty of the Sheriff to hire him out for the best price he can get after having given five days previous notice thereof from month to month; and if no owner shall appear and substantiate his claim before the expiration of the year, the Sheriff shall give a certificate to such black or mulatto person who on producing the same to the next Circuit Court of the county, may obtain a certificate from the Court, stating the facts and the person shall be deemed a free person, unless he shall be lawfully claimed by his proper owner or owners hereafter."

150.   *See*, E. Gertz, *The Black Laws of Illinois*, Journal of the Illinois State Historical Society, 56 (Autumn 1963), p. 454. (Tracing the history of the Black Codes in Illinois from territorial laws in 1807, through various constitutional provisions and laws through 1862.) *See also*, N.D. Harris, *History of Negro Slavery in Illinois* and of the Slavery Agitation in that State, A.C. McClurg & Co. (1904), pp. 9–10.

151.   F. Bordewich, *Bound for Canaan*, Amistad (2005), p. 93.

152.   *Id.*; Dunne, E.F., *Illinois, The Heart of The Nation*, The Lewis Publishing Co. (1933),Vol. 1, pp. 275–76.

153.   Records of the Illinois State Anti-Slavery Society, Chicago History Museum, p. 79 (Minutes of Meeting at Quincy, September 20, 1839).

154.   Blanchard, R., *Discovery and Conquests of the Northwest*, Vol. I (1879) and Vol. II (1900), p. 288. *See also*, E. Gertz, *The Black Laws of Illinois*, Journal of the Illinois State Historical Society, 56 (Autumn 1963) p. 472 (citing Act of February 7, 1865, *Public Laws of Illinois*, 24 G.A. 105).

52   A Slave Is Sold at Auction – in Chicago!

155.   S. Currey, *Chicago: Its History and Its Builders*, S.J. Clarke (1912), pp. 410–11.

156.   J. Kirkland, *The Story of Chicago*, Dibble Publishing Co. (1892), p. 225.

53   Illinois Hears about Slave-Catchers in Pennsylvania

157.   *Western Citizen*, August 5, 1842.

54   The Slave-Catchers Come to Illinois

158.   F. Cook, *Bygone Days in Chicago*, McClurg & Co. (1910), p. 64.

159.   *Fergus' Directory of Chicago*, Fergus Printing Co. (1839); *Fergus' Directory of Chicago*, Fergus Printing Co. (1843); J.W.Norris, *A Business Advertiser and General Directory of the City of Chicago for the Year 1845–46*, J. Campbell & Co. Publishers (1845); J.W.Norris, *A Business Advertiser and General Directory of the City of Chicago for the Year 1848–49*, Eastman & McClellan (1848); *Danenhower's Chicago City Directory for 1851*, W.W. Danenhower (1851). In 1857, Dr. Dyer moved his residence to "Green Bay Road near Toll Gate" which would probably be in the vicinity of Clark and Wrightwood Streets today. *Gager's Chicago City Directory for the Year Ended June 1, 1857*, John Gager & Co. (1857).

160.   The story is told in a number of histories of Chicago. Upton, G.P. and Colbert, E., *Biographical Sketches of the Leading Men of Chicago*, Wilson & St. Clair (1868), pp. 76–7; E. Dedmon, *Fabulous Chicago*, Antheneum (1981), p. 50; *The Chicago Times*, April 25, 1878 (Obituary of Dr. Dyer). The cane is now at the Chicago History Museum. It was donated by Dr. Dyer's son-in-law, Adolf Heile in 1884.

55   **De Tocqueville's Observations on Slavery and Racism**

161. B.L. Pierce, *A History of Chicago*, A.A. Knopf (1937), p. 245.

162. A. De Tocqueville, *Democracy in America*, 1835, Folio Society ed. (2002), p. 304.

163. *Id.*, p. 326.

164. *Id.*, p. 329.

165. *Id.*, p. 329.

166. A. Lincoln, Debates, Springfield 1857, quoted in Z. Eastman, *The Anti-Slavery Agitation in Illinois*, p. 672. Lincoln also stated he was not advocating equal treatment in 1854: "Let it not be said I am contending for the establishment of political and social equality between the whites and the blacks. I have already said the contrary." A. Lincoln, *Speeches and Writings*, Library of America (1989), p. 329.

56   **Lincoln and the Underground Railroad**

167. Z. Eastman, *History of the Anti-Slavery Agitation, and the Growth of the Liberty and Republican Parties in the State of Illinois* (undated), p. 670.

57   **Lincoln's Early Encounters with Slavery**

168. A. Lincoln, *Speeches and Writings, 1832–1858*, Library of America (1989), p. 74.

169. *Id.*, p. 360.

58   **The Disrupted Trial – An Armed Negro Riot?**

170. A. Andreas, *History of Chicago*, Arno Press (1975), p. 607. Andreas tells Eastman's version recounted in later years. Eastman recalled only one black being on trial. Contemporary reports make it clear there were two men on trial. *See Western Citizen*, November 3, 1846, letters of J.H. Collins, R.P. Hamilton, and Calvin De Wolf.

171. A. Andreas, *History of Chicago*, Arno Press (1975), p. 607.

172. G.P. Upton and E. Colbert, *Biographical Sketches of the Leading Men of Chicago*, Wilson & St. Clair (1868), p. 77.

59   **The First Public Meeting to Discuss "That Affair"**

173. *Western Citizen*, November 3, 1846.

174. *Id.*

175. *Western Citizen* reported that they sang two songs but did not identify what songs were sung. This apparently was an activity that punctuated speeches in this type of gathering.

60   **Activists, Pacifists and the Quest for a Third Path**

176. *The Liberator*, no. 1, January 1, 1831.

177. Resolution of the Anti-Slavery Society, January 27, 1843.

178. D.S. Reynolds, *John Brown, Abolitionist*, Knopf (2005), p. 65.

179. A. Lincoln, *Speeches and Writings 1832–1858*, Library of America (1989), pp. 31–32.

180. J. Niven, *John C. Calhoun and the Price of Union*, Louisiana State University Press (1988), pp. 187–88.

61   **The Second Public Meeting**

181. *Western Citizen*, November 3, 1846.

182. *Western Citizen*, November 10, 1846.

183. *Id.*

184. *Western Citizen*, November 3, 1846.

185. *Id.*

62   **The Backlashes**

186. *Western Citizen*, December 29, 1846.

187. S. Currey, *Chicago: Its History and Its Builders*, S.J. Clarke (1912), p. 414.

63   **Thornton's Case**

188. *Thornton's Case*, 11 Ill. 332 (1849).

189. The text of the statute is set forth above at n. 150.

190. *Prigg v. Pennsylvania*, 16 Peters 627, 41 U.S. 539 (1842). (This is the same decision discussed in *Eells v. Illinois*, discussed above).

191. *Thornton's Case*, 11 Ill. at 335.

64   **The Little Giant**

192. R. W. Johannsen, *Stephen A. Douglas*, Oxford University Press (1973), p. 15.

193. R. W. Johannsen, *Stephen A. Douglas*, Oxford University Press (1973), p. 19.

194. J. Sheahan, *The Life of Stephen A. Douglas*, Harper & Brothers (1860), p. 17.

195. *Id.*, p. 18.

196. R. W. Johannsen, *Stephen A. Douglas*, Oxford University Press (1973), p. 4.

197. J. Sheahan, *The Life of Stephen A. Douglas*, Harper & Brothers (1860), p. 48.

198. Prior to 1913, Senators were elected by the legislatures of the States, pursuant to Article I, Section 3 of the Constitution. This provision was changed by the Seventeenth Amendment which was ratified in 1913.

65 Douglas Makes His Mark in Congress

199. G.M. Capers, *Stephen A. Douglas, Defender of the Union*, Little, Brown (1959), pp. 18–19.

200. C.E. Carr, *Stephen A. Douglas*, A.C. McClurg (1909), pp. 18–19 and pp. 160–161.

201. R.W. Johannsen, *Stephen A. Douglas*, Oxford University Press (1973), p. 499.

202. G.M. Capers, *Stephen A. Douglas, Defender of the Union*, Little, Brown (1959), p. 15.

68 Mormons, Welcoming Free Blacks, Are Ejected from Missouri

203. Under Joseph Smith, the Mormons ostensibly embraced blacks. Smith ordained Elijah Abel, the first black ordained as a priest. After Smith's death, under the leadership of Brigham Young, Young banned blacks from being ordained in 1852, a ban that was not repealed until 1978. *Chicago Tribune*, July 26, 2005 at Section 1, pp. 1, 17.

204. S. Black and R. Bennett, *A City of Refuge – Quincy, Illinois*, Millennial Press (2000), p. 1. See, http://www.angelfire.com/mo2/blackmormon/q2.htm, visited June 28, 2004.

205. I. S. Davis, *The Story of the Church*, Herald Publishing House (1977), pp. 276–78; A. Abanes, *One Nation Under Gods*, Four Walls Eight Windows (2002) pp. 161–64.

69 Dr. Dyer Prods the Mormons

206. Bennett had his own version of plural marriage. He sought to persuade young women to submit to him without the benefit of marriage and told those who hesitated that Joseph Smith had ordered them to submit. This led to his excommunication. A.F. Smith, *The Saintly Scoundrel*, University of Illinois Press (1997), p. 81.

207. *Times and Seasons*, Vol. 3, no. 10 (1842), reprinting the letters between Dyer and Bennett and Smith's editorial comment.

70 Judge Douglas Presides Over a Mormon Trial

208. It also included Quincy, which is why Douglas presided over the trial of Richard Eells.

71 The Mormon Wars and the Murder of Joseph Smith, Jr.

209. http://www.angelfire.com/mo2/blackmormon/q2.htm (visited April 29, 2004).

210. N. G. Bringhorst, *Saints, Slaves and Blacks*, Greenwood Press (1981), pp. 55–56.

72 John Hossack

211. J.H. Ryan, *A Chapter from the History of the Underground Railroad in Illinois*, Journal of the Illinois Historical Society, Vol 8 No. 1 pp. 25–30 (April 1915).

212. G. Manierre, *The Manierre Family in Early Chicago History*, Journal of the Illinois Historical Society, Vol. 8, No.1, p. 448 (April 1915).

72 The Exclusion of Free Negroes from Illinois

213. J. Cornelius, *Constitution Making in Illinois 1818–1970* (1972), p. 40 (citing Journal of the Convention (1847), pp. 470, 475–76).

214. J. Sheahan, *The Life of Stephen A. Douglas*, Harper & Brothers (1860), p. 156.

215. The provision was mooted by the passage of the Fourteenth Amendment after the Civil War which recognized "all persons born or naturalized in the United States" as "citizens" and provided that "no State shall make or enforce any laws which shall abridge the privileges and immunities of citizens of the United States…." U.S. Constitution, Amendment XIV.

73 The Prevalence of Racism

216. Letter of Andrew T. Judson to the *Brooklyn Advertiser Press*, March 29, 1833, quoted in K.C. Julius, *The Abolitionist Decade, 1829–1838*, McFarland & Co. (2004), p. 108.

74 The Union before 1850

217. G.M. Capers, *Stephen A. Douglas, Defender of the Union*, Little, Brown (1959), p. 45.

218. E.F. Dunne, *Illinois, The Heart of the Nation*, The Lewis Publishing Co. (1933), p. 277.

219. See http://geography.about.com/library/weekly/aa041999.htm and http://freespace.virgin.net/john.cletheroe/usa_can/usa/mas_dix.htm (visited June 16, 2004).

220. The "Mason-Dixon Line" is often used colloquially to delineate a boundary that separated the Free and Slave States or the Union and Confederate States fighting in the Civil War. However, the surveyed line does not do that since Delaware, a Slave State below the line stayed in the Union and Illinois, Indiana and Ohio were always Free States even though parts of their respective territories would fall below an extension of the surveyed line.

221. "Unjust laws exist…. Under a government which imprisons unjustly, the true place for a just man is also in prison. The proper place today, the only place which Massachusetts has provided for her freer and

less dependent spirits, is in her prisons…. It is there that the fugitive slave, and the Mexican prisoner on parole [can be found]…. A minority is powerless while it conforms to the majority; it is not even a minority then; but it is irresistible when it clogs by its whole weight. If the alternative is to keep all just men in prison, or give up war and slavery, the State will not hesitate which to choose."

222. J. Sheahan, *The Life of Stephen A. Douglas*, Harper & Brothers (1860), pp. 92–93.

76   The Deadlock Prior to the Compromise of 1850

223. R.W. Johannsen, *Stephen A. Douglas*, Oxford University Press (1973), pp. 238–39.

224. On November 19, 1832, South Carolina held a convention and passed its "Ordinance of Nullification," a measure providing that the State would not enforce the Tariff of 1832, commanding all office holders to uphold the Ordinance or forfeit their office. John C. Calhoun, then Vice President in Andrew Jackson's presidency, was widely acknowledged to be the designer of the ordinance. President Jackson immediately issued a Proclamation stating his intent to enforce the Tariff, by force if necessary. The crisis was averted when Congress modified the Tariff. *See*, K.C. Julius, *The Abolitionist Decade, 1829–1838*, McFarland & Co. (2004), pp. 95–101.

76   Dr. Dyer Pushes the Liberty Party Forward

225. N.D. Harris, *History of Negro Slavery in Illinois and the Slavery Agitation in that State*, A.C. McClurg & Co. (1904), p. 159 (citing *Western Citizen*, June 30, 1846).

226. *Western Citizen*, June 30, 1846.

227. N. D. Harris, *History of Negro Slavery in Illinois and the Slavery Agitation in that State*, A. C. McClurg & Co. (1904), p. 159.

78   The Free Soil Party

228. E. Magdol, *Owen Lovejoy, Abolitionist in Congress*, Rutgers University Press (1967), p. 88; A. C. Cole, *The Era of the Civil War 1848–1870*, Illinois Centennial Commission (1919), p. 59.

78   Dr. Dyer Runs for Governor as the Free Soil Candidate

229. J. Cunningham, *Historical Encyclopedia of Illinois*, Vol. 1 (1905), p. 143.

230. http://www.rootsweb.com/~ilhistory/governors/french.html (visited March 11, 2007).

231. C.A. Church, *History of the Republican Party in Illinois 1854–1912*, Wilson Bros. (1912).

79   The Wilmot Proviso in Illinois

232. R.W. Johannsen, *Stephen A. Douglas*, Oxford University Press (1973), pp. 252–53.

79   Famine and Immigration

233. *Western Citizen*, February 23, 1847.

79   Slavery in the Nation's Capitol

234. F. Bordewich, *Bound for Canaan*, Amistad (2005), p. 300 (citing D.H. Donald, *Lincoln*, Simon & Schuster [1995], p. 135.)

235. D.H. Donald, *Lincoln*, Simon & Schuster (1995), p. 135.

PART II
1850–1860:
Restraining Slavery Becomes the Issue

82   The Compromise of 1850

236. F.M. Bordewich, *Bound for Canaan*, Amistad (2005), p. 313.

237. R.W. Johannsen, *Stephen A. Douglas*, Oxford University Press (1973), p. 277.

238. W.H. Herndon, *Life of Lincoln*, World Publishing Co. (1942), p. 374.

239. J. Sheahan, *The Life of Stephen A. Douglas*, Harper & Brothers (1860), p. 130.

240. *Id.*, p. 139. Webster argued that slavery was excluded from California and the New Mexico territories by a "law of nature" making the Wilmot Proviso unnecessary.

241. Clay tried to finesse the slavery issue by arguing that Mexico had not allowed slavery in the territory ceded by Mexico and that Mexican law carried forward until changed. In other words, Congress did not need to address slavery in those territories. This rational allowed Clay to oppose the Wilmot Proviso as unnecessary, though for slightly different reasons than Webster's.

242. In many respects Douglas's approach was not very different from Clay's Omnibus Bill approach. Clay did not succeed in large part because President Taylor and his loyalists saw Clay as a potential rival. Taylor's death changed that equation. R. Johannsen, *Stephen A. Douglas*, Oxford University Press (1973), p. 295.

243. J. Sheahan, *The Life of Stephen A. Douglas*, Harper & Brothers (1860), p. 169.

244. R.W. Johannsen, *Stephen A. Douglas*, Oxford University Press (1973), p. 280.

245. *Id.*, p. 278.

246. *Id.*, p. 297.

83   Douglas and Slavery

247. G.M. Capers, *Stephen A. Douglas, Defender of the Union*, Little, Brown (1959), p. 98.

248. J. Sheahan, *The Life of Stephen A. Douglas*, Harper & Brothers (1860), p. 11.

249. G.M. Capers, *Stephen A. Douglas, Defender of the Union*, Little, Brown (1959), p. 44.

84   The Fugitive Slave Act

250. Von Holst, *Constitutional History of the United States*, Callahan and Co. (1888), Vol. III, p. 548.

251. D.S. Reynolds, *John Brown, Abolitionist*, Knopf (2005), p. 112.

85   Dr. Dyer and Friends Defy the New Fugitive Slave Act

252. A.T. Andreas, *History of Chicago*, Arno Press (1975), p. 606.

253. R.W. Johannsen, *Stephen A. Douglas*, Oxford University Press (1997), p. 300.

254. C. Winslow, *Historical Events of Chicago*, Manuscript at Chicago History Museum (undated) Vol. I, p. 64.

255. *Id.*

256. R. Blanchard, *Discovery and Conquests of the Northwest*, Vol. I (1879) and Vol. II (1900) p. 298.

257. C. Winslow, *Historical Events of Chicago*, Manuscript at Chicago History Museum (undated) Vol. I, p. 64.

258. *Id.*

259. 41 U.S. 539 (1842).

260. J. Sheahan, *The Life of Stephen A. Douglas*, Harper & Brothers (1860), p. 183.

261. Remarks of Stephen A. Douglas, October 23, 1850, reprinted in J. Sheahan, *Stephen A. Douglas*, Harper & Brothers (1860), p. 184.

262. *Id.* p. 185.

263. *Id.* p. 186.

264. *Id.*, p. 225.

87   Escaping Via the Coal Hole

265. *The Free West*, December 15, 1854.

266. R. Blanchard, *Discovery and Conquests of the Northwest*, R. Blanchard and Co., Vol. II (1900), pp.285–86.

267. The Underground Railway, *The Stentor*, May 1890, p. 185.

268. *Id.*

269. *Id.*, p. 185.

270. *Id.* at 187.

88   Dr. Dyer Gets Even with the "Officious" Henry Rhines

271. *The Chicago Times*, April 25, 1878 (Obituary of Dr. Dyer).

272. *Id.*

273. *Id.*

88   Uncle Tom's Cabin

274. D. Appelton, *Cyclopedia of American Biography*, Vol. 2 (1888), p. 285.

275. C. Sandburg, *Abraham Lincoln, The Prairie Years*, Harcourt Brace (1926), p. 132.

276. *Western Citizen*, December 1, 1846; December 15, 1846.

277. F.M. Bordewich, *Bound for Canaan*, Amistad (2005), pp. 254, 371–72.

278. Beveridge, A.J., *Abraham Lincoln 1809–58*, Vol. II, Houghton Mifflin (1928), p. 138.

279. The stereotyping critique may better be directed to the later theatrical productions of *Uncle Tom's Cabin*. The story also enjoyed a long life as a play.

90   Religion and Slavery

280. M. Dillon, *Lovejoy, Abolitionist Editor*, University of Illinois Press (1961), p. 51. While Lovejoy is rightly revered for his martyrdom for speaking out against slavery, the record would not be complete without also noting that Lovejoy's religious inspiration did not give him 20–20 eyesight on all issues. At the same time that he preached and wrote to condemn slavery, he regularly bashed Catholicism. The anti-Catholics of his era worried that there was a conspiracy afoot: the Pope was supposedly in league with unnamed European Princes to claim the American west.

281. M. Dillon, *Lovejoy, Abolitionist Editor*, University of Illinois Press (1961), p. 77.

282. A motion to postpone the subject indefinitely was carried by a vote of 154 to 87. Lovejoy and twenty-seven others presented a formal protest. M. Dillon, *Lovejoy, Abolitionist Editor*, University of Illinois Press (1961), p. 78.

283. *Id.*, pp. 117–18.

284. In the 2004 Presidential election battle, Missouri was awash in competing claims as to which party best represented religious values. Honey Pickren of Rockaway Beach made this observation when asked to explain how it was that her own family was split with her father and brother unable to see how the

other could support a given position and still claim to be a Christian. *Chicago Tribune*, August 25, 2004, pp. 1, 18.

285. B.L. Pierce, *A History of Chicago*, A.A. Knopf (1937), p. 245.

286. J.S. Currey, *Chicago, Its History and Its Builders*, S.J. Clarke (1912), p. 405.

287. *The Free West*, September 14, 1854.

288. Magdol, E., *Owen Lovejoy, Abolitionist in Congress*, Rutgers University Press (1967), p. 33.

91   Frederick Douglass

289. F. Douglass, *The Frederick Douglass Papers*, J.W. Blassingame (ed.), Yale University Press (1979), p. 3.

92   The Election of 1852

290. Pierce was nominated out of the blue on the thirty-fifth ballot, dashing the hopes of Stephen Douglas to be the Democrats' standard bearer.

291. A. Beveridge, *Abraham Lincoln 1809–58*, Vol. II, Houghton Mifflin (1928), p. 156.

292. Z. Eastman, *Anti-Slavery Agitation in Illinois*, Chicago History Museum (undated), p. 669.

293. *Id.*

294. *Id.*

295. A. J. Beveridge, *Abraham Lincoln 1809–1858*, Houghton Mifflin Company (1928), Vol II, p. 223 n.1.

93   Building Out Chicago

296. G. Manierre, *The Manierre Family in Early Chicago History*, *Journal of the Illinois Historical Society*, Vol 8, No.1, p. 448 (April 1915).

297. J. Kirkland, *The Story of Chicago*, Dibble Publishing Co. (1892), p. 230.

298. C. Winslow, *Historical Events of* Chicago, Soderlund Printing (1937), p. 95.

299. L. Wendt, *Chicago Tribune, The Rise Of A Great American Newspaper*, Rand McNally (1979), p. 69.

300. *The Chicago Times*, April 25, 1878 (Obituary of Dr. Dyer).

301. A.T. Andreas, *History of Chicago*, Arno Press (1975), p. 522.

302. *Chicago Daily Democrat*, June 21, 1855, November 10, 1855.

94   The Free West

303. *The Free West*, December 1, 1853.

304. *The Free West*, September 7 and 28, 1854.

305. http://www.greatriverroad.com/Cities/Alton/Lovejoy.htm.

306. *The Free West*, December 8, 1853.

95   Nebraska Becomes the Dominant Issue

307. *The Free West*, October 26, 1854.

308. *The Free West*, October 26, 1854.

96   The Nebraska Act

309. J. McPherson, *Battle Cry of Freedom*, Oxford University Press (1988), p. 122.

310. J.W. Sheahan, *The Life of Stephan A. Douglas*, Harper & Brothers (1860), pp. 193–94.

311. *Id.* at 193.

312. *Id.* at 193.

313. *Id.*, p. 222.

314. *Id.*, p. 225.

98   The Chicago Tribune

315. L. Wendt, *Chicago Tribune: The Rise of a Great American Newspaper*, Rand McNally (1979), p. 69.

316. P. Kinsley, *The Chicago Tribune, Its First Hundred Years*, Alfred A. Knopf (1943), p. 7.

317. *Id.*, p. 44.

318. *Id.*, p. 47.

98   Douglas Gets Mobbed in Chicago

319. A. Beveridge, *Abraham Lincoln, 1809–1858*, Vol. 2, Houghton Mifflin (1928), p. 233, n.4.

320. *The Free West*, September 7, 1854.

321. A. Beveridge, *Abraham Lincoln, 1809–1858*, Vol. 2, Houghton Mifflin (1928), p. 232.

322. *Chicago Journal*, quoted in *The Free West*, September 7, 1854. *See also*, J.W. Sheahan, *The Life of Stephen A. Douglas*, Harper & Brothers (1860), pp. 271–74.

323. C. Sandburg, *Abraham Lincoln, the Prairie Years*, Vol. 2, Harcourt, Brace and World, Inc. (1926), p. 10.

324. J.W. Sheahan, *The Life of Stephen A. Douglas*, Harper & Brothers (1860), p. 264.

325. *Id.* p. 274.

100   Birth of the Republican Party

326. A.F. Gilman, *The Origin of the Republican Party*, 1914, reproduced at www.wisconsinhistory.org/turning-points/search.asp?id=137 (visited March 25, 2006).

327. A. Beveridge, *Abraham Lincoln, 1809–1858*, Vol. 2, Houghton Mifflin (1928), p. 264.

328. *The Free West*, September 7, 1854.

329. A. Beveridge, *Abraham Lincoln, 1809–1858*, Vol. 2, Houghton Mifflin (1928), p. 264.

330. *Daily Register* (Springfield, Illinois), October 6, 1854.

331. A.C. Cole, *The Era of the Civil War 1848–1870*, Illinois Centennial Commission (1919), p. 128.

332. Selby, P., *Genesis of the Republican Party in Illinois*, Paper read at a Meeting of the Illinois Republican Editorial Association, Decatur, Illinois, September 14, 1904. Chicago History Museum.

333. *Id.*, p. 140.

101 Lincoln Re-Enters Politics

334. A. Beveridge, *Abraham Lincoln, 1809–1858*, Vol. 2, Houghton Mifflin (1928), p. 164.

335. J.P. Frank, *Lincoln as a Lawyer*, University of Illinois Press (1961), p. 1.

336. A. Beveridge, *Abraham Lincoln, 1809–1858*, Vol. 2, Houghton Mifflin (1928), p. 243, (citing Herndon's letter to Weik, October 28, 1885).

337. A. Lincoln, *Speeches and Writings 1832–1858*, Library of America (1989), pp. 1–5.

102 Lincoln Prepares to Do Battle

338. *Id.*, p. 238.

339. J.P. Frank, *Lincoln as a Lawyer*, University of Illinois Press (1961), pp. 99–100; A. Lincoln,. *Speeches and Writings 1832–1858*, The Library of America (1989), p. 177.

340. A. Lincoln, *Speeches and Writings 1832–1858*, The Library of America (1989), p. 83; *See*, Wilson, D., *Lincoln's Sword: the Presidency and the Power of Words*, Alfred A. Knopf (2006).

341. John Calhoun was an Illinois Democrat with whom Lincoln debated. *See*, A. Lincoln, *Speeches and Writings 1832–1858*, The Library of America (1989), p. 866 n. 306.6.

342. A. Beveridge, *Abraham Lincoln, 1809–1858*, Vol. 2, Houghton Mifflin (1928), pp. 238–239 (quoting the *Illinois Journal*, September 11, 1854).

343. J.P. Frank, *Lincoln as a Lawyer*, University of Illinois Press (1961), p. 28.

104 Douglas and Lincoln Meet at the State Fair in Springfield

344. A. Beveridge, *Abraham Lincoln, 1809–1858*, Vol. 2, Houghton Mifflin (1928), p. 243 (citing *Illinois State Register*, October 4, 5, 1854).

345. *Id.*, p. 262.

346. *Daily Register* (Springfield, Illinois), October 6, 1854.

347. *Id.*, p. 244. The text of the "Peoria Speech" can be found in A. Lincoln, *Speeches and Writings 1832–1858*, The Library of America (1989), p. 307, which reprinted the texts from *The Collected Works of Abraham Lincoln*, edited by Roy P. Basler, Abraham Lincoln Association (1953).

105 The "Peoria Speech"

348. A. Lincoln, *Speeches and Writings 1832–1858*, Library of America (1989), pp. 307–308. (The capitalizations are Lincoln's, reflecting words he emphasized.)

349. A. Beveridge, *Abraham Lincoln, 1809–1858*, Vol. 2, Houghton Mifflin (1928), p. 244.

350. A. Lincoln, *Speeches and Writings, 1832–1858*, Library of America (1989), p. 308.

351. *Id.*, p. 316.

352. *Id.*, p. 309.

353. *Id.*, p. 312.

354. *Id.*, p. 325.

355. *Id.*, pp. 325–26.

356. *Id.*, p. 326.

109 Lincoln's First Run for the Senate in 1855

357. C. Winslow, *Historical Events of* Chicago, Soderlund Printing (1937), p. 95.

358. G. Capers, *Stephen A. Douglas, Defender of the Union*, Little, Brown (1959), p. 113.

359. D. Goodwin, *Team of Rivals, The Political Genius of Abraham Lincoln*, Simon & Schuster (2005), pp. 170–71.

360. A. Lincoln, *Letter to Elihu B. Washburne*, February 9, 1855, reprinted in *Speeches and Writings 1832–1858*, Library of America (1989), pp. 355–56.

361. D. Goodwin, *Team of Rivals, The Political Genius of Abraham Lincoln*, Simon & Schuster (2005), pp. 170–71; A. Beveridge, *Abraham Lincoln, 1809–1858*, Vol. 2, Houghton Mifflin (1928), p. 286.

362. A. Lincoln, *Letter to Elihu B. Washburne*, Feb. 9, 1855, reprinted in *Speeches and Writings 1832–1858*, Library of America (1989), pp. 355–56.

110 Bloody Kansas and Beecher's Bibles

363. Eastman, *Anti-Slavery Agitation in Illinois*, Chicago History Museum, p. 674 (undated) (quoting Lincoln's Springfield speech).

364. Kansas Army National Guard website, http:/// www.ks.ngb.armmy.mil/34star/34star.htm, visited February 15, 2007.

365. D. Reynolds, *John Brown, Abolitionist*, A. Knopf (2005), p. 140.

366. http://www.kshs.org/portraits/beecher_bibles.htm

111 A Second Effort to Form an Illinois Republican Party Succeeds

367. C.A. Church, *History of the Republican Party 1854–1912*, Wilson Bros. (1912), pp. 24–25.

368. *J. Abraham Lincoln Association*, Vol 22, Issue 1; citing, D.E. Fehrenbacher, *Prelude to Greatness*, Stanford University. Press (1962), pp. 44–45.

369. L. Wendt, *Chicago Tribune, The Rise Of A Great American Newspaper*, Rand McNally (1979), p. 68.

370. *Id.*, p. 69.

371. C.A. Church, *History of the Republican Party 1854–1912*, Wilson Bros. (1912), p. 29.

372. A. Cole, *The Era of Civil War, 1848–1870*, University of Illinois Press (1987), p. 126.

112 Lincoln's "Lost Speech"

373. L. Wendt, *Chicago Tribune, The Rise Of A Great American Newspaper*, Rand McNally (1979), p. 76.

374. R.J. Norton, *Abraham Lincoln's Lost Speech*, http://members.aol.com/RVSNorton1/Lincoln63.html (visited January 19, 2008); see also A. Cole, *The Era of the Civil War 1848–70*, Illinois Centennial Commission (1919), pp. 145–46; D. Fehrenbacher, *Prelude to Greatness*, Stanford University Press (1962), p. 46; E. Magdol *Owen Lovejoy: Abolitionist in* Congress, Rutgers University Press (1967), pp. 143–47; A. Beveridge, *Abraham Lincoln, 1809–1858*, Houghton Mifflin (1928), p. 379.

113 Dr. Dyer and the Abolitionists "Fuse" to Become Republicans

375. *Free West*, September 21, 1854.

376. *New York Times*, February 26, 1856.

377. E. Magdol, *Owen Lovejoy: Abolitionist in Congress*, Rutgers University Press (1967), pp. 137–38.

114 Foiling the Recapture of Fugitives

378. *The Free West*, September 14, 1854.

379. A.T. Andreas, *History of Chicago*, Arno Press, Vol III (1975), pp. 394, 482–83; R. Blanchard, *Discovery and Conquests of the Northwest*, Vol. II (1900), pp. 275–76.

380. *The Biographical Dictionary and Portrait Gallery of Representative Men of Chicago, Minnesota Cities and the World's Columbian Exposition*, American Biographical Publishing Co. (1892), pp. 350–53.

381. *Western Citizen*, October 1 and 17, 1853.

382. *Western Citizen*, October 15, 1853.

383. *Id.*

115 John Brown's Raids in Kansas

384. D. Reynolds, *John Brown, Abolitionist*, A. Knopf (2005), p. 113.

385. Blanchard, R., *Discovery and Conquests of the Northwest*, Vol. I (1879) and Vol. II (1900), pp. 298–99.

386. www.ohiohistorycentral.org/images/943.jpg.

387. D. Reynolds, *John Brown, Abolitionist*, A. Knopf (2005), p. 136.

388. Kansas Army National Guard web site, http://www.ks.ngb.army.mil/34star/34star.htm, visited February 12, 2007.

389. *See*, http://www.answers.com/topic/lecompton-constitution.

390. L. Wendt, *Chicago Tribune, The Rise Of A Great American Newspaper*, Rand McNally & Co. (1979), p. 65.

391. D. Reynolds, *John Brown, Abolitionist*, A. Knopf (2005), p. 157.

392. *Id.*, pp. 171–72.

393. *Id.*, pp. 172–73.

394. *Id.*, p. 204.

395. *Id.*, p. 207.

396. *Id.*, p. 237.

397. *Id.*, pp. 243–44.

398. *Id.*, 267.

118 The Dred Scott Decision – The Not-So-Final Word

399. *Scott, a man of color v. Emerson*, 15 Mo. 576 (1852).

400. J. Simon, *Lincoln and Chief Justice Taney*, Simon & Schuster (2006), p. 119.

401. *Scott v. Sandford*, 60 U.S. 393 (1857). (The case was published as *Scott v. Sandford* due to a clerk's error in recording John Sanford's name.) *See*, W. Rehnquist, *The Supreme Court, How It Was, How It Is*, William Morrow and Co. (1987), at 134.

402. *New York Tribune*, December 19, 1855.

403. W. Rehnquist, *The Supreme Court, How It Was, How It Is*, William Morrow and Co. (1987), p. 138. Because justices spent part of the year sitting as trial judges in the various circuits, they were expected to be familiar with the law of the State in which they sat. The nine circuits were configured as follows: 1st (Maine, NewHampshire, Massachusetts, Rhode Island), 2nd (New York, Connecticut, Vermont), 3rd (Pennsylvania, New Jersey), 4th (Delaware, Maryland, Virginia), 5th (Alabama, Louisiana), 6th (North Carolina, South Carolina, Georgia), 7th (Ohio, Illinois, Indiana, Michigan), 8th (Kentucky, Tennessee, Missouri), and 9th (Mississippi, Arkansas). *Id.*, p. 140.

404. *Scott v. Sandford*, 60 U.S. 393, 403 (1857).

405. *Id.* at 407.

406. *Crandall v. State*, 10 Conn. 339 (1834).

407. *See,* http://www.constitution.org/cons/kent1798.htm (visited January 20, 2008).

408. *Strader v. Graham*, 51 U.S. 82 (1851).

409. *Id.* at, 93–94.

410. Scott was actually freed shortly after the decision of the Supreme Court. Mrs. Emerson had remarried and her second husband was a member of Congress. He sold Scott and Scott's family to Blow, who freed them. A. Beveridge, *Abraham Lincoln, 1809–1858*, Houghton Mifflin, Vol. II (1928), pp. 455–56.

411. J. Simon, *Lincoln and Chief Justice Taney*, Simon & Schuster (2006), p. 127.

124   The Dissenters

412. *Id.*

413. *See, Scott v. Sandford*, 60 U.S. 393, 587.

414. *Id.* at 618–19.

415. *Id.* at 532–33.

416. *Id.* at 559.

125   Repercussions from the Dred Scott Decision

417. L. Wendt, *Chicago Tribune, The Rise Of A Great American Newspaper*, Rand McNally (1979), p. 79.

418. The decision also did damage to the Supreme Court as an institution for years to come. Justice Curtis resigned and went back to the private practice of law. The Court was now viewed as a partisan institution, a rabid defender of slavery. Two later Chief Justices had this to say about the decision: Chief Justice Charles Evans Hughes aptly called the Dred Scott decision "a self-inflicted wound." And Chief Justice William Rehnquist criticized the decision for violating two judicial canons. First, the ruling on the constitutionality of the Missouri Compromise was *unnecessary* because the case could have been disposed of on non-constitutional grounds; and, second, the declaration that the Missouri Compromise was unconstitutional did not meet the high threshold for declaring an act of Congress unconstitutional. Chief Justice Taney could not point to an explicit provision in the Constitution or a well recognized construction of the Constitution that supported his conclusion. The use of the Fifth Amendment and the claim of "unfairness" to slaveholders rationale–that it was unfair to prevent slaveholders from taking their property to the territories–had no precedential support and could not be supported by the explicit language of the Amendment. W. Rehnquist, *The Supreme Court, How It Was, How It Is*, William Morrow and Co. (1987), p. 143.

125   Lincoln Deconstructs Dred Scott

419. A. Beveridge, *Abraham Lincoln, 1809–1858*, Houghton Mifflin, Vol. II (1928), p. 500.

420. A. Lincoln, *Speeches and Writings 1832–1858*, Library of America (1989), p. 392.

421. *Id.*

422. *Id.*

126   Douglas and Lincoln Spar over Negro Equality

423. A. Beveridge, *Abraham Lincoln, 1809–1858*, Houghton Mifflin, Vol. II (1928), p. 505.

424. A. Lincoln, *Speeches and Writings 1832–1858*, Library of America (1989), p. 397.

425. *Id.*, pp. 397–98.

426. *Id.*, p. 398.

427. *Id.*

428. *Id.*, p. 400.

127   The Illinois Republicans Slate Lincoln to Unseat Douglas

429. Dr. Dyer is listed as a delegate in the (Springfield) *Daily Illinois Journal*, June 17, 1858.

430. A. Beveridge, *Abraham Lincoln, 1809–1858*, Houghton Mifflin, Vol. II (1928), p. 549.

431. See http://mrlincolnandfriends.org/content-inside.asp?pageID=17&subjectID=1. Visited January 26, 2008.

432. L. Wendt, *Chicago Tribune, The Rise Of A Great American Newspaper*, Rand McNally (1979), p. 84–85.

433. *Id.*, pp. 90–91.

434. *Id.*, pp. 90–91.

435. Some scholars are skeptical of the Wentworth threat story. *See*, D. Fehrenbacher, *Prelude To Greatness, Lincoln in the 1850s*, Stanford University Press (1962), p. 50.

128   The "House Divided Speech"

436. A. Beveridge, *Abraham Lincoln, 1809–1858*, Houghton Mifflin, Vol. II (1928), p. 576.

437. A. Lincoln, *Speeches and Writings 1832–1858*, Library of America (1989), p. 426.

438. *Id.*, p. 427.

439. *Id.*, p. 433.

440. *Id.*, p. 431.

441. *Id.*, p. 432.

130　The Lincoln-Douglas Debates

442. C. Sandburg, *Abraham Lincoln, The Prairie Years*, Harcourt Brace (1926), p. 138.

443. D. Fehrenbacher, *Recollected Words of Abraham Lincoln*, Stanford University Press (1996), p. 99.

444. *Id.*

445. A. Lincoln, *Speeches and Writings 1832–1858*, Library of America (1989), p. 479.

446. D. Fehrenbacher, *Recollected Words of Abraham Lincoln*, Stanford University Press (1996), pp. 100–01.

447. *Id.*, pp. 101–02.

448. L. Wendt, *Chicago Tribune, The Rise Of A Great American Newspaper*, Rand McNally (1979), p. 100.

449. Douglas's opening speech in the first debate, reprinted in A. Lincoln, *Speeches and Writings 1832–1858*, Library of America (1989), p. 495, 503.

450. *Id.*, 497.

451. *Id.*, p. 500.

452. *Id.*, p. 501.

453. *Id.*, p. 504.

454. *Id.*, p. 556.

455. *Id.*, pp. 538–39.

456. L. Wendt, *Chicago Tribune, The Rise Of A Great American Newspaper*, Rand McNally (1979), pp. 99–100.

457. A. Lincoln, *Speeches and Writings 1832–1858*, Library of America (1989), p. 542.

458. J. Cunningham, *The Bloomington Convention of 1856 and Those Who Participated In It*, Springfield (1906), Transactions of the Illinois Historical Society (1905–1906).

459. A. Lincoln, *Speeches and Writings 1832–1858*, Library of America (1989), p. 545.

135　The Freeport Doctrine

460. *Id.*, pp. 551–52.

135　Lincoln and White Supremacy

461. *Id.*, p.636.

462. *Id.*, p. 765.

463. *Id.*, p. 770.

464. *Id.*, p. 770.

465. *Id.*, p. 793.

466. *Id.*, pp. 801–02.

137　Lincoln Is Defeated by Douglas

467. A. Beveridge, *Abraham Lincoln, 1809–1858*, Houghton Mifflin, Vol. II (1928), pp. 695–96.

137　Was Lincoln a Racist?

468. *Webster's II New College Dictionary*, Houghton Mifflin Co. (1995), p. 912.

469. N.D. Harris, *History of Negro Slavery in Illinois and the Slavery Agitation in that State*, A.C. McClurg & Co. (1904), p. 235.

470. *Id.*

471. *Id.*, p. 238.

472. *Id.*

473. *Id.*, p. 239.

138　John Brown Ignites the Powder Keg

474. D. Reynolds, *John Brown, Abolitionist*, A. Knopf (2005), p. 279.

475. *Id.*, pp. 283–85.

476. *Id.*, p. 286.

477. *Id.*, p. 287.

478. Blanchard, R., *Discovery and Conquests of the Northwest*, Vol. I (1879) and Vol. II (1900), p. 300.

479. *Id.*, p. 302.

139　Dr. Dyer – An Ambassador for Chicago

480. *Chicago Press and Tribune*, February 28, 1859.

481. *Chicago Press and Tribune*, February 26, 1859.

482. *Id.*

483. *Id.*

484. *Chicago Press and Tribune*, February 28, 1859.

485. *Chicago Press and Tribune*, June 22, 1859.

486. *Chicago Press and Tribune*, August 4, 1859.

487. *Id.*

141　Lincoln's Cooper Union Speech

488. D. Fehrenbacher, *Prelude To Greatness*, Stanford University Press (1962), pp. 143–44.

489. *Id.*, p. 164.

490. *Press and Tribune*, February 16, 1860.

491. *Id.*

492. A. Lincoln, *Speeches and Writings 1859–1865*, Library of America (1989), p. 120.

143　Lincoln Becomes the Favorite Son of Illinois

493. Dyer is listed as a delegate to both the 1858 and 1860 Illinois Republican Conventions in the Springfield newspaper *Illinois Journal*. *Illinois Journal*, June 17, 1858; May 12, 1860.

494. A. Lincoln, *Speeches and Writings 1832–1858*, Library of America (1989), p. 517.

495. D. Fehrenbacher, *Prelude To Greatness*, Stanford University Press (1962), pp. 148–49.

496. L. Wendt, *Chicago Tribune, The Rise Of A Great American Newspaper*, Rand McNally (1979), p. 115.

144   The "Second Choice" Strategy

497. *Id.*, p. 146, citing R. Basler, *The Collected Works of Abraham Lincoln*, Vol IV, p. 34.

498. D.K. Goodwin, *Team of Rivals*, Simon & Schuster (2005), p. 216.

499. L. Wendt, *Chicago Tribune, The Rise Of A Great American Newspaper*, Rand McNally (1979), p. 118.

500. *Id.*, pp. 117, 120.

501. *Id.*, p. 121.

502. King, Willard L., *Lincoln's Manager David Davis*, Harvard University Press (1960), p. 139; The counterfeit ticket story is told in Baringer, William, *Lincoln's Rise to Power*, Little Brown and Co. (1937) p. 267.

145   The Cameron Club

503. Minute Book of the Cameron-Lincoln Club 1859–1860, (Chicago History Museum Archives), September 29, 1859.

504. *Id.*, November 24, 1859.

505. *See*, Simon Cameron Papers, Historical Society of Dauphin County, Harrisburg, PA.

506. Minute Book of the Cameron-Lincoln Club 1859–1860, (Chicago History Museum Archives), December 1, 1859.

507. *Id.* , November 17, 1859.

508. Dr. Dyer's "close personal friendship with Lincoln" is mentioned in Biographical Encyclopedia of Illinois of the Nineteenth Century (1875) and in *New York Times*, April 25, 1878, Obituary of Dr. Dyer. Dr. Dyer is listed as a delegate to the Illinois Republican Convention held in Decatur May 9 and 10, 1860 in the Daily Illinois State Journal (Springfield), May 12, 1860, p. 2 as reported by Wayne C. Temple in Journal of the Illinois Historical Society, Autumn (1999).

509. R.O. Davis, "Dr. Charles Leib: Lincoln's Mole?," *Journal of the Abraham Lincoln Society*, Vol. 24, No. 2, p. 20.

510. *Id.*, pp. 23–24.

511. *Id.*, p. 25.

512. See, Letter of Dr. Charles Leib to Simon Cameron, September 2, 1859, Simon Cameron Papers, Historical Society of Dauphin County, Harrisburg, PA.

513. *Id.*

514. *Id.*

515. Letter of Dr. Charles Leib to Simon Cameron, March 24, 1860, Simon Cameron Papers, Historical Society of Dauphin County, Harrisburg, PA.

516. *Id.*

148   Pennsylvania Switches to Lincoln

517. King, Willard L., *Lincoln's Manager David Davis*, Harvard University Press (1960), p. 139.

518. *Id.*

519. *See for example*, Baringer, William, *Lincoln's Rise to Power*, Little Brown and Co. (1937), pp. 213, 267.

520. King, Willard L., *Lincoln's Manager David Davis*, Harvard University Press (1960), p. 140.

521. Minute Book of the Cameron-Lincoln Club 1859–1860, (Chicago History Museum Archives), May 25, 1860.

522. R.O. Davis, "Dr. Charles Leib: Lincoln's Mole?," *Journal of the Abraham Lincoln Society*, Vol. 24, No. 2, p. 27.

523. *Chicago Tribune*, March 9, 1888.

149   Dr. Dyer and the "Wide-Awakes" Campaign for Lincoln

524. http://en.wikipedia.org/wiki/Wide_Awakes, visited February 26, 2008.

525. *The Chicago Press and Tribune*, July 24, 1860.

526. *The Chicago Press and Tribune*, September 7, 1860.

527. *The Chicago Press and Tribune*, October 9, 1860.

528. *The Chicago Press and Tribune*, October 15, 1860.

529. *The Railsplitter*, June 23, 1860.

530. *The Railsplitter*, July 7, 1860.

151   Lincoln Wins the Presidency

531. *Declaration of the Immediate Causes Which Induce and Justify the Secession of South Carolina from the Federal Union*, http://americancivilwar.com/documents/causes_south_carolina.html (visited December 13, 2007).

532. *Id.*

533. *Secession Declaration of Georgia*, Approved, January 29, 1861. http://americancivilwar.com/documents/causes_georgia.html (visited December 13, 2007).

PART III
1860–1865:
Emancipation – Triumph of the Abolitionists

154   The Road to the Extinction of Slavery

534.   Letter of Horace Greeley to Abraham Lincoln, 1864, quoted in J.M. McPherson, *Drawn With The Sword*, Oxford University Press (1996), p. 133.

535.   L. Bennett, *Forced Into Glory: Abraham Lincoln's White Dream,* Johnson Publishing Co. (2000). Another criticism depreciating Lincoln's role in ending slavery is the "self-emancipation" thesis, the proposition that the slaves freed themselves. It is true that slaves flooded into military camps hastening the need to establish a policy on emancipation, the self-emancipation thesis overweighs this phenomenon. *See,* J.M. McPherson's essay "Who Freed the Slaves" in *Drawn with the Sword*, Oxford University Press (1996) p. 192.

154   Lincoln's Record Opposing Slavery before his Inauguration

536.   4 Ill. 71 (1841).

537.   A. Lincoln, *Speeches and Writings 1832–1858*, Library of America (1989), p. 363.

538.   *Id.*, p. 315.

539.   A. Lincoln, *Speeches and Writings 1859–1865*, Library of America (1989), p. 190.

155   The "Hands Off" Policy of Lincoln's First Inaugural Address

540.   A. Lincoln, *Speeches and Writings 1832–1858*, Library of America (1989), p. 215.

541.   A. Lincoln, *Speeches and Writings 1859–1865*, Library of America (1989), p. 218.

542.   A. Lincoln, *Speeches and Writings 1859–1865*, Library of America (1989), p. 293.

156   First Steps

543.   Hill, Walter B. Jr., "Living with the Hydra," *Prologue Magazine*, Winter 2000, Vol. 32, No. 4 (National Archives and Records Administration), p. 9 n. 31.

544.   *New York Times*, November 17, 1862.

545.   A. Lincoln, *Speeches and Writings 1859–1865*, Library of America (1989), p. 290.

157   The Confiscation Acts of 1861 and 1862

546.   *Id.*, p. 291; Confiscation Act of 1861, 12 Stat. at Large, 319.

158   Frémont's Blunder

547.   L.H. Harrison, *Lincoln of Kentucky*, University Press of Kentucky (2000), p. 135.

548.   A. Lincoln, *Speeches and Writings 1859–1865*, Library of America (1989), p. 293.

158   Recognizing Haiti and Liberia

549.   J. Niven, *John C. Calhoun and the Price of Union: A Biography*, Baton Rouge: Louisiana State University Press (1988), p. xv, 324.

550.   A. Lincoln, Message to Congress, April 16, 1862, A. Lincoln, *Speeches and Writings 1859–1865*, Library of America (1989), p. 282.

159   Abolishing Slavery in the District of Columbia

551.   A. Lincoln, Message to Congress, April 16, 1862, A. Lincoln, *Speeches and Writings 1859–1865*, Library of America (1989), p. 316.

160   Exhausting the Peaceful Extinction of Slavery Option

552.   A. Lincoln, *Speeches and Writings 1832–1858*, Library of America (1989), pp. 359–60.

553.   A. Lincoln, *Speeches and Writings 1859–1865*, Library of America (1989), p. 319.

554.   *Id.*, p. 310.

555.   L. Bennett, *Forced into Glory: Abraham Lincoln's White Dream,* Johnson Publishing Co. (2000).

556.   M. Vorenberg, "Abraham Lincoln and the Politics of Black Colonization," *Journal of the Abraham Lincoln Association*, Vol. 14, No. 2 (1993).

557.   A. Lincoln, *Speeches and Writings 1832–1858*, Library of America (1989), p. 271.

558.   R. Basler, *The Collected Works of Abraham Lincoln*, Vol. IV, p. 561.

559.   A. Lincoln, *Speeches and Writings 1859–1865*, Library of America (1989), pp. 291–92.

560.   *Id.*, p. 368.

561.   A. Lincoln, *Speeches and Writings 1859–1865*, Library of America (1989), p. 395.

162   Arming the Slaves – Cameron Rebuked

562.   J. Nicolay and J. Hay, *Abraham Lincoln*, Vol. V, The Century Co. (1886) p. 124.

563.   *Id.*, p. 126.

564.   *Id.*

565.   *Id.*, p. 128.

566.   E. Bradley, *Simon Cameron Lincoln's Secretary of War*, University of Pennsylvania Press (1966).

163   An Insurrection or a War?

567.   United States Constitution, Article I, § 8.

568.   *Id.*, Article II, § 2.

569.   *Id.*, Article II, § 3.

570.   *Id.*, Article IV, § 4.

571.   *The Brig Amy Warwick; The Schooner Crenshaw; The Barque Hiawatha; The Schooner Brilliante*, 67 U.S. 635, 668 (1863).

164   The Trent Affair – Keeping the Lion at Bay

572.   N. Graebner, "Northern Diplomacy and European Neutrality," in *Why the North Won the Civil War*, edited by D.H. Donald, Simon & Schuster (1966), pp. 60–61.

166   Lincoln Appoints Dr. Dyer to Be a Judge

573.   *Message Of The President Of The United States Transmitting A Copy Of The Treaty Between The United States And Her Britannic Majesty For The Suppression Of The African Slave Trade*, 37th Congress, 2nd Session, Senate Executive Document No. 57, Abraham Lincoln Presidential Library and Museum.

574.   A. Lincoln, *Speeches and Writings 1859–1865*, Library of America (1989), p. 538.

575.   Lincoln, A., *Basler's Collected Works of Abraham Lincoln*, first supplement (1953), p. 178.

576.   D. Fehrenbacher, *Recollected Words of Abraham Lincoln*, Stanford University Press (1996), pp. 146–47; Wilson, D.L., *Herndon's Informants*, University of Illinois Press (1998), pp. 149–50 (Zebina Eastman's letter of January 2, 1866 to William H. Herndon).

167   Republicans from Illinois Serving the Lincoln Administration

577.   *Id.*, p. 30.

167   Dr. Dyer Goes to Africa

578.   *The Chicago Tribune*, April 25, 1878, p. 7 (Obituary).

579.   *The Chicago Tribune*, April 25, 1878, p. 7 (Obituary).

580.   *Id.*

168   Lincoln's Reply to Greeley

581.   *New York Tribune*, August 19, 1862.

582.   A. Lincoln, *Speeches and Writings 1859–1865*, Library of America (1989), p. 358.

169   Timing – The Reply to the Chicago Emancipation Memorial

583.   *New York Times*, September 26, 1862.

584.   A. Lincoln, *Speeches and Writings 1859–1865*, Library of America (1989), p. 361.

585.   *Id.*, p. 363.

586.   *Id.*, p. 365.

587.   *Id.*, pp. 364–65.

588.   *Id.*, p. 366.

170   The Emancipation Proclamation

589.   *Id.*, p. 425.

172   Arming the Slaves

590.   *Id.*, p. 497.

591.   *Id.*

592.   P. Selby, *Abraham Lincoln and the Evolution of his Emancipation Policy*, Chicago Historical Society (1906).

173   Thirteenth Amendment

593.   *Id.*, p. 501.

594.   C. Dana, *Recollections of the Civil War*, D. Appelton and Co. (1898), pp. 174–77.

173   The Persistence of Racism

595.   33 Ill. 390, 1864 Ill. LEXIS 88 (1864).

596.   *People v. Nelson*, 33 Ill. 390, 394 (1864).

597.   *Id.*, 33 Ill. at 396, citing *Eells v. The People*, 4 Scam. 498, 5 Ill. 498 (1843).

175   Dr. Dyer Learns of Lincoln's Assassination in Rome

598.   G. Upton, and E. Colbert, *Biographical Sketches of the Leading Men of Chicago*, Wilson & St. Clair (1868), p. 75.

599.   *Id.*, p. 79.

600.   *Id.*

176   Has Chicago Forgotten the Abolitionists?

601.   *The Chicago Times*, April 25, 1878.

602.   R. Blanchard, *Discovery and Conquests of the Northwest*, R. Blanchard and Co., Vol. I (1879) and Vol. II (1900), p. 305.

603.   *Id.*

604.   R. Varon, *Street Talk: Walk Down Halsted*, ABC7 Chicago, reprinted on http://abclocal.go.com/wls/news/streettalk/print_110403_streettalk_halsted-street.html (visited April 29, 2004).

605.   I. Bach, *A Guide to Chicago's Public Sculpture*, University of Chicago Press (1983).

606.   A.T. Andreas, *History of Cook County, Illinois*, A.T. Andreas Publishers (1884), pp. 288–89.

{ BIBLIOGRAPHY }

Andreas, A.T., *History of Chicago*, Arno Press (1975).

Abanes, R., *One Nation Under Gods*, Four Walls Eight Windows (2002).

Appleton's Cyclopedia of American Biography, Vol. 2, D. Appleton & Co. (1888).

Arnold, Isaac N., *The History of Abraham Lincoln and the Overthrow of Slavery*, Clarke & Co. (1866).

Arnold, Isaac N., *The Life of Abraham Lincoln*, A.C. McClurg & Co. (1887).

Bach, Ira J. *A Guide to Chicago's Public Sculpture*, University of Chicago Press (1983).

Baringer, William, *Lincoln's Rise to Power*, Little Brown and Co. (1937).

Basler, Roy P., *The Collected Works of Abraham Lincoln*, Rutgers University Press (1953).

Basler, Roy P., *The Collected Works of Abraham Lincoln*, First Supplement, Rutgers University Press (1953).

Bateman, N. and Selby, P. *Historical Encyclopedia of Illinois with Commemorative Biographies*, Munsell Publishing Co. (1926).

Bennett, L., *Forced Into Glory: Abraham Lincoln's White Dream*, Johnson Publishing Co. (2000).

Beveridge, A. J., *Abraham Lincoln, 1809–1858*, Houghton Mifflin (1928).

The Biographical Dictionary and Portrait Gallery of Representative Men of Chicago, Minnesota Cities and the World's Columbian Exposition, American Biographical Publishing Co. (1892).

Biographical Encyclopedia of Illinois of the Nineteenth Century (1875).

Black, S. and Bennett, R., *A City of Refuge: Quincy, Illinois*, Millennial Press (2000).

Blanchard, R., *Discovery and Conquests of the Northwest*, R. Blanchard and Co., Vol. I (1879) and Vol. II (1900).

Bordewich, F.M., *Bound for Canaan*, Amistad (2005).

Bradley, Erwin Stanley, *Simon Cameron Lincoln's Secretary of War*, University of Pennsylvania Press (1966).

Bringhurst, N. G., *Saints, Slaves and Blacks*, Greenwood Press (1981).

Burton, Orville V., *The Age of Lincoln*, Hill and Wang (2007).

Capers, G., *Stephen A. Douglas, Defender of the Union*, Little, Brown (1959).

Carr, C. E., *Stephen A. Douglas*, A.C. McClurg & Co. (1909).

Chicago American, January 8, 1841.

The Chicago Times, April 25, 1878.

Chicago Tribune, July 26, 2005, section 1, pp. 1 and 17; August 25, 2004, pp. 1, 18.

Church, C.A., *History of the Republican Party in Illinois 1854–1912*, Press of Wilson Bros. (1912).

Cole, Arthur C., *The Era of the Civil War 1848–70*, Illinois Centennial Commission (1919).

Cook, F.R., *By Gone Days of Chicago*, McClurg & Co. (1901).

Cornelius, J., *Constitution Making in Illinois 1818–1970*, University of Illinois Press (1972).

Currey, S., *Chicago: Its History and Its Builders, A Century of Marvelous Growth*, S.J. Clarke Publishing Co. (1912).

Crozat, R.C., *Illinois and Louisiana under French Rule* (1893).

Cunningham, J., *The Bloomington Convention of 1856 and Those Who Participated In It*, Springfield (1906), Transactions of the Illinois Historical Society (1905–1906).

Daily Register (Springfield, Illinois), October 6, 1854.

Dana, C., *Recollections of the Civil War*, D. Appelton and Co. (1898).

Danenhower, W., *Danehower's Chicago City Directory for 1851*, W.W. Danenhower (1851).

Davis, I. S., *The Story of the Church*, Herald Publishing House (1977).

Declaration of the Immediate Causes Which Induce and Justify the Secession of South Carolina from the Federal Union, http://americancivilwar.com/documents/causes_south_carolina.html (visited December 13, 2007).

Dedmon, E., *Fabulous Chicago*, Antheneum (1981).

De Tocqueville, A., *Democracy in America*, 1835, Folio Society Edition (2002).

Dillon, M., *Elijah P. Lovejoy, Abolitionist Editor*, University of Illinois Press (1961).

Donald, D.H., *Lincoln*, Simon & Schuster (1955).

Douglass, F., *The Frederick Douglass Papers*, J.W. Blassingame (ed.), Yale University Press (1979).

Dunne, E.F., *Illinois, The Heart of The Nation*, The Lewis Publishing Co. (1933).

Eastman, Z., *Anti-Slavery Agitation in Illinois*, Chicago History Museum (undated).

Eastman, Z., *History of the Black Codes of Illinois*, Chicago History Museum (undated).

Fehrenbacher, D.E., *Prelude to Greatness*, Stanford University Press (1962).

Fergus, R., *Fergus' Directory of Chicago*, Fergus Printing Co. (1839).

Fergus, R., *Fergus' Directory of Chicago*, Fergus Printing Co. (1843).

Frank, J.P., *Lincoln as a Lawyer*, University of Illinois Press (1961).

Franklin, J. H. and Schweninger, L., *Runaway Slaves*, Oxford University Press (1999).

Free West, December 1, 1853; December 8, 1853; October 26, 1854; December 15, 1854; September 7, 1854; September 21, 1854; September 28, 1854; September 14, 1854.

Gager, J., *Gager's Chicago City Directory for the Year Ended June 1, 1857*, John Gager & Co. (1857).

Gale, E.O., *Reminiscences of Early Chicago and Vicinity*, Revell Co. (1902).

Gara, L., *The Liberty Line: The Legend of the Underground Railroad*, University of Kentucky Press (1961).

Gara, L., *A Glorious Time: The 1874 Abolitionist Reunion in Chicago*, Journal Illinois State Historical Society, Vol. lxv, No. 3 (Autumn 1972).

Gertz, E., *The Black Laws of Illinois*, Journal of the Illinois State Historical Society, 56 (Autumn 1963).

Gilbert, P. and Bryson, C.L., *Chicago and Its Makers: a Narrative of Events from the Day of the First White Man to the Inception of the Second World's Fair*, F. Mendelsohn (1929).

Gilman, A.F., *The Origin of the Republican Party*, A.F. Gilman (1914).

Goodwin, D.K., *Team of Rivals*, Simon & Schuster (2005).

Graebner, N., "Northern Diplomacy and European Neutrality," in *Why the North Won the Civil War*, edited by D.H. Donald, Simon & Schuster (1966).

Grunwaldt, D.C., *Quincy, Illinois and the Underground Railroad*, (unpublished), Historical Society of Quincy and Adams County (1961).

Hagadorn, Ann E., *Beyond the River*, Simon & Schuster (2002).

Harris, N.D., *History of Negro Slavery in Illinois and the Slavery Agitation in that State*, A.C. McClurg & Co. (1904).

Harrison, L.H., *Lincoln of Kentucky*, University Press of Kentucky (2000).

Herndon, W.H., *Herndon's Life of Lincoln*, World Publishing Co. (1942).

Highlander, March/April 2004; September/October 2004.

Hughes, D. *The Mormon Church, A Basic History*, Deseret Book Company (1986).

Illinois State Register, June 19, 1840.

Journal of the American Medical Association, May 20, 1968.

Johannsen, R.W., *Stephen A. Douglas*, University of Illinois Press (1997).

Julius, K.C., *The Abolitionist Decade, 1829–1838*, McFarland & Co. (2004).

King, Willard L., *Lincoln's Manager David Davis*, Harvard University Press (1960).

Kinsley, P., *The Chicago Tribune, Its First Hundred Years*, Alfred Knopf (1943).

Kirkland, J., *Chicago Yesterdays*, Daughaday and Co. (1919).

Kirkland, J., *The Story of Chicago*, Dibble Publishing Co. (1892).

Lamon, Ward Hill, *The Life of Abraham Lincoln*, James R. Osgood and Co. (1872).

Landrum, C.A., *Quincy in the Civil War*, Carl Landrum (1966).

Lincoln, A., *Speeches and Writings 1832–1858*, Library of America (1989).

Lovejoy, J.C. and O., *Memoir of the Rev. Elijah Lovejoy*, 1838 (with introduction by John Quincy Adams), J.S. Taylor (1838).

Magdol, E., *Owen Lovejoy: Abolitionist in Congress*, Rutgers University Press (1967).

Manierre, G., *The Manierre Family in Early Chicago History*, Journal of the Illinois Historical Society, Vol 8, No.1 (April 1915).

McPherson, J. M., *Battle Cry of Freedom*, Oxford University Press (1988).

McPherson, J.M. "Who Freed the Slaves" in *Drawn with the Sword*, Oxford University Press (1996).

Message Of The President Of The United States Transmitting A Copy Of The Treaty Between The United States And Her Britannic Majesty For The Suppression Of The African Slave Trade, 37th Congress, 2nd Session, Senate Executive Document no. 57, Abraham Lincoln Presidential Library and Museum.

Miers, E.S., *Lincoln Day by Day*, Lincoln Sesquicentennial Commission (1960).

Miller, W.L., *Arguing About Slavery*, A.A. Knopf (1996).

Minute Book of the Cameron Club, 1859–60, Chicago History Museum Collection.

Moses, J. and Kirkland, J. *The History of Chicago*, Munsell and Co. (1895).

New England J. of Medicine (April 7, 1933).

New York Times, (February 26, 1856).

New York Tribune, (December 19, 1855).

Newton, Joseph Fort, *Lincoln and Herndon*, The Torch Press (1910).

Nicolay, J. and Hay, J., *Abraham Lincoln*, The Century Co. (1886).

Niven, J., *John C. Calhoun and the Price of Union: A Biography*, Louisiana State University Press (1988).

Norris, J.W., *A Business Advertiser and General Directory of the City of Chicago for the Year 1845–46*, J. Campbell & Co. Publishers (1845).

Norris, J.W., *A Business Advertiser and General Directory of the City of Chicago for the Year 1848–49*, Eastman & McClellan (1848).

Norton, R.J., *Abraham Lincoln's Lost Speech*, http://members.aol.com/RVSNorton1/Lincoln63.html (visited January 19, 2008).

Page, Elwin L., *Cameron for Lincoln's Cabinet*, Boston University Press (1954).

Pierce, B.L., *A History of Chicago*, A.A. Knopf (1937).

Presbyterian Life, (May 30, 1953).

Raymond, Henry J., *The Life and Public Service of Abraham Lincoln*, Derby and Miller Publishers (1865).

Records of the Illinois State Anti-Slavery Society, Minute Book, Chicago History Museum.

Rehnquist, W., *The Supreme Court, How It Was, How It Is*, William Morrow and Company (1987).

Reynolds, D.S., *John Brown, Abolitionist*, A.A. Knopf (2005).

Ryan, J.H., *A Chapter from the History of the Underground Railroad in Illinois*, *Journal of the Illinois Historical Society*, Vol.8, No. 1 (April 1915).

Ricks, M. K. *Escape on the Pearl*, William Morrow (2007).

Sandburg, C., *Abraham Lincoln, The Prairie Years, Vol. 2*, Harcourt, Brace & World, Inc. (1926).

Schurz, Carl, *Abraham Lincoln*, Houghton, Mifflin and Co. (1891).

Selby, P., *Abraham Lincoln and the Evolution of His Emancipation Policy*, Address to the Chicago Historical Society (February 27, 1906), reprinted by Chicago Historical Society (1909).

Selby, P., *Genesis of the Republican Party in Illinois*, Paper read at a Meeting of the Illinois Republican Editorial Association, Decatur, Illinois, September 14, 1904. (Chicago History Museum).

Secession Declaration of Georgia, Approved, January 29, 1861. http://americancivilwar.com/documents/causesgeorgia.html (visited December 13, 2007).

St. Louis Observer (October 1835).

Sandburg, C., *Abraham Lincoln, The Prairie Years*, Harcourt Brace (1926).

Sheahan, J., *Stephen A. Douglas*, Harper & Brothers (1860).

Simon, J., *Lincoln and Chief Justice Taney*, Simon & Schuster (2006).

Simon, P., *Lincoln's Preparation for Greatness, The Illinois Legislative Years*, University of Oklahoma Press (1968).

Simon, P., *Lovejoy, Martyr to Freedom*, Concordia (1964).

Smith, A. F., *The Saintly Scoundrel, The Life and Times of Dr. John Cook Bennett*, University of Illinois Press (1997).

Snay, M., *Abraham Lincoln, Owen Lovejoy, and the Emergence of the Republican Party in Illinois*, Journal of the Abraham Lincoln Association, vol 22, Issue 1.

Stentor, The Underground Railway, Lake Forest College Archives (May 1890).

Tarbell, I., *In the Footsteps of the Lincolns*, Harper & Bros. (1924).

Thomas, B.P., *Theodore Weld, Crusader for Freedom*, New Brunswick (1950).

Tillson, J., *History of the City of Quincy, Illinois*, S.J. Clarke Publishing Co. (1900).

Times and Seasons, 1842.

Upton, G.P. and Colbert, E., *Biographical Sketches of Leading Men of Chicago*, Wilson & St. Clair (1868).

Varon, R., *Street Talk: Walk Down Halsted*, ABC7 Chicago, http://abclocal.go.com/wls/news/streettalk/print-110403streettalkhalstedstreet.html (visited April 29, 2004).

Von Holst, *Constitutional History of the United States*, vol. III, p. 548. Callahan and Co. (1888).

Vorenberg, M., "Abraham Lincoln and the Politics of Black Colonization," *Journal of the Abraham Lincoln Association*, Vol. 14, No. 2 (1993).

Web sites visited:

http://alabamamaps.ua.edu/historicalmaps/usstates/indiana/index.html

http://abclocal.go.com/wls/news/streettalk/print110403streettalkhalstedstreet.html (visited April 4, 2004)

http://www.altonweb.com/history/lovejoy/a01.html

http://www.angelfire.com/mo2/blackmormon/q2.htm

http://www.answers.com/topic/lecompton-constitution

http://www.constitution.org/cons/kent1798.htm (visited January 20, 2008)

http://freespace.virgin.net/john.cletheroe/usacan/usa/masdix.htm

http://geography.about.com/library/weekly/aa041999.htm

http://ngeorgia.com/history/why.html (visited January 7, 2004)

http://www.greatriverroad.com/Cities/Alton/Lovejoy.htm

http://www.ilsos.net/departments/archives/servant.html

http://www.kshs.org/portraits/beecher_bibles.htm

http:///www.ks.ngb.armmy.mil/34star/34star.htm (visited February 15, 2007)

http://mrlincolnandfriends.org/content_inside.asp?pageID=17&subjectID=1.

http://www.papersofabrahamlincoln.org/narrative_overview.htm

http://www.rootsweb.com/~ilhistory/governors/french.html (visited March 11, 2007)

http://www.spartacus.schoolnet.co.uk/USACWcameron.htm (visited March 25, 2007)

http://www.spartacus.schoolnet.co.uk/USASlovejoy.htm

Wendt, L. *Chicago Tribune, The Rise Of A Great American Newspaper*, Rand McNally & Co. (1979).

Western Citizen, July 26, 1842; August 5, 1842; October 13, 1846; November 3, 1846; November 10, 1846; November 14, 1846; December 1, 1846; December 29, 1846; May 2, 1848; June 20, 1848; June 27, 1848; July 11, 1848; August 22, 1848.

Whittier, J.G., *Justice and Expediency or Slavery Considered with a View to its Rightful and Effectual Remedy, Abolition*, New York (1833).

Wilson, D. and Davis, R, *Herndon's Informants*, University of Illinois Press (1998).

Wilson, D., *Lincoln's Sword: the Presidency and the Power of Words*, Alfred A. Knopf (2006).

Winslow, C., *Historical Events of Chicago*, Soderlund Printing (1937).

Winslow, C., *Historical Events of Chicago*, Manuscript at Chicago History Museum, Vol. I (undated).

{ INDEX }

Tom Campbell is an attorney in Chicago who specializes in the trial of business disputes. He has always nurtured a thirst for Illinois history, especially the trials and tribulations of the Chicagoans who helped get Lincoln elected. The fact that Illinois had a form of slavery and that, before the Civil War, the courts of Illinois were called upon to decide cases involving the rights of slave owners, their creditors, and fugitives from slavery, is a chapter in the history of Illinois that largely has gone unexplored to date.

While Lincoln and Douglas could exchange humorous barbs, many of which are memorable, the substance of the Lincoln-Douglas debates is the clash of visions for the future of America as its territory expanded and its population and economy grew. This battle was fought by two of the foremost lawyers in the country who took carefully constructed legal arguments to the electorate, explaining them in plain terms. These arguments are best understood by knowing the precedents that their reasoning employed.

One of the skills of a trial lawyer is the ability to express complicated ideas in a simple way. This was something Lincoln excelled at and something Tom Campbell has emulated in explaining his arguments. Campbell is a graduate of Dartmouth, received his J.D. from Cornell University and has been named among The Best Lawyers in America. He lives and works in Chicago.